Contents

THE ACOUSTIC GUITAR GUIDE

THE ACOUSTIC GUITAR GUIDE

Everything
You Need to Know
to Buy and Maintain
a New
or Used Guitar

Larry Sandberg

a cappella books

Library of Congress Cataloging-in-Publication Data

Sandberg, Larry.
    The acoustic guitar guide : everything you need to know to buy and
maintain a new or used guitar / Larry Sandberg.
        p.   cm.
    Includes bibliographical references.
    ISBN 1-55652-104-9 : $14.95
    1. Guitar. 2. Guitar—Maintenance and repair. I. Title.
ML1015.G6S3   1991
787.87'19'0296—dc20   90-28593
                                                        CIP
                                                            MN

Published 1991 by a cappella books, Incorporated
Editorial offices:
PO Box 380
Pennington, NJ 08534

Business/sales office:
814 N. Franklin St.
Chicago, IL 60610

Cover photograph courtesy J. W. Gallagher and Son Guitars
Cover design by Fran Lee
Line art by Fred Hickler, based on computer drawings
  by Larry Sandberg

How to Use This Book

Scope

This book will help you buy a steel-string acoustic guitar and will help you understand how it works once you have bought it. Even if you already own a guitar and have no intention of looking for a new one, you'll find lots of information that will help you get the best out of it--and out of yourself as well.

The main focus is on flattop acoustic guitars with six strings--the kind of instrument that most people think of when they think of the guitar. Other kinds of guitars are described a little, but this book is not really about them.

Redundancy

You're welcome to read through this book cover-to-cover if you care to, but I assume you won't. It seems to me the kind of book that you'll treat more like a business consultant than like a steady date. On the theory that you'll be going to it from time to time to look up specific details, I haven't hesitated to mention things more than once if you're likely to need to know about them in more than one place. (Or, to paraphrase the old saw, anything worth saying is worth saying twice.)

Money

Except through luck or trickery, a really good guitar is going to cost you a fair bunch of money—money that's hard to earn, or that you are reluctant to spend, or that you just may not have right now. Since the ideal is one thing and reality is another, I've tried to offer sensible, balanced advice and recommendations for entry-level and midrange buyers.

The prices given in the instrument guide section were accurate at the time this book went into production, but are probably no longer so by the time you're reading this. Prices from all manufacturers can be expected to rise relative to each other, so you can still use the figures in this book for comparisons and ball park budgeting. Once you narrow down your interest to several brands, I suggest you write to the manufacturers for their catalogs and price lists.

In any case, you'll find once you get into the market that dealers usually discount, so street prices may vary considerably from list.

Words

There are lots of reasons why one guitar is different from another. Size, shape, wood, and design all play a part; so, in fine guitars, does the magic of the individual craftsperson's touch. The way you learn about guitars is not by reading books, but by playing and handling lots of instruments until you come to hear the difference between rosewood and mahogany, between a boomy guitar and a balanced one. A book can never teach you to hear the difference between a played-in old guitar, a brand-new guitar with a sound that hasn't opened up yet, and a new guitar that will *never* open up. What a book can do is to tell you that these differences do exist, and why they exist, and that you need to learn to recognize them.

So don't try to memorize a lot of words out of this book. Use it to teach yourself what to look for when you visit music stores to try out various guitars. Make it your business to do so. Memorize the feel and sound of the guitars instead of my words about them.

You'll also come to understand that what makes a guitar play and feel the way it does is not just the bracing, or the choice of wood, or the strings, or the instrument's size, but rather the way all these factors combine and relate to each other in each individual instrument.

Because so many factors are interdependent, it's not always easy to explain something without referring to something else that doesn't get explained until a later section. For that reason, I've included a hefty and detailed glossary at the end of the book, so you can check up on any terms you may not know. Use it! In fact, you can probably learn a lot about the guitar, or review what you've learned from this book, just by reading through the glossary.

Generalizations

The more you know about a field, the more difficult it becomes to make any statement, because all the exceptions and anomalies that you've encountered flood your mind. It can lead to paralysis. It can also lead to bad writing, with an abundance of hedging and ambiguity, and the proliferation of "usually," "as a rule," and "generally speaking."

I've indulged quite heartily in "generally speaking," but even so, this book contains plenty of blanket statements to which there are numerous exceptions. This is especially true of the many specifications concerning the dimensions of parts and adjustments. Always remember that general information is for your guidance, but that the instrument you hold in your hand may be unique.

Acknowledgments

Many thanks for help along the way to Richard Carlin (who asked me to write this book, and then edited it with aquiline eye), Harry Fleishman, Dennis Kercher, Max Krimmel, Eileen Niehouse, Robin Rockley,

John Rossi, Charles Sawtelle, Dennis Stevens, Steve Wiencrot, and the many luthiers and guitar manufacturers who helped supply information and illustrations.

But after all this fine help, the buck still stops here: with the author. If there are any errors of fact in this book I would like to hear about them for future correction. Please write me in care of a cappella books, Box 380, Pennington, NJ, 08534.

Larry Sandberg

PART I

All About the Guitar

The Guitar from Then to Now

Ancient History

Sound is produced by motion, and the stringed instruments almost certainly owe their origin to the twang heard in the motion of the ancient hunter's bowstring. It must have been that one day an early artistic genius, too impractical to invent the wheel, instead discovered that the sound of the bowstring could be enhanced by attaching a resonating chamber—most likely a tortoiseshell—to the bow. From the bow come the three main types of stringed instruments that are recognized by musical instrument scholars: the *harp family* (where the sound of plucked strings is indirectly transmitted to an attached sound chamber), the *lyre family* (where strings of fixed pitch are attached directly to the sound chamber), and the *lute family* (where the pitch of the strings is altered by pressing them against a neck that is attached to the sound chamber). Being the analytical sorts that they are, scholars divide the lute family into lutes proper (with round backs) and guitar-type instruments (with flat backs)—not to mention banjos, mandolins, the Japanese samisen, the Chinese pyiba, the Greek bouzouki, the West African kora, or any other of the manifold shapes of plucked stringed instrument that human ingenuity has created.

Anthony Rooley of the Consort of Musicke, playing the lute. *Photo courtesy Byers, Schwalbe & Associates.*

The earliest stringed instrument we know of seems to be the one that ultimately gave the guitar its name, even though it was a member of the lyre family: the Assyrian *chetarah* of about 2000 BC, with five strings fixed to a tortoise shell resonator. The first documentation we have of an instrument in the lute family comes from about 700 years later. By then, Egyptian tomb-carvings and pottery paintings showed men and women playing the *nefer*, which looks something like a loaf of bread with a broomstick for a neck. Presumably it sounded better than it looked, or at least tasted better. Perhaps it was this instrument that inspired Jimi Hendrix to eat his guitar.

From about the same time we also have Hittite carvings from Turkey showing an instrument much more guitar-like in appearance. Later on, the ancient Greeks came up with their own version of the lute. Called the *pandoura*, it was never as popular with them, or with their successors the Romans, as were the *kithara* (harp) and *lyra* (lyre).

The Dark and Light Ages

We don't know much about what went on during the Dark Ages after the fall of Rome—after all, there's a reason we call them the Dark Ages. But by the time we get into the Middle Ages, we have ample evidence of many exciting changes: a proliferation of bowed instruments, and the musical and technological development of the lute in the high Arabic culture of Spain and North Africa. (Arabic *al-'ud*, meaning "the wood," is where our word "lute" comes from.) And the Arabic term for a flatbacked lute, *qitara*, seems to have been the immediate source for the Spanish word *guitarra*.

While the roundback lutes became courtly professional instruments, the fiddles and the flatbacked guitars became the instruments for ordinary folks. Illustrated manuscripts, church frescoes, and stone carvings from the 14th through the 16th centuries show men, women, biblical figures, and angels performing on instruments of the guitar and violin families with names like *gitterns, citterns, citharas, fidels, rebecs, viols, vielles,* and *vihuelas*. Some of the actual players of the day, it seems, were less than angelic. In a blast from the 14th century, the English preacher John Wycliffe complained of musicians who used "veyn songis and knackynge and harpynge, gyternynge and dauncynge, and othere veyn triflis to geten the stynkynge love of damyselis." Some things never change.

The Renaissance and Baroque periods were a time of continuing variety in stringed instruments, with all sizes and shapes of lutes, guitars, and fiddles moving in and out of fashion. The *Syntagma Musicum* of Michael Praetorious and *Musurgia Universalis* of Athanasius Kircher, which for all practical purposes you may think of as the *Buyer's Guides to the Musical Instrument Industry* for the years 1620 and 1650, showed page after page of drawings of lute- and guitar-like instruments. In these catalogs, the various roundback lutes still outnumbered the flatbacked guitar-family instruments, which had names like *quinterna, cythara,* and *mandora*. This is not surprising considering the lute's courtly preeminence and the fact that some of the greatest music of the time—the lute works of John Dowland, for example—had been written for it.

Like the lute, most of the guitar-family instruments of this time were *double-strung*: that is to say, they were fitted with pairs of closely-placed strings as on today's 12-string guitar, tuned at the unison or, in the case of some bass strings, at the octave. (One finger pressed down both strings at the same time. Such groups of strings are called *courses*, a handy term that can apply to any grouping of strings from one up to three—or even more in theory, though I can't recall ever hearing of an instrument with more than three strings to a course.)

Often the highest course was a single string, for greatest melodic clarity. (This is the normal way lutes are strung.) There was little stand-ardization of instrument configurations, or even of their names, at this time. At the beginning of the 1500s in Spain, two instruments emerged: the *vihuela*, with six courses of strings, and the simpler *guitarra*, with only four courses (which corresponded to the four inside courses of the vihuela). Because the vihuela, with its two extra courses, was more apt for the expression of composed counterpoint, this instrument was generally associated with professional court musicians and their noble patrons. The music of Narvaéz, Mudarra, de Milán, and other such 16th-century *vihuelistas* is still regularly performed and recorded in transcription by concert guitarists. The easier-to-play guitarra, on the other hand, was a more popular instrument associated with minstrels and the lower classes. It was common to see a guitarra hanging in a barbershop for the use of waiting customers, and the instrument ap-pears in the hands of tavern musicians and peasant folk in the work of painters like Velazquez and the Brueghels.

Instruments at this time had strings made of sheepgut. Sheepgut was also used for frets, which were tied around the neck and fingerboard. The vihuela was typically tuned (low to high) GCFADG and the guitar CFAD. But by around 1600, guitars were being made with five courses of strings tuned ADGBE, which has remained the standard tuning for the guitar's five highest strings ever since. Guitars at this time (and into the 19th century) were smaller in size and less full-figured in shape than they are today.

The lute, during this period after 1600, acquired many more strings—even extra bass strings attached to an extra neck—and became increas-ingly complex, unwieldy, and temperamental. It was a well-worn witticism that lutanists only tuned, never actually played. Meanwhile, the five-course guitar, known in Spain as the *guitarra castellana* ("Cas-tilian guitar") and throughout the rest of Europe by its Italian name of *chitarra spagnuola* ("Spanish guitar"), was played so much by all classes of society that eventually it drove the lute and vihuela players out of business. The guitar's currency extended throughout all Europe by the end of the 15th century, and even such exalted personages as King Louis XIV of France and King Charles II of England were devotees. (What an allstar band *that* would have made! Unfortunately, their managers didn't get along.)

Development of the
Modern Classical Guitar

The guitar remained popular in Spain during the 1700s, but it declined in other parts of Europe as the harpsichord became more fashionable. (At one point, the guitar experienced a brief resurgence among English gentlewomen, who almost brought the harpsichord industry to bankruptcy when they sold off their instruments in droves. The shrewd harpsichord manufacturers put short shrift to the fad by distributing cheap guitars among shop-girls, ballad-singers, and other such vulgar lowlifes, soon driving the embarrassed gentry back to their keyboards.)

Although occasional guitars with six courses of strings had begun to appear in France and Spain, it wasn't until almost 1800 that the sixth (low E) course really caught on. About the same time, guitarists began to abandon double-stringing, resulting in the six-string EADGBE configuration that remains standard to the present day. (Other historical offshoots include the 12-string guitar, and the amazing variety of guitars of all sizes and shapes with single, double, and even triple-strung courses that are used in Spain and Latin America.)

The 19th century saw a new trans-European revival of the guitar, even in Germany, the last stronghold of the lute. Almost everyone took it up: the composers von Weber, Schubert, Rossini, and Berlioz; the songwriter Thomas Moore; the writer and activist Giuseppi Mazzini; the violinist Niccolò Paganini; all manner of lords and ladies, budding romantic poets, young lovers, and even plain folks like you and me. The Duke of Wellington's officers brought home guitars from Spain and France after the Napoleonic Wars, and so once more they became fashionable in England. Paris, Vienna, and Berlin were seized during the second and third decades of the century by what the French called *la guitaromanie*, and there was plenty of work for a new crop of international teachers and performer-virtuosos like Matteo Carcassi, Dionysio Aguado, Ferdinando Carulli, Mauro Giuliani, and Fernando Sor. Their concert and teaching pieces are still in standard use today.

Though the guitars they played had the 12-fret neck that is still standard on classical guitars today, they were small in body size and in voice as well. They were typically constructed with tops reinforced by several braces (wooden struts) running laterally under the top, parallel to the bridge. This *transverse bracing* pattern fulfills a basic function of keeping the guitar from warping or pulling apart under pressure from the strings, but it doesn't contribute much to sound. Even Sor, who encouraged luthiers to experiment with lighter woods in order to achieve greater resonance, only had transverse-braced guitars to play.

But fashions come and go. By 1850 the guitar had once more retreated

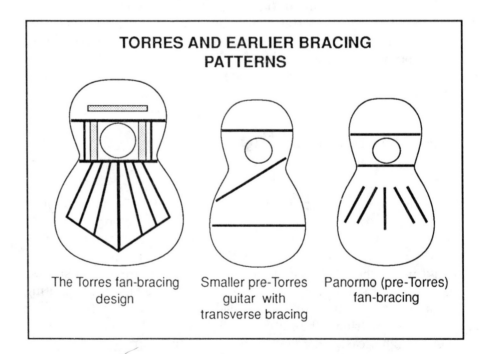

TORRES AND EARLIER BRACING PATTERNS

The Torres fan-bracing design

Smaller pre-Torres guitar with transverse bracing

Panormo (pre-Torres) fan-bracing

to its traditional refuge, Spain. It was vanquished in the rest of Europe by a new and domineering fad: the modern piano, and its new stars, Chopin and Liszt. And it was fitting that in Spain, the guitar's spiritual home, it should be reborn in modern form.

The basic form of the classical guitar as we know it today was achieved by a carpenter-turned-luthier named Antonio Torres (or, more formally, Antonio de Torres Jurado; 1817–1892). By 1850, Torres had developed a revolutionary seven-strut fan-shaped bracing pattern for the guitar's top, and enlarged its body size and fingerboard length. The result was an astounding improvement in projection, dynamic range, and tone quality. Visually, he established for the instrument's shape a set of proportions that has never been surpassed for grace of line, and cut down on the excessive inlay and ornamentation that had burdened many earlier instruments. He was also the first important maker to routinely use geared tuning pegs, rather than violin-style wooden pegs held in place by friction.

We owe the present state of classical guitar music to Francisco Tárrega (1852–1909), the guitarist, composer, and transcriber who laid the foundation of contemporary technique, and to the late Andrés Segovia (1894–1987), who established the contemporary standards of repertory and performance. It's likely that neither of them would have been able to make their contributions had it not been for the design achievements of Torres. While modern luthiers continue to develop and diverge from the Torres design, it's still accepted as the root from which all other flowers have sprung.

C. F. Martin and the American Guitar

The guitar was present in America from colonial times. Benjamin Franklin and the first Secretary of the Navy, Francis Hopkinson, both played. In Latin America, of course, the Portuguese and Spanish settlers brought over all manner of guitars and vihuelas from Iberia. They were readily adopted by the native peoples, who developed them into many new breeds and species.

A small following for the classical guitar was present in America during the 19th century, and the names of the leading teachers of the era are still known to us. They lived mainly in cities like New York, Philadelphia, and Cincinnati, where the traditions of upper middle-class European culture were actively preserved. Probably most of the guitar music played and taught in 19th-century America was in the now-forgotten "parlor guitar" genre, which featured light classical arrangements of European and popular American melodies.

The 19th century also saw the emergence of C. F. Martin & Co. (now called the Martin Guitar Company) as the leading manufacturer of American guitars, a position it retains to the present day. A more complete history of the Martin company appears in Part II of this book, but since the history of the American guitar is in large part the history of the Martin guitar, it's important to mention a few details here as well.

Guitar-maker Christian Frederick Martin emigrated from Saxony to the United States in 1833, bringing with him a mastery of pre-Torres

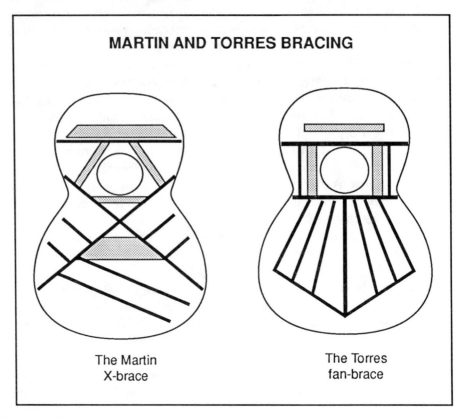

MARTIN AND TORRES BRACING

The Martin
X-brace

The Torres
fan-brace

guitar design in the Viennese style. By the 1850s, though, he developed a new bracing pattern based on two large struts that crossed, like an X, slightly below the bridge. Like the Torres fan-brace, it was an improvement over the transverse-braced sound of the German and French guitars, and by the end of the 19th century it was copied by many other American makers.

As it turned out, Martin's X-brace wasn't as effective for the classical guitar sound as the Torres design. Meanwhile, though, something else was happening in American music that made the Torres guitar irrelevant. Beginning around 1900, steel strings, with their brighter sound and their response more suitable for strumming, began to replace gut in popular use. The Martin X-brace could withstand the higher tension of steel strings, and enhanced their brighter sound. By the end of the 1920s, steel strings had almost completely replaced gut except among classical guitarists, and the X-brace had been adopted as an industry standard.

The Early Years of the Steel-String Guitar

The guitar was a relative newcomer to American popular and folk music (following the banjo by several decades and the fiddle by several centuries), but once steel strings came in, its place was assured. By the time disk recording began in the twenties, blues singers had already developed a number of brilliant regional and personal guitar styles. The guitar had also by then achieved a place in southern white stringband music.

The first few decades of this century saw guitars getting larger and larger. 19th-century guitars were tiny by today's standards, and even the largest ("auditorium-size") guitars of the late twenties are now thought of as small by most guitarists. But thanks to pioneers like the early country music singer Jimmie Rodgers, the guitar was increasingly being used as a solo accompaniment for the voice.

Bigger Guitars for the Thirties

As the guitar began to find a place in the new musical styles of this century, musicians wanted instruments with powerful, booming bass notes in order to provide a strong bottom for vocal accompaniments, and to provide bass runs and fills in stringband music. Martin and Gibson, as well as long-gone makers like the now-classic Bacon & Day, Prairie State, and Euphonon companies, turned increasingly to the production of larger instruments during the decades from 1900 to 1930. Bigger guitars, as a rule, mean that the sound balance of the instrument becomes bottom-heavy and the quality of the high notes gets sacrificed, but that's what people wanted (and still do).

In 1931 Martin first introduced a deep, wide-bodied, broad-waisted model that they named the *dreadnought* after a famous battleship of the time. Few guitars since have equalled the power and bass projection of the classic dreadnoughts that came out of the Martin factory during the first decade of their production. The dreadnought shape (like Martin's other innovation, the X-brace) is so widely copied that it's now an industry standard. (Martin had made dreadnought-style guitars for other marketers before 1931, but it was not until that year that they aggressively marketed the style under their own name. For more on the dreadnought, see chapter 13 in Part II.)

The other major manufacturer, Gibson, developed a large-bodied but narrow-waisted design called the jumbo, which eventually evolved into the classic J-200 model. Eventually Gibson also developed its own versions of the dreadnought, which were also somewhat confusingly catalogued as "jumbo" guitars. But Gibsons have always had a completely different sound from Martins: sweeter, less boomy, usually not as loud.

But while the tastes of early country music singers and guitarists were turning toward bottom-heavy sound balance, blues guitarists continued to favor instruments with sound balanced toward the high end. The twenties and thirties saw the flowering of the great country blues stylists whose influence pervades today's music. Their music was based mostly on melodies and licks played on the high strings while the bass strings supplied a rhythmic undercurrent, so it was important that the sound of the bass strings not dominate the high strings. A combination of taste and racial economics joined together in leading blues guitarists to prefer the thicker high notes and thuddy basses of Gibsons and of lower-priced instruments like the Regals and Stellas of that time, rather than the clearer, brighter, and more expensive Martin sound. Many blues players even used *resophonic* guitars, in which metal resonators produce strong highs ranging in character from throaty and twangy to thick and syrupy. (See chapter 2 for more on resonator guitars.)

Around 1930, it became fashionable to make guitars whose bodies began at the fourteenth rather than the twelfth fret. (In other words, there were two extra frets that could be reached by the player's fingers because the body was no longer in the way. Classical guitars and a very few steel-string models are still made with 12-fret necks.) The designers did this by flattening out the shoulders to shorten the body a little, rather than by adding frets or making the neck longer. This takes a bit of cubic volume out of the upper bout.

The extraordinarily powerful Martin dreadnoughts of the thirties are the most sought-after guitars on the market today, but superb instruments of other shapes and sizes also came out of the Martin factory during this time. The Gibson product line was more varied in quality level (their low end was lower than Martins and their high end not generally as high), but many great instruments also came out of their factory in Kalamazoo, Michigan. Those who prefer the old Gibson sound to the old Martin sound, among whom are many country blues players, can also find exciting instruments from this era.

The Forties and Fifties

The late forties and the fifties were the low point in the recent history of the acoustic guitar. Even the classical guitar world could support only one performer, Segovia, as a full-time concert artist of international stature—and even so, he was viewed as something of an oddity. Mainstream pop had some use for archtop guitars (and they were mostly electrified), but almost none for the acoustic flattop guitar. In Nashville, the acoustic guitar was used for the most part for rhythmic texture or informal accompaniment, but in the studios and on the road the electric guitar and pedal steel ruled the lead and solo roost. In blues, in jazz, in rockabilly and early rock, the electric guitar was experiencing a healthy and vital period of development.

Electric guitar was in; acoustic guitar was out. It survived only in isolated rural pockets, among the few professional practitioners of bluegrass and acoustic country music who could make a living in those days, and in the small urban folk music scene, mostly affiliated with left/labor politics and songmaking, which was lying underground ready to burst forth in the sixties.

Martin deserves a lot of credit for holding the acoustic guitar fort during the late forties and early fifties. The Martin company was really the only game in town for new high-quality acoustic guitars in those days. The people at Gibson had their minds on electric guitars. The Guild company started up in the early fifties and eventually made good flattops, but their business at first was concentrated on archtops and electrics. Decent sounding, more poorly made guitars were also available at this time from lesser makers like Favilla and the Swedish Goya firm. Cheapies came from makers and distributors who used names like Harmony, Kay, and Regal—names that had been around for decades, and are still used by marketers today for Asian import lines. And don't forget the Silvertone guitars from Sears and Roebuck, which were usually made by Kay, Harmony, or other factories. There are thousands of good guitarists out there whose first instrument was a Silvertone.

The Folk Boom and Beyond

At the end of the fifties, the Kingston Trio achieved mainstream commercial success singing more-or-less folk songs while strumming a guitar, banjo, and tenor guitar. They demonstrated to the entertainment industry that there was a buck to be made with acoustic guitars. Guitar sales began to pick up. Changing demographics and a shift in the tastes and social standards of the college generation created a strong base of support for the new trend, which tapped into the latent folk music underground for ideas and inspiration. Young talents emerged, old talents were dragged out of the woodwork, and singers with guitars in their hands began to appear regularly on the college circuit. Folk festivals became popular. Suddenly, guitars were making lots of bucks, and lots of friends, too. Guitars meant freedom and sex. Everybody wanted to play. Even the classical guitar market began to expand, reaching proportions today that would have been thought impossible in 1960. The folk boom and subsequent development of rock put guitars into millions of hands, and moved the mainstream sound of American pop music from the piano-, band-, and orchestra-oriented 32-bar song form (conceived mostly in the flat keys) to guitar-oriented, blues- and folk-song forms conceived mainly in sharp keys. It has been a major revolution.

Musicians used a motley assortment of guitars in those days. If you were just starting out, you could pick up a used Harmony or Kay for next to nothing, or, if you had a little more change in your jeans, a Goya or Favilla. You could get used Martins and Gibsons at prices that would make you laugh (or maybe cry) today. You could always count on finding a dependable guitar to play when you went visiting. Whether new or used, Martins and Gibsons were the guitars most professionals and aspirants wanted in those days, though a few were attracted to instruments from the relatively new Guild company.

The music of the Beatles divided the folk music community. Traditionalists, their numbers swelled, returned underground. Protest song remained in the forefront because it was so important to the civil rights and antiwar movements. But Bob Dylan went electric, and a lot of folkies went with him. (He'd always been interested in rockabilly and country music, but to have admitted that in the purist folkie circles that gave him his start would have been bad politics.) Many of the brightest developing talents of the folk music boom turned to electric music, giving birth to hybrid groups like the Buffalo Springfield which profoundly influenced the sound of music today. (At the same time many rockers also became influenced by acoustic music: witness John Lennon's acoustic sound on songs like the Beatles' "Norwegian Wood." And many of the brightest developing talents coming from non-"folk" markets also began to play a hybrid music influenced by the folk movement. Witness what happened to the group that was backing up barroom rockabilly singer Ronnie Hawkins, now a minor cult figure. They went to work for Bob Dylan and, for want of a better name, eventually started calling themselves The Band.)

Ironically, it was probably the electronic impact of the Beatles that permitted the acoustic guitar to maintain its position as a separate but equal partner to the electric guitar. The new sound mixing technologies used in multitrack recording and stadium-level amplification permitted the acoustic guitar (miked or with a pickup) to still remain part of an electric band. Without that technology, the acoustic guitar might have been relegated to amateur and cult use. Instead it has remained an important part of the musical mainstream. We'll see whether it stays so as synthesizers and samplers become more common in the next few years.

The sixties brought about a renewed interest in making guitars as well as playing them. Many youngsters began to explore the art of luthiery, with the result that they were able to produce instruments of fine quality by the seventies, and to establish their reputations by the eighties. Today's proliferation of guitarists with money to spend gives the luthiers a strong enough market to survive, helped out by repair work on the hundreds of thousands of instruments that have found their way into people's hands over the past 25 years. (For more about what contemporary luthiers have to offer, see chapter 15.) The increasing number of skilled craftspeople has also made it possible for newer American companies (like Santa Cruz, Taylor, and Gibson's Montana Division) to compete with Martin by staffing factories capable of turning out production-line instruments of high quality.

New styles of music have also brought about changing tastes in instruments. A generation of players used to the fast, smooth feel of electric guitar necks and fingerboards have caused many manufacturers to offer similar-feeling acoustic guitars, while the technical and stylistic demands of ragtime, contemporary Celtic, new-age, and other "new acoustic" fingerpicking styles have called for a new breed of fast, resonant instruments with response characteristics close to those of a classical guitar. Preconceptions and prejudices have almost entirely killed off the small-bodied guitar in the marketplace, with the result that many people simply don't know what they're missing. And, of course, the increased demand for electric sound has brought about the invention of the electro-acoustic guitar with built-in electronics, designed entirely for an amplified environment.

The demand for more guitars, coupled with changing economics, has also led to a growing import market. The Japanese jumped in as demand grew during the sixties, at first with inexpensive plywood student guitars. A familiar pattern of development followed: the quality of Japanese products improved, cheaper products of lower quality started coming out of Taiwan and Korea, and now the quality of these products has begun to improve as well.

As the guitar market moves closer to the 21st century, it must—along with the rest of the world—deal with the question of diminishing natural resources. Already we are several decades past the point where fine grades of the favored traditional guitar woods—rosewood from Brazil, spruce from the subalpine regions of Europe—have become too rare to be used on any but limited-production guitar models. The same may happen soon to today's standards: Sitka (Pacific Northwest) spruce and Indian rosewood. Woods unheard of a few years ago are now in common use: for example, nato instead of mahogany for guitar necks. Veneers and laminates (in other words, plywoods) have replaced solid woods on all but the most expensive guitars, and in fact are so typically used by the guitar industry that it's hard to tell from catalogs, merchandise labels, and dealers' sales raps exactly what it is you're buying. The Ovation company has been in the unique marketing position of offering guitars made of synthetic materials for many years, and it's hard to imagine that all the traditional manufacturers, even those with the most conservative image, aren't also casting an experimental eye in the direction of synthetics. If they're not doing so now, they will be in the future. They'll have to.

We've seen that the guitar first began to achieve the form in which we know it today during the 1700s, and since then has been bouncing in and out of fashion every few generations. Its enduring appeal seems to lie in its intimacy, its relative simplicity, and musical fullness. A single person can get more music out of a piano, but at extreme cost of money, space, and portability. Only a few people ever learn to play the guitar really well, but most people can learn to coax satisfying music out of it with only a short learning curve. It may be the friendliest of musical instruments.

2

It Takes All Kinds

Folk Guitars

This book is about the steel-string acoustic flattop guitar. Some people also call it the folk guitar. It's versatile, it's accessible, and it sounds good whether you strum chords or play individual notes, whether you use a flatpick, fingerpicks, or bare fingers. You can use it to play country songs, traditional folk songs, blues, and new-age music. You can use it to express in its own voice many styles of pop, jazz, and rock. You can learn to accompany your singing, you can strum rhythms, or you can play solos. It comes in different sizes and shapes, each with a slightly different character. It's probably the kind of guitar you want. It's the kind of guitar most people want. But let's take a quick look at some other kinds of acoustic guitars, just to make sure you won't be happier with one of these instead.

The 12-String Guitar

If six strings aren't enough for you, you can always try more. The 12-string guitar is played just like a 6-string, except for the small adjustments in touch, style, and concept that you may have to make. Its 12 strings are mounted in six pairs ("courses"). In each of the two highest courses, the strings are tuned to the unison (the same as each other), but in the lowest four courses the strings are tuned in octaves. Even though I2-string guitars are built for extra sturdiness, they're usually tuned a whole tone (two frets) lower than 6-strings in order to help reduce the amount of tension on the instrument's neck and body. Some players even like to tune yet another tone lower, which can make for a bassy, growly sound.

The sound of the 12-string is full, resonant, and apt to be a bit messy in the wrong hands. It can be very rich-sounding for accompanying singing with simple strumming (John Denver), it adds an important texture to many styles of Hispanic music, and it can be a uniquely

A typical folk guitar; in this case, a Saga BR-85 dreadnought. *Photo courtesy Saga Musical Instruments.*

A Martin 12-string guitar. *Photo courtesy Martin Guitar Co.*

expressive instrument in the hands of a skilled stylist (Leadbelly, Willie McTell, Marc Silber, Pete Seeger, Michael Cooney, Leo Kottke).

Many of the old bluesmen adapted the 12-string to their own sounds by using only nine, ten, or eleven of the possible strings, in one or another combination. By leaving one, two, or three of the upper courses strung singly, it's possible to achieve a clearly expressed melody on top and a rich, highly-textured bass accompaniment.

If you admire the music of the 12-string guitar then there may be one in your future, but I'd advise you to get a 6-string first— it's much easier to learn on. Almost everyone who enjoys the 12-string enjoys it as a second instrument. And remember that, although the 12-string has only twice as many strings as the 6- string, it seems to take four times longer to get one in tune.

Part II of this book lists a variety of models in all price ranges that are now available from most of the the important manufacturers. But it wasn't always so. Apparently a fair number of 12-strings were made by low- and midrange American manufacturers in the late 19th century, and Martin made a handful of experimental prototypes in the thirties, but Gibson, Martin, and Guild didn't turn out production-model acoustic 12-strings until 1962–64.

The great classic country blues guitarists who used 12-strings, like Leadbelly and Willie McTell, played instruments made in the thirties and forties by lesser manufacturers like Stella and Regal. In the fifties and early sixties, 12-string players had to make do with cheap, undependable Mexican models, or have custom conversions made on sturdy 6-strings. Today the sixties folk boom has faded, but good 12-strings are easier to come by now than ever before because their sound has become an accepted texture in contemporary music. The instrument itself has changed as well. Some models are like the 12-strings of old: heavy, brash, hard-to-play monsters that boom and jangle and handle like a jeep. But others are more like sports cars: airy-sounding, meant to be responsive to light strings, with slender, more comfortable necks.

The Classical Guitar

The history and nature of the classical guitar are described in the first chapter of this book. If you're serious about learning to play the music of Bach, Sor, and Tárrega, this is the instrument to have. It's built and braced to work with nylon strings. Steel strings aren't right for playing classical guitar music. People who think otherwise are kidding themselves.

On the other hand, the classical guitar's nylon strings don't provide the tonal resources that the blues, country, traditional, and new acoustic idioms demand. They don't have a bright ring when strummed; they just aren't designed to do this. A few stylists with a highly individual touch—Chet Atkins, Guy van Duser, Willie Nelson, and (sometimes) Jerry Reed among them—have found ways of using nylon strings in these kinds of music, but they're really not for most people. I wouldn't recommend you get a classical guitar unless you have very good reason to think you'll be happy with one. Or unless, of course, you want to play classical guitar music. (There is an exception, though. If you're looking for a cheap kid-size instrument for your youngster to start on, it's easier to find, and afford, one of the off-brand Korean-made classical instruments than to get a steel-string model. For most kids, nylon strings will do just fine for starters.)

Classical guitars are smaller than most steel-string guitars, and have broader fingerboards. Good ones are much more lightly built than steel-string guitars. Necks aren't reinforced the way steel-string necks need to be. Nylon strings don't put as much energy into the top, so the top and bracing have to be much lighter in order for the strings to set them vibrating. Don't *ever* put steel strings on a classical guitar. They just can't take it. You'll destroy the instrument, and quickly, too.

Fine steel-string guitars are in their prime by the time they reach 50 years of age, but fine classical guitars, because of their lightness, tend to burn out their voices by then and have to be retired.

The Flamenco Guitar

These are essentially a subspecies of classical guitar, adapted especially for the Spanish Gypsy music called flamenco. They're often built a bit more shallow than classical guitars, with some other minor structural differences. They are usually equipped with wooden violin-style friction pegs to make the headstock lighter. This makes it easier to balance the instrument on the player's lap in the traditional flamenco playing position, where the guitar is held more erect than it is for classical or folk playing.

The traditional body wood for flamenco guitars is Spanish cypress, a softwood, rather than the rosewood or other hardwoods used for classical instruments. This gives flamenco guitars a sharp, brittle sound that cuts right through hands clapping, castanets tapping, bottles clinking, shouts of "olé!," and dancers' feet pounding on the floorboards. The essence of flamenco rhythm is in the forceful strumming patterns called *rasgueados*. Flamenco guitars are made to sound tight and punchy when you strum them hard—just the opposite of classical guitars, which sound airy, messy, and generally untogether when you ask them to do the same job. (In fact, the better a classical guitar is at producing plucked sounds, the worse it sounds when strummed.)

Flamenco guitars are special-purpose instruments. They're superb at what they do best, but not many people like them for other kinds of music. And, like classical guitars, they burn out in the course of their careers. Even faster. It must be the flamenco spirit.

Archtop and Electric Guitars

How Archtops Work

The archtop guitar owes its design to the violin. Instruments of the violin family have tops and backs that are carved from a thicker board into an arched shape, rather than cut flat. A master builder will tune the top and back while carving them, tapping them from time to time to judge the

Archtop guitar by Linda Manzer.
Photo © 1990 by Mark Brickell,
courtesy Linda Manzer.

sound and determine where and how much the wood should be graduated (thinned). On cheaper mass-produced guitars, the sides and back are plywood that is steamed and pressed into shape.

Most archtop guitars now use violin-like f-shaped soundholes, which were popularized in the 1920s on the Gibson company's classic L-5 guitars and F-5 mandolins. Before that, archtop guitars and mandolins followed Orville Gibson's original design with a round or elliptical soundhole.

Flattops and archtops both look like guitars and walk like guitars, but they quack like two entirely different animals. Underneath the top of the flattop is a complicated system of bracing struts, while archtops use only two long struts called *tone bars*. The strings of flattop guitars are held in place by pins in the bridge, whereas the strings on archtops merely rest on the bridge, and then run into a holding bracket called the *tailpiece* that screws into the end of the guitar.

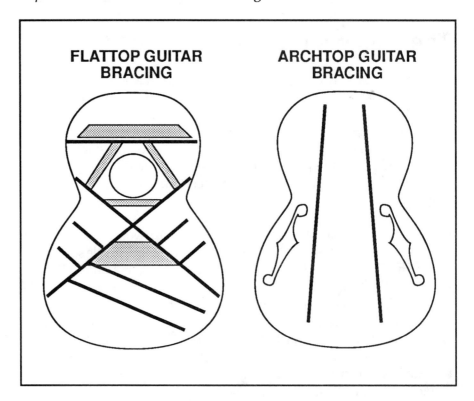

FLATTOP GUITAR BRACING   **ARCHTOP GUITAR BRACING**

As a result of these structural differences, the soundboards move according to different physical principles. An archtop soundboard moves up and down, whereas a flattop soundboard moves in complicated twisting patterns that vary depending on the pitches being produced. As a result, the sounds produced by either instrument have different characters and occupy completely different musical spaces in ensembles. In addition, the pressure of the strings on archtop guitars (and violin-family instruments, for that matter) is implosive, forcing the body joints in on themselves. But on flattops, the string tension is explosive, pulling the instrument apart rather than compressing it.

The original function of the archtop guitar was to provide a punchy, supportive beat in the rhythm section of big bands—a beat more felt by the other players than heard by the audience. It accomplishes this not by overwhelming the other instruments, but by projecting cannonballs of compressed sound that find their way into spaces between the other instruments.

The Great Archtop Guitars

The archtop guitar replaced the 4-string banjo in jazz rhythm sections. As American music moved out of the twenties, the sound of the banjos used in early jazz bands was too clanky and unpliable to keep up with the new textures and rhythms. Yet the original round-hole archtop guitars were too slow to speak, too wooly-sounding, too lacking in clarity and projection to provide an effective substitute. When the Gibson company's designers Lewis Williams and Lloyd Loar perfected the f-hole archtop guitar in the twenties, it was the right instrument in the right place at the right time.

In their heyday, the great archtop guitars came from the Gibson and Epiphone factories and from the workshops of John D'Angelico and Charles and Elmer Stromberg. Most Gibsons and some D'Angelicos are good for jazz single-line and chord-style solo playing. Epiphones (a product line of mixed quality and characteristics), Strombergs, the Gibson Super-400 models and some others, and many D'Angelicos are generally more suited for punchy rhythm section work.

F-hole guitars of one sort and another were also made by other companies, including not only the cheapie producers like Harmony and Kay, but also high-quality manufacturers like Martin, Prairie State, and Vega. Some of these instruments had arched tops but flat backs. Most of these instruments have a sound which did not achieve great favor in their day or in more recent days; they are more sought after as collectibles and curiosities than as player's instruments.

Electric Archtops

As electrified instruments became increasingly more popular from the 1940s on, the factories let the quality of their acoustic guitars become inconsistent (though some very fine instruments continued to be made). Gibson and Epiphone began to mount pickups in the top of the guitar. This cut down on the top's projection, which didn't matter if the instrument was going to be played amplified all the time. But once you start doing this, you then start asking yourself: Why bother to do a fine job of top-carving in the first place? (If you want to electrify a finely-made acoustic archtop guitar without messing up the top, the way to do it is with a *floating pickup*. This mounts on the end of the fingerboard or on the pickguard, without interfering with the top.)

While the electric archtop depends more on its pickups and amplifier to determine its sound, it still has a character and clarity that makes it sound quite different from contemporary-style solidbody electric guitars. The mainstream jazz and fifties rockabilly sounds (especially the rockabilly sounds of Gretsch guitars) are both creatures of the electric f-hole guitar, and you can't really get them on solidbodies.

Solidbody Electrics

In the late forties, the Fender company pioneered solidbody electric

Albert Collins. *Photo by Larry Sandberg.*

guitars. In a solidbody guitar, the sound is totally electric. The body, being solid wood, offers no acoustic resonance, but its mass promotes sustain. Vibrational energy, not being dissipated into the top or an air chamber, tends to stay in the string. Gibson soon followed Fender with its own solidbody lines, including the classic Les Paul design. Gibson also pioneered a series of semi-hollowbody guitars, like B. B. King's Lucille, which combine a solid wood strut down the middle of the body with small air chambers on either side.

Modern Archtop Guitars

As we move into the 1990s, there are a handful of luthiers still making high-quality acoustic archtop guitars, and a number of formerly electrified jazz guitarists, notably the great Jim Hall, have cultivated the beauties of the pure acoustic sound. In addition, there's a renewed curiosity in round-hole carved arch-tops, and a few luthiers now offer such models. You'll also find several round-hole archtop models offered by the mass manufacturers in their electro-acoustic series, but these generally have pressed wood tops with flat backs, flattop-style bracing, and no tailpiece, so their response is essentially that of a regular flattop guitar.

Among the well-reputed North American luthiers and shops making acoustic f-hole guitars today are Steven Andersen, Bob Benedetto, James D'Aquisto, Linda Manzer, John Monteleone, the Santa Cruz Guitar Company, Dennis Stevens, and John Zeidler. The Gibson, Guild, and Heritage companies are sources of well-made factory acoustic and electric archtops.

Is an Archtop the Guitar for You?

If you have to ask, the answer is probably *no*. The archtop guitar simply doesn't sound right with most forms of contemporary acoustic music. To today's ears, it doesn't find a sonic space within most contemporary ensembles. It doesn't seem to surround or support the voice properly when accompanying modern song styles. It doesn't ring enough, and it speaks too thickly and too slowly. But it's still unsurpassed for recreating the authentic sounds of swing, and for clarity and elegance in executing mainstream jazz styles. Many professional flattop guitarists own an archtop model that they play when it's called for, or for a change of pace. Someday someone will probably readapt the archtop guitar to contemporary music, or contemporary music to the archtop guitar, but it hasn't happened yet.

Hawaiian and Other Lap-Style Guitars

The instrument called the Hawaiian guitar may be any guitar, just as long as it's played face up flat across your lap, with raised strings and a slide. Koa and mahogany, sweet-sounding woods that are also favored for ukuleles, are the body woods of choice for the true Hawaiian sound. Resophonic guitars like the bluegrass Dobro (see the section on Resophonic Guitars a bit further on) may also be held and fretted in the

Hawaiian *manner*, but most Hawaiian *people* who play Hawaiian *music* seem to find that an all-wood guitar is better suited to their style.

It's common to use medium or heavy gauge strings on these instruments, so as a rule they're sturdily built and may have square necks for maximum strength. Since they're intended to be played exclusively with a heavy steel slide, they usually have an extra-high nut and saddle to keep the strings well away from the fingerboard even when weighed down by the slide.

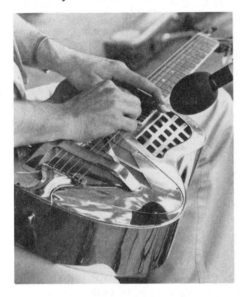

Hawaiian-style playing position; note metal slide bar in left hand. The guitar shown is a National tri-cone (see section on resophonic guitars). *Photo by Larry Sandberg.*

If you'd like to try out a lap-style guitar, you can satisfy your curiosity cheaply. An old ten-dollar junker from the flea market or music store basement will do for experiment, just as long as it doesn't explode when you put the strings on. Because you'll be playing with a steel slide, it doesn't matter how bad the action is. In fact, the worse it is, the better. If it's still not bad enough, a couple of bucks will buy you a removable gadget called a *nut extender*, a grooved metal collar that sits over your nut and raises the action to a height suitable for slide playing. You'll also need a slide. A heavy glass bottle or length of metal tubing will get you started, but ultimately you'll find a store-bought one more satisfying. For decades most players' favorite slide was the Stevens Steel™ with its comfortable grooved finger-holds, but recently the Shubb company has marketed a similar version with a rounded end that makes it easier to move from string to string. Most acoustic-guitar players prefer to keep away from the large, heavy "bullet" steels that work better on electric pedal steel guitars (see below).

Sometimes it's worth the effort to convert a good-quality Hawaiian guitar back to a regular one. Just get the high nut replaced with one of regular height. If you're lucky, the neck will be straight and you'll be ready to play. However, many of these instruments may also need fairly extensive surgery to be playable. Often, after enduring years of heavy string tension, they'll need to have the neck taken off and reset at the proper angle. And if they've got square necks, a luthier will have to recarve them to a standard contour. Why go to this trouble and expense? Because some of the better Hawaiian instruments from before World War II turn into superb country blues guitars when they're rebuilt!

Cyndi Cashdollar playing a Dobro. *Photo by Larry Sandberg.*

The Pedal Steel Guitar

Sometime in the thirties somebody got the bright idea of building a solidbody amplified Hawaiian-style guitar and adding one or two extra strings. These instruments are called *lap steels*.

Then someone else got the bright idea of mounting lap steels on legs so they could be played standing up. (Steel virtuoso Waldo Otto calls his instrument the "electric table.") Then others got the idea of shortening the legs so the table could again be played sitting down, this time with a bunch of knee levers and foot pedals to change the pitch of different strings as the instrument was being played. And of course, there was now enough room on the tabletop to include two completely different necks, each with eight or more strings, and each in completely different tunings with different knee-lever and pedal configurations.

The result is the modern *pedal steel*, which has evolved so far away from the guitar that it's a completely different instrument. It's a specialized, challenging, and highly virtuosic instrument requiring the soul of a musician mated with the mind of a chess master.

Resophonic Guitars

The twangy resophonic guitar gets its sound from a metal resonator built into the body. In a regular flattop guitar, the vibration of the strings sets the entire top in motion. In a resophonic guitar, the vibrations pass instead into what is basically a glorified pieplate mounted under the bridge. It's called the *cone*, and like the cone of a loudspeaker it amplifies the vibrations it receives. Since it's metal, it adds a metallic twang and a somewhat echoey quality to the sound. Resophonic guitars are usually quite loud—the concept of the cone resonator was intended by its designers primarily as an amplifying device, and its distinctive tone was strictly secondary. These days it's the tone that's highly valued. If it's merely loud you want, you can get it by turning a knob. A resonator guitar is a poor choice for a first guitar, unless you're absolutely sure it's what you want. But later on in your development, it could be a stimulating second instrument—especially for playing blues.

In order for the cone to amplify most effectively, a good deal of string energy has to be transmitted to it. Therefore resophonic guitars are usually strung with medium to heavy strings, and solidly built to withstand their tension. In fact, they're usually so thick and solid that the tops have a negligible acoustic function—it's the cone that does all the work. Because there's not much you can do to the body that would affect the instrument's sound, resophonic guitars are the perfect candidates for inlay designs, engravings, paint jobs, and other kinds of ornamentation, some of which have extended the boundaries of taste.

You can play resophonic guitars with a slide or just like a regular guitar, but a slide brings out the best in them. In fact, the combined sound of slide and resonator cone is, like shrimp and garlic, a marriage made in heaven.

The best known resophonic guitar is the Dobro model played lap-style with a slide in bluegrass and sometimes in country music. (The

Ron Mesing with a wooden-bodied Dobro-style resonator guitar. *Photo courtesy Flying Fish Records.*

Dobro name, a trademark of Original Musical Instruments [OMI], comes from the company's founders, the DOpyera BROthers. "Dobro" has become the generic term for lap-style resophonic guitar, though other companies also make such guitars, and the Dobro company also makes resophonic guitars designed to be held the usual way.)

The other resophonic archetype is the all-metalbodied instrument originally sold under the National brand name. While bluegrass and country players mostly prefer the Dobro sound, blues players mostly prefer Nationals.

The original Dobros and Nationals were made from 1927 through 1941. (Electric guitars and the shortages of the war years combined to bring sales to a halt.) In the ensuing years, a few odd resophonic-style models were marketed by the companies which purchased OMI's parts and stock.

As usual, the story gets a little more complicated. Thanks to tangles in the corporate history of the two brands, there are some older metal-bodied instruments labelled "Dobro" and woodenbodied instruments labelled "National." And when OMI cranked up operations again in 1959, it started producing both wooden and metal instruments under the Dobro name. So when you hear the words "Dobro" or "National," it could mean that they are being used specifically to refer to the manufacturer, or generically to refer to the type of instrument.

The history of OMI in its post-1959 incarnation has been speckled, with several changes of brand name ownership and manufacturing procedures, but the company has stabilized and since the seventies has again established itself as the major manufacturer of resophonic guitars.

Dobros and Nationals differ not only in having wood versus metal bodies, but also in details of cone design which have an effect on tone. Not only are the cones themselves differently shaped, but in Dobros the cone is connected to the bridge indirectly by a strutwork apparatus called a "spider," which looks like a skinny cousin of the fitting you rest a pot on over a gas burner. Dobros also have an ornamental covering called a *cover plate*—another pieplate, but this time with perforations— that fits over the resonator cone and spider. (When you look at a Dobro, the metal plate you see is the cover plate. You have to take it off, or look through its holes, to see the actual cone.) Nationals may have one large or three small cones.

Because resophonic guitars are strung heavily, they're usually pluck-ed with fingerpicks rather than bare fingers, and are often built with rather stout necks. On instruments intended to be played lap-style, the tuning pegs may be mounted with the pegs facing up for convenience, and the necks may be square for maximum strength. It's safest not to go heavier than medium-gauge strings on any but the square-necked models.

New resophonic instruments are available from Original Musical Instruments, the Emmons Guitar Company, the National Resophonic Company, Bob Jones, the Shot Jackson Guitar Center, and other domes-tic manufacturers. You can find Asian imports from Saga and other importers.

With a little luck and elbow grease, you can find a used resophonic guitar made by OMI in its post-1959 incarnation at a reasonable price.

Bob Brozman performing with a steel-bodied National resophonic guitar. *Photo by Larry Sandberg.*

Sixties models made by Gretsch under the Gretsch and Sho-Bro names, using genuine Dobro parts, can also be good. Seventies models from R. Q. Jones are fine instruments, but they usually have asking prices to match. Unless you happen across an uninformed seller, instruments from the original 1927–40 period are pricey collectors items, subject to the forces of an expert market that values cosmetic condition, and ornamentation, as well as minor historical and design features too specialized to go into here.

Other excellent instruments from the 1930s include those made by the Regal company, otherwise a maker of mostly nondescript guitars, under license from OMI. (Note that Saga now uses the Regal name for its contemporary imports.) Minor companies also made lower-quality resophonic-style instruments during the thirties. Others have continued to make instruments of varying degrees of quality through the present day.

Resophonic instruments are sturdy on the outside, but the cones and spiders are fairly fragile and may easily be damaged by shock or heavy-handed adjustment. What with all the nuts, bolts, pieplates, spiders, and other unusual creatures that inhabit them, they're also subject—much more than regular guitars—to all sorts of irrational buzzes and rattles. These problems are best sorted out by dealers or repairpeople who are experienced in resophonic instruments. You can learn in time to do your own servicing. In fact, you'll have to; I guarantee it. But get some advice along the way.

The Maccaferri ("Django") Guitar

This distinctive instrument was the brainchild of an eccentric Italian luthier and guitarist named Mario Maccaferri. It was marketed during the thirties by the Henri Selmer company of Paris, better known as a manufacturer of fine wind instruments, and is best recognized as the instrument which contributed to the unique sound of the great Gypsy jazz guitarist, Django Reinhardt. Django was the quintessential Maccaferri player.

The original Maccaferri guitar of 1930 had a wooden inner sound chamber within its lower bout—a body within the body, as it were—and a soundhole shaped like a D in order to accommodate the sound chamber. The interior sound chamber was open at the end next to the soundhole, but a saucer-like sound deflector bounced the sound around inside the body for a while before it actually got to the hole. Four longitudinal straight braces supported the top (similar to the two straight braces of archtop guitars), and the strings were supported archtop-style by a tailpiece rather than a pin bridge. The result was a brilliant, throaty, highly sustained single-line sound, and a compressed, punchy chord sound with little separation.

In 1937 Maccaferri bowed to consumer pressure and went from a 12- to a 14-fret neck. This resulted in a reproportioned body shape which compelled him to omit the inside sound chamber. The 14-fret guitars, produced until Maccaferri came to the United States in 1940, are still Maccaferri-sounding, but not as Maccaferri-sounding as the original

One of Saga's current versions of the Maccaferri design: the maple-bodied DG-250 model. *Photo courtesy Saga Musical Instruments.*

models with the sound chamber. In all, about 750 12-fret and 350 14-fret Maccaferris were made, which makes them prime collectors' items.

Although Maccaferri began his career as a concert artist, his mind had primarily a technological bent. He was among the first makers to use laminate backs and sides. In his later years he became infatuated with plastics and turned to the invention and production of plastic wood-wind reeds, in addition to pretty much sewing up the market on plastic guitars and ukeleles. If you remember the rows of plastic novelty ukes, guitars, and miniature instruments hanging in dime stores during the fifties and sixties, then you've seen Maccaferri's work. At one time, he even made some full-size plastic guitars.

The Maccaferri guitar has been of interest mainly to players working in the Django Reinhardt style. There's really no reason why it shouldn't be extended imaginatively into more modern styles, but I've never heard it done. In any case, it's a specialized sound and a specialized instrument, and not one to choose unless you know exactly what you're doing. If you're interested in a contemporary Maccaferri-style guitar, look for the Asian import models available from Saga at several price levels (including high quality instruments at the top of the line). Some luthiers, including John Monteleone, make fine handmade versions.

Harp Guitars and Other Oddballs

7-Strings, 10-Strings, and More

Toronto luthier Linda Manzer once, on a commission from jazz guitarist Pat Metheny, constructed a guitar with 42 strings strung on four necks (one 6-string and three 12-strings) running every which way out from the body. She called it the "Pikasso guitar" because it looks like one of those multiperspective guitar renderings the Cubists were so fond of.

If your tastes are less extravagant, maybe you'll settle for only seven strings. Usually the seventh is an extra bass string tuned to B or A, which

The "Pikasso" guitar by Linda Manzer, commissioned by Pat Metheny. *Photo © 1986 Brian Pickell, courtesy Linda Manzer.*

gives you the opportunity to add a lot more bottom to your playing. A few guitarists, like swing player Bucky Pizzarrelli, Nashville jazz player Lenny Breau, and the incomparable cocktail-jazz virtuoso George van Eps, have mastered the seventh string, and in their footsteps have followed a handful of acoustic flattop guitarists working with custom-made instruments or instruments adapted from wide-necked or 12-string guitars. But most players find that six strings are quite enough trouble to master and, once mastered, they do the job just fine, thank you.

The 7-string guitar actually goes back over 150 years. At the peak of European *guitaromanie* around 1830, all kinds of experiments with novelty guitar shapes were going on, but there was also a lot of interest, especially in Russia, in ordinary guitars with anywhere from one to nine extra bass strings. (Such instruments were known in their time as "bass guitars.")

Today, the 10-string guitar is experiencing a small revival. Classical guitarist Narciso Yepes and Latin/jazz guitarist Egberto Gismonti, for example, are known for their 10-string instruments, which look like a regular nylon-string guitar with a neck almost twice as broad and busy as usual. To the best of my knowledge, no one has made a similar instrument for steel strings. Not yet, anyway.

To play this kind of instrument, you conduct business as usual on the highest six strings. The remaining four strings are all tuned to such extra bass notes as might come in handy in the piece you're playing, so that, whenever you want some extra bottom to the piece, you can just reach up with your thumb and pick one of them. Sometimes it may be convenient to fret one of them to get the note you want, but for the most part they simply provide extra open notes. In addition, they're great showbiz.

The Harp Guitar

New acoustic stylist Michael Hedges has revived the 19th century oddity known as the harp guitar, in which extra bass strings (and sometimes sympathetic strings) are added onto an extra neck or a lyre-like extension of the body. The idea actually goes back to lute-family instruments of the 16th century called the archlute and theorbo, but it wasn't until the 1790s that the idea was applied to the guitar. The 1790 model was called by its maker a "harp guitar" because the extension for the extra strings looked like a small harp grafted onto the guitar body, and the name stuck.

Harp guitars had enough of a following to survive through the 19th century and into this one. Gibson turned out over 400 of them between 1900 and 1920, and the Larson brothers, important manufacturers early in this century, turned out a number of them under the Dyer and Stahl brand names. Even Martin made a few special-order models. But when the twenties roared in, they pushed harp guitars out of the way, and there they remained, until recently mere curiosities.

On harp guitars the extra bass strings are unfretted. The player just plucks the appropriate open strings. On some contemporary custom models there are also extra open high strings added below the high end of the fingerboard. (This, in essence, is a reinvention of the zither.)

An old Gibson harp guitar. *Photo by George Gruhn, courtesy Gruhn Guitars, Inc.*

If you're motivated to learn to play such an instrument, you'll either have to locate an old collectors'-item harp guitar, or have a luthier make a custom instrument for you. In either case, you'd better start saving your pennies right now. You're unlikely, at least as of the time this book goes to press, to find an inexpensive Korean import model at your local music store.

All this could change, though, if a harp guitar gets used in the next Madonna or Michael Jackson video.

Multineck Guitars

Guitars with more than one neck, each one tuned its own way, also began to appear during the 1830s. They persist, in one form or another, to the present day. Nowadays you're more likely to find them made as electrics, but you can find acoustics too—though only as custom models. Most multi-neck guitars are ordered by professionals for very specific purposes. One player may need to go rapidly back and forth between 6- and 12-string, another between a regular neck and a high-action slide neck, others between guitar and mandolin, or regular and open guitar tunings, and so on. They also look real sharp on stage, which is probably the main reason to have one.

The Bass Guitar

Perhaps you've seen a *guitarrón* in a Mexican *mariachi* band. It's the instrument that looks like a jumbo guitar on steroids. In recent years several American manufacturers, including Martin, Guild, and the

Martin acoustic-electric bass guitars. *Photo courtesy Martin Guitar Co.*

Acoustic bass guitar by Harry Fleishman. The cutaway and fretless fingerboard would make such an instrument especially congenial to players used to a conventional bass viol. *Photo courtesy Harry Fleishman.*

Ernie Ball String Company, have been turning out somewhat more manageably-proportioned versions of these acoustic bass guitars. Like regular string basses, they have four strings tuned in a relationship corresponding to the lowest four strings of the guitar. As a rule they come with pickups, since they're rather weak sounding. (You really need an instrument with the cubic volume of a string bass to get a big bass sound.)

If you're interested in playing bass and have a commitment to acoustic sound you might enjoy trying one of these instruments, although in my own opinion a real string bass or a regular electric bass would probably be more satisfying for most people in terms of sound. Electric basses are also tuned like the lowest four strings of the guitar, and since they're held the same way, most guitarists find them fairly easy to adjust mechanically. (Adjusting to them conceptually is another story; the bass requires its own way of thinking and of relating to other instruments.)

Air Guitars

Since air guitars are invariably electric, they are outside the scope of this book and are not included here. However, because of its low cost, ease of playing, and quick learning curve, you should seriously consider whether the air guitar is the instrument for you.

3

Guitar Sound

Guitar makers design guitars the way they do in order to get a certain sound out of them. Or else, they decide what sound qualities they're going to compromise in order to build a cheaper guitar. Before we look at how guitars are built, we'd better learn how to describe the sounds the makers are aiming for when they build them.

I think we need to acknowledge at the outset that learning about sound from words is an impossible task. I can't teach you what "balance" or "full-sounding" means—not with just a typewriter. This is something that can only be taught by example.

But maybe I can help you teach yourself. The way to teach yourself is to play as many different guitars as you can. And the way I can help is by giving you a vocabulary you can use to sort out what you hear. Some of these words overlap. Some are used differently by different people. Some seem to be inconsistent or contradictory. Eventually they will fall into place.

Tone

"Tone" refers to the precise color of a note: the qualities that make your guitar sound different from my guitar, and even more different from a bassoon or a trumpet. Tone quality is what people try to describe when they use words like "dark," "bright," "throaty," "harsh," "transparent," or "sweet." At best they're only grasping at metaphors, but that's what metaphors are for.

Tone differences come about because musical instruments, just like the rest of us, obey the laws of physics whether we like them or not. When a string (or, in the case of other instruments, an air column or drum head or whatever) is set into motion, it does more than vibrate along its entire length. It also splits up into smaller vibrating portions that give off their own sounds. The big, underlying vibration of the whole string is called the *fundamental,* and the smaller vibrations are called *overtones.* Each instrument has its own way of splitting up the smaller vibrations, of giving greater prominence to some of them rather than to others, and of leaving some out. This is what gives each instrument its unique tone quality.

All guitars share some combinations of fundamental and overtones in common. That's what make them all sound like guitars. But depending on how it's built, and what it's built of, each individual guitar also has its own personal combination of fundamental and overtones. And that's why my guitar doesn't sound exactly the same as your guitar, even though they both sound like guitars.

The main factor in a guitar's tone color is the material of its back and sides. To an experienced ear, rosewood compared to the other major body woods is soulful and it growls or shouts. Mahogany is sweeter and softer; it sighs or hums and, in the finest mahogany guitars, it sounds plump and round and beautifully balanced. Maple is as projective as rosewood but more brittle and astringent in tone and with less bass resonance.

Tone, Timbre, and Pitch

I try to use everyday language in this book as much as I can. But you should be aware that, in formal discourse, musicologists don't use the term *tone* quite the way we do in ordinary speech. They prefer the terms *tone color* or *timbre* for what we call *tone*. (*Timbre* comes from French and is pronounced tám-brah.) In correct scholarly talk, *tone* actually means what the rest of us usually call a *note*, meaning a sound you hear. *Note* in correct scholarly talk refers only to the dot on the printed page, not to what you hear. *Pitch* refers to the actual frequency of vibration of a given tone (or note, depending on whether you're speaking to me or to a musicologist.)

Volume

Volume is how loud your guitar is. At its simplest, volume is an objective standard that audio engineers call *sound pressure level* (or SPL), and measure with a decibel meter to tell them how loud a guitar *is*. But in real life there's more than meets the meter, because subjective perception of other qualities such as balance and presence also play a part in how loud a guitar *seems*.

Volume is mainly a function of how freely the top of the guitar moves when driven by the strings, but a combination of factors is involved:

- The quality of the top wood, and the way it's planed, braced, and finished, determines the guitar's loudness potential. Quality of the back and sides also plays a part, because their rigidity determines how efficiently the air chamber of the body works.
- Heavier strings usually sound louder because they put more energy into the top than lighter strings do. (However, some guitars—usually but not necessarily light, delicately built ones—seem to be able to absorb only so much string energy, and produce diminishing returns if you string them too heavily.)
- Of course, you have to *play* loud by applying your own energy to the strings to get them moving enough to move the top.

- All other things being equal, larger guitars sound louder. There's more top to vibrate and a larger sound chamber to reinforce the vibrations. But, because in the guitar world all other things are never equal, you can find dynamic small guitars that overwhelm big ones with stodgy tops.
- Finally, an instrument's capacity to absorb energy from the strings is affected by the mass of the neck and headstock. An odd but interesting phenomenon is that every so often you'll find an instrument that can be improved by putting heavier tuning machines on the headstock.

Volume may also differ from high strings to low. It's cheaper and easier to make a guitar with relatively loud bass strings, but high strings that have only a weak, false jangle to them. Beginners are sometimes attracted to this sound, but they become dissatisfied as their ear, taste, and musicianship become more sophisticated. An instrument that's genuinely loud is loud all across its range, not just in the low notes. (For more on this subject, see *Balance* below.)

Presence

Presence is another mysterious, subjective quality. It can make a guitar *seem* louder even though it may not actually read so on a meter. It makes the guitar sound full and *all there*.

The kind of volume that can be metered affects how far away you can move from a guitar and still hear it, and is an index of whether or not one instrument can overwhelm another. But presence is more of a psychological factor that will make you and your friends feel surrounded by sound when you play in an intimate setting. Having to play too loud is a poor way to compensate for an instrument with insufficient presence.

A good measure of presence is how satisfying an instrument sounds when you play it softly. In a good guitar, softly played notes will have the same degree of authority as loud ones: Tone quality won't fall off along with the volume level. This sensation of fullness is closely related to balance and sustain, and implies good tone quality as well.

As I understand presence, it comes from the efficiency of the guitar's top. It seems to me that a guitar sounds fuller and more honest in proportion to the degree it depends on its top, rather the resonance of its air chamber, to produce its total volume.

Dynamic Range

You'd think that in order to get the guitar to play more softly or more loudly, all you'd need to do is strum or pluck it softer or harder. But that's true only to a point. A great guitar goes from very, very soft to very, very loud, responding to every nuance of your touch. An ordinary guitar only goes from soft to loud, if that.

The concept of dynamic range overlaps somewhat with those of volume and presence, and, as with those qualities, it's primarily a function of the guitar's top. An instrument without a full dynamic range will frustrate you when you want to add strong accents, or emphasize the meaning of a song through loud and soft sections.

Cutting Power

Cutting power is the ability of an instrument to insert itself into spaces in an ensemble with other instruments, as opposed to overwhelming them through sheer volume. Therefore it depends also on the nature of the ensemble and the music being played. A swing band with horns, a bluegrass band, an old-time music band, and a band with a keyboard or an accordion or a cittern all leave completely different spaces to be filled, and each may call for a very different-sounding kind of guitar.

Since cutting power depends on the sum of the qualities of the instrument and how they relate to the sum of the qualities of the ensemble you're playing in, it can only be judged from personal experience and as a matter of personal utility.

Separation

Separation is the ability of an instrument to express simultaneously played notes so that they are perceived distinctly and individually, rather than as a homogeneous whole. In other words, when you strum an open E chord, is what you hear more like one glob of sound or six separate ingredients? An analogy might be to the flavors that make up a fine sauce.

Separation is hard to learn how to hear and harder to express in words, but it's an important factor in determining the "sound" of an individual stylist. How much separation you want is a matter of personal preference. However, it's harder to build a guitar with good separation, and luthiers generally consider it an achievement.

Separation is also a function of the player's individual touch.

Balance

Balance is the relationship between the high and low notes in point of fullness and volume. In a balanced guitar, the notes have equal authority throughout the entire range of the instrument.

Guitars that are overbalanced toward the bass are called *boomy*. This may be a desirable quality depending on your style. If your main goal is to punch out bass notes in a bluegrass band, such an instrument might still be best for you. Bass-heavy guitars also provide an extremely full sound when being played in a bass-note/strum style as the sole accompaniment to a singer. The total effect sounds much fuller when the bottom gets filled up with those big bass notes.

If you want to play by yourself in a quiet room, or do a lot of melodic fingerpicking, you may find that you prefer a guitar that's balanced more toward the high strings. Instruments that sound this way are usually called just plain "balanced," notwithstanding the fact that, to today's predominant tastes, a slightly bass-heavy instrument is actually the norm.

The ideal, perfectly balanced guitar is one that gives you the opportunity to control the relative volume of the high and low strings through touch. To a beginner's ear, a well-balanced guitar may sound flat and dry compared to a boomy one. Such guitars are harder to make and harder to find than imbalanced ones—especially bass-heavy ones. They're also harder to play, since they put more of the responsibility for how they sound squarely on *you*.

Balance is mostly a function of size. If all other factors are equal, as they never are, larger guitars tend to be bass-heavy (with dreadnoughts the boomiest of all), while smaller instruments tend to bring out the highs more strongly. Body wood also plays a part (mahogany is less boomy than rosewood), and a larger soundhole also tends to balance toward the highs. Balance is also a quality of the individual instrument, so that one rosewood dreadnought may be better balanced than another, apparently identical, one.

Sustain

Sustain is the measure of how long a note keeps sounding after you initiate it. (Acoustic scientists divide the sound into two components: attack and decay. If the sound decays too fast, you have poor sustain.) Instruments that have poor sustain lack a singing quality, and make it impossible to hold long notes or chords. Generally sustain is a quality of fine guitars and is something you want, but it may be more or less important to you than to the next person depending on your style. I can even imagine a guitarist feeling that a given guitar has too much sustain.

The vibration of the top is what gives you an honest, clean sustain that preserves all the components of the tone throughout its duration. Echoey sustain that depends more on the air chamber makes for a cheaper, less clean sound. You can learn to hear the difference. Sustain is also affected by many other factors including the lightness of the body, the mass of the neck and headstock, and the quality of the saddle and bridge.

It's hard to judge sustain on high notes if you're a beginner, because you need to build up enough strength to hold the string firmly against the fret in order to let the note sing for as long as the guitar will let it. Experienced players also play with vibrato, which adds extra energy to the note and increases the sustain and singing quality. Factors outside the acoustics of the guitar itself, such as condition of the frets and the age and gauge of the strings, may also alter the instrument's intrinsic sustain.

Sustain is one of the most important factors in creating the immediate impression—even to the unsophisticated ear—that a guitar does or does not sound good.

Voice

Voice is the way the instrument projects its sound. It's possible to describe different instruments as slow or quick to speak, and to say (for example, of a brand-new instrument that has not yet been played in) that its voice sounds "contained."

Note that the term "voicing" is used in a somewhat different sense to refer to the way a luthier listens to the sounds of the top and bracing as they are being carved into final shape on a fine handmade guitar. This—along with the body woods and the rigidity of the body—are the main factors in voice.

You

Ultimately, the sound of the guitar will also be *your* sound. It's a function of your personal touch, your decisions about string gauge, the kinds of picks you use (if any), the way you shape your fingernails, and so on. Instead of thinking of a guitar as having a certain sound in and of itself, it's best to think of it as having a sound that comes from an interaction between you and it. It's hard for a beginner to judge this. Experienced players can pick up a guitar and be able to say, almost immediately, "This guitar is for me. It does what I want it to do. It says what I want it to say."

Facts and Impressions

Most of the qualities we've discussed can be reduced to quantitative measurements. If they can't, it's only because our technology isn't good enough yet. We can measure volume with a decibel meter. We can see the relationship between fundamental and overtones on an oscilloscope. We can analyze the vibration patterns of a moving top by sprinkling graphite dust over it, or through holography.

Some of these measurements are useful to the quality-control engineers whose mass-produced guitars need to be as standardized as possible. Some luthiers also use this kind of quantitative data, though most prefer to work by touch and intuition. How they do it is their business. But your business is to go by sound only. As a musician, your first duty is to listen, for the simple reason that to listen is the *only* duty of your audience.

4

Wood, Finish, and Glues

Plywood and Solid Wood

Most Guitars Are Plywood

Most of the guitars made nowadays—just about *all* new guitars with a list price under $1000—have plywood backs and sides. The real cheapies even have plywood tops. If this comes as a surprise to you, it's because the guitar industry has not exactly been trumpeting the news around. In fact, the guitar industry, by and large, should be ashamed of the essentially deceptive way it skirts the issue in its advertising and sales literature.

In the guitar world, plywood goes by the hifalutin' name of *laminate*, which implies (for the most part correctly) a higher class of goods than the stuff you get at the lumberyard. It boils down to the same thing, though: several layers (*plies*) of wood are glued together. The guitar makers would prefer me to use the word *laminate* exclusively, but since I'm not on anyone's payroll at the moment, in this book I use *laminate* and *plywood* interchangeably. Real, honest-to-god wood, the stuff that comes to you in unadulterated planks right off the log as God and Nature made it, is known in the industry as *solid* wood.

The Mystique and Value of Solid Wood

The spirituality of a laminate guitar is another story. Although it may offend you to discover that plywood should be even used, much less standard, in the holy art of guitar making, you'd better remember that plywood is the standard construction material in most homes today, possibly your own. You'd also better remember that almost all dark hardwood furniture these days is laminate (or *veneer*, as they call it in the furniture trade). Just as with guitars, you've got to go either to a prestige maker or buy an antique if you want solid wood—in fact, new solid-wood furniture is probably harder to come by than a new solid-wood guitar, and proportionately more expensive in relation to veneer furniture.

It also seems likely that fine solid-wood guitars will last longer, though solid woods of inferior quality will likely hold up over time no better than laminates.

If you need or want to feel that you own a "real" guitar, though, you'll need solid wood. A real wood guitar of fine quality is something that becomes an heirloom. It sounds better and it gets better with age. But there are a lot of guitarists out their playing away happily—and some of them very well, and some of them for good money—on their laminate guitars.

Laminates

Buyer Beware

Too many guitar manufacturers are careless at indicating that they use laminates, and dealers may not leap to point this out either, unless they're trying to move you up into the all-solid-wood price range. (Many businesspeople's business ethics allow omission, but won't allow a lie in response to a direct question. So ask.) Roughly the same standards seem to apply to the way veneer is treated by furniture dealers. (In the furniture industry, by the way, these terms are used a little differently. The word *veneer* generally implies a true wood surface ply, while *laminate* refers to a synthetic surface ply, usually over a chipboard core.)

When you browse through manufacturers' catalogs or even read the labels on showroom guitars, you'll find that the way solids and laminates are labelled is often confusing. (Some manufacturers are very clear, some inconsistent, and some just plain shoddy.) I suspect that this is due in part to sloppy copy writing and poor communication between copy and marketing departments, in part to ignorance, in part to a desire to play down the term, and in part to deliberate evasion. Standards need to be raised. Not the least of the problem is the way laminates are so often described in ads and catalogs as "fine woods." Well, yes, veneer-grade rosewood and mahogany *are* fine woods, so it's probably legal to describe laminates this way. But don't you get the feeling that someone is trying to play you for a fool? Much guitar advertising operates at the same level of moral validity as slapping a "low-sodium, low-cholesterol" label on a food product laden with artificial flavors and polysyllabic preservatives.

Perhaps you get the feeling by now that it's safest to assume that any wood not specifically labelled as "solid" is laminate. You're right. I'm afraid that you even have to extend this degree of suspicion to the model specs given in Part II of this book, which are based on manufacturer's sales literature.

Even better would be to get the word "laminate" out of the closet. It's become the standard industry material for backs and sides, so why not admit it? As things stand now, the manufacturers are silent about the quality of the wood they use in cores, glues, and other specs. If laminate comes out of the closet, they'll be able to compete with each other in the advertised quality of their materials and we'll all be better off. But for the time being, a great silence hangs over all. Like political candidates who cannot admit that they will raise taxes, no manufacturer seems brave enough to take the first step in acknowledging reality.

Laminate Construction

Guitar laminates are usually 3-ply. The outer ply is a finished veneer of rosewood, mahogany, maple, or whatever else the back and sides are "supposed" to be made of. Veneers are milled by a process called rotary cutting, in which a thin, continuous layer is cut off the log in a way that resembles peeling the skin off an apple. Rotary cutting gives the wood merchant the highest profit per log of any milling method. It also brings out the figure (ornamental grain pattern) of most woods more than other milling methods do. As a result, laminate guitars may be more attractive, on the surface at least, than much finer instruments made of solid wood. (Veneers, of course, vary among themselves in quality and the best looking ones wind up on the more expensive laminates.)

The center ply, or core, is glued crossgrained (with the grain going in a perpendicular direction) to the veneer and inner layer. This imparts strength, in the same way that gluing corrugated plies of cardboard perpendicular to each other imparts strength to cardboard cartons. Ideally the center ply should be of the same wood used in the inner and outer plies, though this may not be the case with inexpensive instruments. In cheapie guitars, it may even be junk wood or (horrors) some kind of chip composition. We don't know. Only the makers know, and they're not telling.

The inner ply, which is what you see when you look through the soundhole, is usually the same wood as the outer ply. In some instruments, especially cheap ones, it obviously isn't. Generally a rather plain-figured cut of wood is used for economy, which is fair enough—beauty is only skin deep, so there's no reason to make the inside of the guitar look ravishing. Some makers do use an inner ply with some figure to it, which usually serves to make it harder to tell by looking whether the wood is plywood or solid.

Stability and Durability

When it comes to stability and durability, laminates come out well in a comparison with solid woods. They don't crack all the way through with dryness as solid wood can, but some (especially if poor quality) may swell up and distort with humidity—though poorly seasoned solid wood may do this too. As a general rule, they hold up very well through climate changes and abusive treatment in the short run, though their behavior over a period of 50 to 100 years is not tested. (Then again, not so many low-range and midrange solid-wood guitars of the past have made it that long, either.)

On the negative side, plywood shatters rather than breaks cleanly when punctured, making it a repairperson's nightmare. In the past most repairpeople advocated only quick-and-dirty work on laminate guitars, but now that they've gone up in price and sound quality, it has become worthwhile to do neat work. But what would be a small patch job on solid wood can mean cutting out and replacing an entire section of laminate. Some repairpeople—the ones who have managed to build up a busy trade exclusively in fine instruments—simply reject repair work on laminates.

The plies in laminate may also separate over a period of time, especially when subjected to abusive changes of temperature and humidity. Sometimes this can lead to a loose section, for example a knot, in the inside ply which creates a hard-to-locate rattle, though once found it's easy enough to fix with a glue injection.

Detecting Plywood

How can you tell if any instrument is plywood? It's not always easy. For starters, ask the dealer or read the merchandise tags and sales literature. Then examine the guitar itself. Try looking for a knot, texture, or pattern in the wood on the back of the guitar and see if it corresponds to an identical pattern on the inside. Or try looking for plies in the wood on the inside edge of the soundhole. (A plastic binding around the inside of the soundhole may be a sign that the maker is trying to cover something up.) The appearance of plies around the edge of the soundhole is least easy to disguise in the area under the end of the fingerboard, where you *may* be able to spot three (or, in very cheap guitars, two) plies. If you have an inspection mirror, take a good look at the underside of the top. Laminate tops generally have an obviously less-finished-looking, courser-grained inside surface. But it's not easy to learn from words. Comparing guitars is the best way to learn, but even so, a clever coverup can be hard to recognize.

Laminate Tops

Only the bottom-line guitars these days have plywood tops. (You may also encounter plywood on the tops of older models from some companies that have switched to all solid tops in the past few years.) Plywood by its very nature is not effective for tops: it just can't vibrate the way a top must in order to sound good. Nonetheless, a properly designed all-plywood guitar can sound adequate for a beginner and would be acceptable if priced fairly. Some makers even believe that it's theoretically possible to build a plywood-bodied guitar that will sound every bit as good as the finest ones' fine solid wood, even as it matures over time. But it hasn't been done.

Solid tops sound better and also improve with age *if* they're made of decent wood to begin with, so most manufacturers, in response to competition, now offer solid tops but compromise on the back and sides to keep costs down.

Laminate Backs and Sides

Plywood back and sides are another story, because back and sides have an entirely different acoustic function from that of the top: they maintain the rigidity of the sound chamber and help project the sound. A good laminate guitar, though offensive to purists, sounds better and is more durable than a poorly-made solid wood guitar.

Plywood has been used on cheapie guitars since I don't know when—the thirties at least. Among American manufacturers, Guild began to use laminates for the backs and sides of some high-range models as early as the mid-seventies, with considerable success. The top-range Korean and Japanese instruments, including the best of the Alvarez-Yairi, Aspen, Washburn, and Yamaha lines with their solid tops and laminate backs and sides, are also widely used by professional musicians—even in the recording studio. Martin has met the Japanese competition by introducing its Shenandoah line of laminate guitars. They look like Martins, they have much of the traditional Martin sound, and to Martin's credit they are kept in a separately-named line. Though the use of laminates in good-quality flattop guitars is a fairly recent development, plywood has also been used on journeyman electric archtop guitars for well over a quarter of a century, and the original Maccaferri ("Django-style") guitars had laminate bodies.

Laminate Fingerboards

On a cheaply made guitar, even the fingerboard may be made of plywood. Sometimes you can spot the lamination by taking a good look at the end of the fingerboard just above the soundhole. Maybe you'll be able to spot the layers of lamination, or a cap of wood glued on over the fingerboard end to hide the layers. But if it's a good dye or cap job and you don't have a good eye, you could be fooled. A laminated fingerboard isn't a good thing: it's potentially unstable, it's weak, and it's a sign of cost-cutting that reflects on the whole guitar. It's acceptable only on the most inexpensive instruments, where you're getting what you pay for.

Laminate Necks and Headstocks

Sometimes necks and headstocks are made of several pieces of glued-together wood. These are also called "laminates," because technically that's what they are, but they're a whole different kettle of fish. Lamination here is a strong, perfectly respectable, time-honored way of constructing these parts of the instrument.

See the sections on necks and headstocks in chapter 5 for more information.

Materials and Tone

As the rest of this chapter discusses in greater detail, each kind of body wood has its own sound: mahogany is sweet, rosewood punchy, maple bright, and so on. But plywood guitars reflect these differences less consistently and strongly than solid woods do—sometimes not at all. Whether or not a laminate accurately reflects the tonal qualities of the wood it's "supposed" to be made of is probably due to the type and quality of woods used for the core and outer ply; you'll find that well-made laminate instruments, like the better Guild and Alvarez-Yairi models, do offer perceptible tone differences between body woods.

But, again, it's hard to say, because the makers don't provide any specifications about the quality of their plywood, and we have no means of comparison.

Seasoning and Milling Solid Wood

Seasoning

This section is not about salt and pepper. Well-seasoned wood is not something that will help your chops or let you play tasty licks. Seasoning, also called "drying" or "aging," is the process by which the wood's natural moisture content is reduced after it is cut. It helps stabilize wood to resist warping, cracking, shrinking, and expanding. How well the wood is seasoned is an important factor in how well your guitar will hold up over the years, and also plays a part in tone quality.

Proper seasoning of fine wood calls for expert skill and sensitivity. Wood is seasoned either by air drying, which may take years, or by slow kiln drying, which may take weeks or months. The faster the kilning, the less stable the wood. At the extreme low end, really quick kiln drying is used only for junk wood like the stuff that's used for tomato stakes and orange crates. The less your guitar wood is like tomato stakes and orange crates, the better off you are.

A lumber kiln is essentially a shed in which you blow warm, dry air through logs or boards stacked so they have some air space between them. Some commercial woods are seasoned by chemical, electrostatic, or dehumidifying (air-conditioning) methods, but these aren't suitable for luthiery.

Many collectors feel that the excellence of fine 19th- and early 20th-century guitars is due in part to the use of wood that was slowly air-dried with a degree of care that would be economically prohibitive today. But this is pure supposition, however reasonable, because no documentation survives of exactly how guitar woods were treated by Martin and other fine makers during that era.

However, almost everyone agrees that air drying is a superior method. Some wood suppliers claim that their kiln-dried woods are indistinguishable by hygrometer readings from air-dried woods; purists counter that hygrometers don't take into account the more gradual evaporation of resins, of the natural glues which hold wood grains together, and of other volatile components, which occurs during the much lengthier air-drying process. Three years is a typical figure for air-drying, though some luthiers air dry for much longer than that. At the minimum, it should take at least one year, so the lumber can go through at least one complete cycle of the seasons.

Whatever the advantages of air-drying, the fact is that most guitar woods today are kiln-dried. Proper seasoning is a patient process that depends on the skill of the kiln operator, since it must achieve a precise balance between the rate at which the moisture evaporates from the surface of the wood, and the rate at which the moisture is drawn to the surface from deeper within the wood. When these two factors are out of balance, the wood cracks or warps from uneven stress patterns. Guitar body wood is only around 3/32-inch thick and it has to withstand the force of string pressure, so it must be free of faults. Only a small part of commercial lumber is kilned finely enough for luthiery use. The better the kilning, the more time and care went into it, so the more expensive it is.

Seasoning doesn't end when the making of the actual guitar begins. In high-quality instrument-making, the wood is allowed to stabilize further for several weeks or even months between assembly stages. In addition, properly climate-controlled shops and factories maintain a relative humidity level of about 40 percent in order to keep the wood at the level to which it has been seasoned.

Nor does seasoning end when the guitar comes out of the factory. Fine instruments continue to mature indefinitely as elements of the wood and finish continue to age, aided by the actual "playing in" of the instrument.

Prime Cuts

Logs are round. Boards, tabletops, and pieces of guitar wood are flat. "Aha," you say, "someone must have cut the log." The process of cutting timber is called milling, as in sawmill, and it's pursued in a considerably more organized and scientific fashion than the Texas Chainsaw Massacre or carving a rump roast. The following few sections cover the subject in a somewhat simplified way, and only consider those points that relate to guitar making.

Grain and Figure

The most obvious visual feature of wood is the surface pattern due to the growth rings that grow outward in concentric circles from the center of the log. Even ring size is a sign of consistent climatic conditions which permit the tree to grow about the same amount each year, while even coloration is a sign that seasonal shifts of humidity within the year have not been extreme. However, each species of wood has its own characteristic cell structure that imparts a unique appearance.

When botanists talk about wood grain, they are referring to specific technical aspects of the alignment of the cellular structure of wood. But when people like you and me talk about grain, we usually mean the visual pattern of the growth rings. *Grain* is used in this colloquial way in this book.

Grain, in this sense, is similar to the woodworkers' term *figure*, which is the overall visual surface pattern of a board. Figure results from a number of factors, including climate and other environmental conditions and the method of sawing, in addition to the character of the grain structure of the wood species.

In addition to the growth rings in their concentric circles, wood also contains tissues called *rays* which radiate outwards from the center in a spokelike fashion, and serve the purpose of storing food over the winter. Rays, as we shall see, are visually present in the wood figure only when certain kinds of sawing are used.

Milling Lumber

Slab Cutting

If you're a wood merchant and want to make the most money per log, you'll rotary cut it for veneer as described earlier in the section on laminates. If you're producing boards, the most economical way to get them out of the log is by the method variously called slab cutting, flat cutting, or plank sawing. This uses up every available bit of the log, so there's no waste.

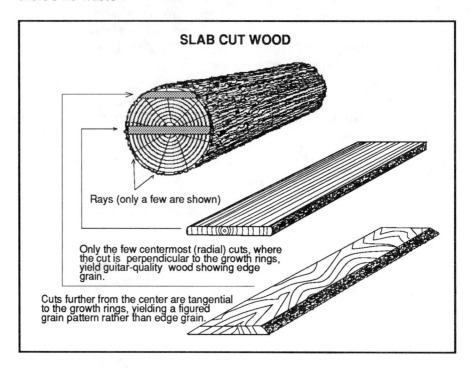

SLAB CUT WOOD

Rays (only a few are shown)

Only the few centermost (radial) cuts, where the cut is perpendicular to the growth rings, yield guitar-quality wood showing edge grain.

Cuts further from the center are tangential to the growth rings, yielding a figured grain pattern rather than edge grain.

In the board cut from the absolute center of the log, the growth rings are perpendicular to the saw cut. This center board is called a *radial cut*. It's the most desirable cut to use in a guitar, because the perpendicular grain pattern makes the wood least likely to warp and distort with climate changes than the pattern of any other cut. It also promotes the best possible vibration patterns in the top.

As the cuts move further from the center, the pattern of the concentric rings becomes less and less perpendicular. These cuts are less desirable for guitars but suitable for less critical applications like furniture-making. (Tabletops and bookcases are considerably thicker than the $\frac{3}{32}$-inch wood used in guitars, so stability is less of an issue.) In addition, the cuts that are further away from the center show the figure of the wood better. In general, wood that you would admire in cabinetry is not as good for guitarmaking as a plain-looking piece of lumber.

Quartersawn Wood

Slab cutting yields only one perfect luthiery-quality board—the radially cut board from the center of the log. Perhaps the next few cuts out from the center might also have grain close enough to perpendicular to be acceptable. But if luthiers and fine woodworkers had to depend on only a few boards per tree at best, their materials costs would be prohibitive. Fortunately, there's another way of running the log through the mill, called *quartersawing*, that results in many more high-quality boards per log.

Quartersawing is so called because the log is first cut into quarters, then milled into boards in a close-to-radial fashion. As with slab cutting, only the center cut is radially-sawn right on the money. But the rest of

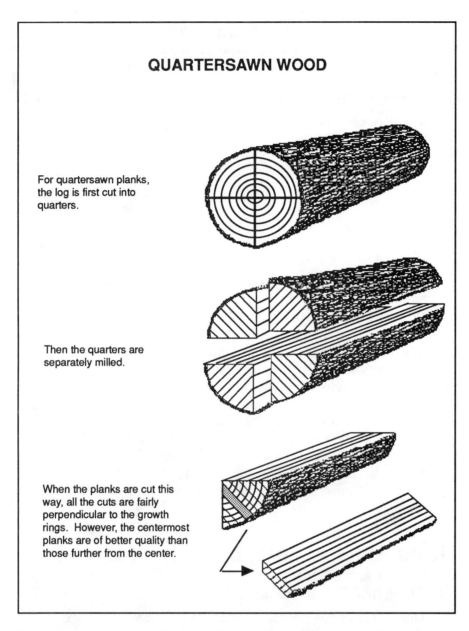

QUARTERSAWN WOOD

For quartersawn planks, the log is first cut into quarters.

Then the quarters are separately milled.

When the planks are cut this way, all the cuts are fairly perpendicular to the growth rings. However, the centermost planks are of better quality than those further from the center.

the cuts come out with the growth ring pattern close enough to perpendicular to be acceptable for luthiery.

Remember, though, that quartersawing does not magically confer fine sound quality on a piece of wood. There are still lots of other things to consider: the tone quality and resiliency of the wood itself, how well it's aged, and how carefully the luthier or factory does the final shaping, thinning, and assembly.

Quartersawn wood, however, is always structurally superior to slab cut wood because it's more stable as it ages. Therefore, it's always the first choice for tops, necks, backs, and sides of fine guitars. Ideally, the bracing struts, bridge blanks, and even the inside blocks should also be quartersawn. But don't expect to find quartersawn woods in any but the most expensive guitars.

Tops should certainly be quartersawn if they are to qualify as fine. So

WOOD WARPING PATTERNS
The degree of warping shown is
exaggerated for visual emphasis.

The outer rectangle in the diagrams below represents the shape of the freshly cut plank before it shrinks over the years.

All wood shrinks over a period of years, but quartersawn wood shrinks evenly as it dries.

Slab cut wood warps as it shrinks, creating additional problems for the guitar.

should back and sides. But some first-class makers use slab-cut wood for back and sides anyway—either for economy or because the maker gives higher priority to beauty of figure than to stability and acoustic value. A finely-made guitar with a well-chosen piece of highly figured slab-cut wood can look stunningly beautiful. But I cannot recommend paying serious money for a supposedly serious instrument in which all woods are not quartersawn. These include the products of some quite accomplished luthiers who have opted for the figure of slab cut wood over the stability of quartersawn wood. It also, surprising, includes recent regular production Martins other than dreadnoughts, for the Martin catalog current at this writing specs quartersawn wood for dreadnought models only.

Tops, Backs, Sets, and Blanks

Bookmatched Tops and Backs

Tops and backs of fine guitars should ideally consist of two sections of wood that are *bookmatched*. This means that they come from a single piece of wood about 3/16 inch thick, which has been cut in half down the narrow dimension into two pieces each about 3/32 inch thick, and then opened out like a book. Bookmatched sections look pretty because they mirror-image each other, but their real importance is the symmetry of grain structure. That means that both sides of the bookmatched joint will expand and shrink at equal and symmetrical rates over the years, and that both sections will be acoustically equal.

Bookmatched veneer sections used on laminates look pretty, but have no structural or acoustic value. In other words, they are essentially a meaningless feature.

Sets

Wood merchants furnish luthiers and factories with the material for

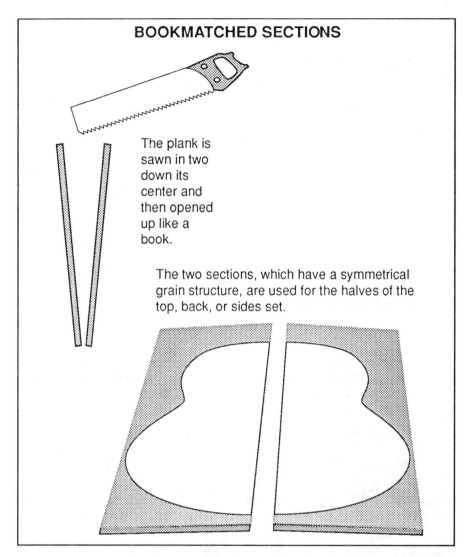

BOOKMATCHED SECTIONS

The plank is sawn in two down its center and then opened up like a book.

The two sections, which have a symmetrical grain structure, are used for the halves of the top, back, or sides set.

back and sides in what is called a *set*: unfinished pieces cut to approximate size and ready for final trimming and shaping. (In mass-production factories, the sets are usually procured and put together by the company's own wood-supply division; in fact, some makers large or small even purchase raw logs and do their own milling.)

In instruments that are made with any degree of care, the backs and sides of a set should be visually and acoustically compatible. But in the very finest guitar making, the ideal set consists of back and sides from the same log. This gives the same advantages that bookmatching does: all sections are acoustically identical, and all will shrink and expand at the same rate because they are matched in raw material and seasoning.

Matched sets from the same log are expensive and hard to come by. Don't expect to find them on any but the most expensive instruments.

Blanks

A roughly-shaped section of wood is called a *blank*. Necks, bridges, heel blocks, and end blocks are all milled to blanks that approximate their final shape. In mass-production guitars, they are machine-cut, but in finer guitars more handwork is used in carving them to final shape.

Tonewoods

The word *tonewood* is used to describe instrument-building woods in general, although some violin-makers use it only to describe spruce for the top. In addition to the large, obvious piece of wood used for the top, back, sides, and neck of the guitar, smaller pieces are used for other structural components as well: the ornamental *binding* strips around the edges of the top, the *lining* strips that reinforce the edge joints of the sides with the back and top from inside the guitar, the *bracing* struts of the top and back, and the massive *heel block* (or *head block*) and *end block* that support the joints where the two sides come together at the top and bottom of the body.

Wood Naming Conventions

Names of woods are confusing even to professionals. The lumber industry uses a hodgepodge of nomenclatures: native and vernacular names, trade names, names that reflect regional origins or ports of shipping, different names for the same wood depending on whether it's been milled or is still on the tree. Guitar makers echo the imprecision, and the names of woods used in instrument making are no less confusing. What violin makers usually call "Swiss pine," for example, is not pine but spruce, and these days it's most likely to come from Romania. "German" spruce might really be from Germany, but it's also an acceptable term for describing European spruce in general. (What isn't acceptable, though, is to ship Sitka spruce to Germany and then import it back as German spruce, and *it's been done*. German spruce sells for enough more than Sitka does that it's worth the trouble. An experienced eye can tell the difference, but can yours?)

The following table lists the major woods used in guitar making. It may help clarify things a little by correlating many of the trade and vernacular names with the Latin botanical names. Don't try to memorize it. Just remember that it's here, so you can flip back to it for reference when you need to.

Spruce

Varieties of Spruce
A resonant softwood of the pine family, spruce is the standard wood for guitar tops. It's also the favored top wood of violin makers, who sometimes refer to it as "Swiss pine."

European spruce is the top wood regarded most highly by guitar and violin makers alike. Mountain-grown logs from Switzerland, Bavaria, and Czechoslovakia have been highly prized in the past, but recently much European spruce for guitars, violins, and piano soundboards has come from Romania. The term "German spruce" may be used generically in the wood industry for any European spruce. What country the

THE MAJOR GUITAR WOODS

Family	Common Name	Botanical Name	Origin & Comments
Cedar (Cupressaceae)	Western red cedar	Thuja plicata	Pacific Northwest. Also called British Columbia cedar, red cedar.
Ebony (Ebenaceae)	Gabon ebony	Diospyros crassiflora	West Africa. Also called African ebony.
	Macassar ebony	Diospyros celebica	Indonesia. Also called Indian ebony.
Mahogany (Meliaceae)	Honduras mahogany	Swietenia macrophylla	Central & South America. Also known as American, Amazon, or "genuine" mahogany, and differentiated commercially by country of origin.
Maple (Aceraceae)	European flame maple	Acer campestre	Parts of Europe.
	Rock maple	Acer saccharum & Acer nigrum	Eastern U.S. and Canada.
Rosewood (Leguminosae)	Brazilian rosewood	Dalbergia nigra	Brazil. Also known as palisander, palo santo, and jacaranda de Bahía. (Do not confuse with other jacarandas.)
	Honduras rosewood	Dalbergia stevensonii	Belize. May be used for bridges and fingerboards; not a body wood.
	(East) Indian rosewood	Dalbergia latifolia	India and Java. "Indian" and "East Indian" are loosely interchangeable.
Spruce (Pinaceae)	Sitka spruce	Picea sitchensis	Pacific Northwest. Also called silver spruce.
	European spruce	Picea abies	Most of Europe. Categories like "German" may be used generically.
	Engelmann spruce	Picea engelmannii	U.S. and Canadian Rockies. Sometimes spelled "Englemann."
	White spruce	Picea glauca	U.S. and Canada. Commercially differentiated as eastern or western white spruce, Québec spruce, Adirondack spruce, etc., depending on origin and port of shipment.
Rosewood family (Leguminosae)	Cocobolo	Dalbergia retusa	Central America. Also called granadillo.
	Jacaranda	Machaerium villosum	Brazil. Also called jacaranda pardo.
	Koa	Acacia koa	Hawaii. The classic ukulele wood.
	Narra	Pterocarpus indicus	South Pacific. Also called amboyna.
	Ovangkol	Guibortia ehie	West Africa.
	Tulipwood	Dalbergia frutescens	Brazil. Also called jacaranda rosa.

piece of wood actually comes from is not as important as its individual qualities.

Sitka spruce, usually somewhat ruddy in complexion, comes from the Pacific northwest and is today the most commonly used wood for guitar tops. Sitka is a bit stronger and stiffer than other spruces, and has a faster growth rate. Some luthiers feel that it lacks the tonal and projective qualities of other, more expensive spruces; others don't share this opinion at all.

Appalachian or Adirondack spruce is found from the Appalachians on into the western states, and north into Québec. Some luthiers regard it as superior to Sitka. It has been suggested that Adirondack spruce (localized eastern white spruce) was the wood used on early Martin guitars, but, according to the Martin company, there are no records to verify or disprove that assertion. Gibson, on the other hand, is said variously to have relied on Michigan or Appalachian white spruce for its prewar guitars.

Another highly regarded spruce is Engelmann spruce (*Picea engelmannii*) from the higher elevations of the Rockies and Pacific Cascades. It's much less common than Sitka spruce, and some feel it gives a more projective, resonant sound. Engelmann, incidentally, is also prized for large Christmas trees because of the perfection of its shape when grown tall.

Spruce is also customarily used for top bracing, though sometimes mahogany or another hardwood is used for the flat brace above the soundhole and beneath the fingerboard spatula. Sometimes other woods are used for bracing, either as an economy measure on cheap guitars or because a luthier just happens to like them. Spruce (or mahogany) may also be used for the end block and heel block.

Spruce Mystique

There are people who swear they can distinguish the sound of German or Adirondack or Sitka spruce blindfolded. I can't claim to hear what they do. (Could it be because I've never tried the blindfold?)

Here's my problem. I have certainly heard a magic in some German spruce tops that I've heard nowhere else. It's a special clarity, a strength and transparency in the high overtones, and a sense that it's the wood, rather than the resonating air chamber, that's doing all the work. But I can't swear that I can always spot German spruce because I've also heard German spruce tops—on instruments from the finest makers, mind you—that have been absolute dogs.

On the other hand, there are hundreds, if not thousands, of Sitka-topped guitars made every year that sound good and better than good. Certainly better than a dog of a German-spruce instrument. And often enough you'll find a Sitka top that's a real knockout.

So just remember that the magic is in the wood, not the name. The finest German spruce may be the best of the lot, but not all German spruce is the finest. Good Sitka is better than bad German. Good German is better than bad Engelmann. Good Engelmann is better than bad Adirondack. Good Adirondack is better than bad Sitka. Good Sitka is better than bad German . . . the circle is complete. Listening to the instrument is what tells you whether it's got a good top or not. Reading the catalog specs will not.

Selecting Spruce for a Top

How well a guitar sings is determined by how well its top vibrates due to the quality and shaping of the surface and of the bracing. The sound of the top will improve with playing and with age. While it may take a decade or two for the top to really mature, you can hear the top of a brand new instrument begin discernibly to "open up" after only a few hours of playing.

You can learn to spot quartersawn tops by the appearance of the rays (see the *Grain and Figure* section above), since rays only appear clearly in the wood figure in quartersawn or radial cuts. They impart a certain lustrous sheen across the texture of the grain when you hold the wood against the light. It can be shown by example but it's impossible to teach by words.

What a guitar maker looks for in spruce is a light color and a fine, straight growth ring pattern. The lighter and darker parts of the grain lines, which represent the tree's spring and summer growth, should not be too highly differentiated in shade. (Extremes of shading indicate excessive differences in humidity between the wet and dry seasons of the growing year.) An edge grain structure of no fewer than 12 to 15 lines per inch at the widest-grained portion of the board is considered the minimum standard for first-class timber. This ideal tends to occur in trees from near the treeline that have experienced healthy, consistent patterns of rainfall and temperature during their lifetime.

The edge grain widens somewhat across the width of the board, reflecting the fact that the outside growth rings of the tree get wider as the log increases in diameter. After the two halves of the top are split and bookmatched, it's conventional to join them with the narrower edge grain at the center seam. However, on some guitars—many vintage Martins in particular—the wider grain is at the center. Both methods seem to work equally well, though each undoubtedly has strong partisans.

However, a good guitar maker will judge the quality of timber not only by sight, but even more importantly by how it rings when tapped, and by its resilience and feel. A fine top requires a unique blend of stiffness and resilience that only the best woods provide. Therefore, in spite of everything said about appearances in the preceding paragraph, you'll occasionally find a quite undistinguished-looking top on a great instrument, and, even more often, a good-looking top on a mediocre one. So again: learn to use your ears! The luthier does.

Cedar and Redwood

Over the past few years, makers have increasingly turned to western red cedar for tops on both steel-string and classical guitars. Redwood, a similar wood, has also been used, though more on classical guitars than on steel-strings.

These woods may have a more brilliant tone than spruce on new guitars, but it seems to stay where it is for the life of the guitar, and not grow richer with time as spruce does. To my ear, the tone is more cutting but less delicious and sustaining in the highs than that of good spruce. Of course, the sound of a good piece of cedar can certainly be preferable to that of bad piece of spruce, no matter what the characteristic qualities of each wood.

Cedar and redwood tops are not to my taste on steel-string guitars, but you should make up your own mind. Some excellent players use guitars with tops made of these woods.

Cedar from Europe and the Middle East is used as well as mahogany for the necks of classical guitars by many of Spain's foremost luthiers. It's the wood of choice for flamenco guitar necks, where both its color and light weight go better with the cypress body. 19th-century guitars, including some Martins, had cedar necks, but mahogany and maple hold up better under the tension of today's steel strings. Cedar is also sometimes used for linings.

Rosewood

Rosewood is a resinous, dense, very hard wood that is usually considered the most desirable material for the back and sides of classical and steel-string flattop guitars. It gets its name because the resins of the freshly cut tree give off a sweet, rose-like fragrance. (Get your nose out of your instrument! The fragrance is long gone by the time the log has become a guitar.)

Rosewood has greater resonance than any other hardwood when struck, which makes it the wood of choice for xylophones and marimbas. It has a brilliant and highly projective sound, with both a dark and bright side to it, with a bit of bark. It's most guitar players' wood of choice, for many excellent reasons. But there are also good reasons to like the sounds of the other major body woods, maple and mahogany, so it's important that you form your own opinion. For maximum projection, the back and sides of the guitar need to reflect sound rather than absorb it. This is why very hard woods like rosewood and maple give a bright sound, while the softer mahogany gives a sweeter sound.

From the builder's point of view, rosewood has excellent structural as well as acoustic properties. It may be cut very thin without sacrificing rigidity (the most important factor in back and sides), and it lends itself to the heat-bending process by which the sides are shaped. However, rosewood splits fairly easily along its grain if subject to climate changes. Regluing split sides and backs is a fairly common repair job, and not much to worry about. Because it's a fairly open-grained (porous-looking) wood, it's usually treated with a filler before staining and finishing.

Quartersawn, straight-grained, evenly colored, and simple-looking rosewood is best for guitars. Rosewood with a purplish cast, plank-sawn with a highly figured grain pattern, can be gorgeous in furniture, but is less suited for a guitar.

Brazilian rosewood is also known as palisander or by its Spanish name, palo santo. (In Brazil it is also sometimes called jacaranda de Bahía, not to confused with other jacarandas.) Until the 1960s, it was imported in the form of uncut logs. Martin and other manufacturers then milled it in their own U.S. factories. But in the late sixties, the Brazilian government, in an effort to develop its own milling industry, decreed that only milled lumber could be exported. Because sawmills find it much more profitable to mill lumber in forms more suitable for furniture than guitars, guitar-quality Brazilian rosewood became rare and expensive. It can still be found on custom and limited-production instruments, but expect to pay a good deal more for it.

But while luthiers and small shops still may use Brazilian rosewood, the large companies found its cost prohibitive. Martin switched to the lighter-colored East Indian rosewood for its standard production models in 1970. (Now, 20 years later, the Indian wood is getting hard to come by as well. The Indian government prohibited shipping of whole logs in the mid-seventies, also in order to stimulate the growth of its own domestic milling industry. In addition, India's forest-growth rosewood has been significantly depleted, and most Indian rosewood we see these days is a lighter plantation-grown variety). Note that the terms "Indian" and "East Indian" rosewood are used interchangeably in the guitar industry.

Most guitar makers feel that Indian and Brazilian rosewood sound the same. Some conservative purists, on the other hand, prefer the appearance of Brazilian wood, and feel (whether or not out of mystical preconceptions) that it does sound somehow better. It may be a moot point, because the accepted standard of comparison is to a 50- or 60-year-old Martin, and all of them were Brazilian. To someone like me who grew up with Brazilian rosewood, the Indian stuff just doesn't look right and that's all there is to it. I expect I'll go to the grave with this bias.

Rosewood is hard enough to be used for bridges and fingerboards, though the more expensive ebony, being harder still, is a better choice and is used on more expensive steel-string guitars (classical luthiers prefer rosewood bridges, which sound sweeter). Rosewood is also used for bridge plates, as is maple.

Honduras rosewood (also called nogaed), a slightly different species, is also used for bridges and fingerboards as well as marimba bars, guitar laminates, and furniture making. But it's generally not used as a solid wood for guitar bodies, because it doesn't like to be bent to shape for the sides.

The various rosewoods are also in great demand not only as furniture veneers but also for turned bowls and trinkets (rosewood lends itself well to lathe-work), and for fine knife handles. For these uses, too, Brazilian rosewood is highly sought after because of its beauty.

Rosewood Substitutes

The following woods are similar to rosewood, and in some cases relatives. For the most part they are inferior to rosewood either acoustically or structurally (for example, some exude pockets of sap when the wood is steam-bent for sides). Therefore they are not generally used for solid-wood guitars, but instead as veneers for laminates, where they are attractive and sometimes even look like real rosewood.

Amboyna (another name for narra).
Bubinga (African rosewood).
Cocobolo (also called granadillo; from Mexico). May be used as a solid wood; some luthiers think highly of it for back and sides.
Jacaranda (also called jacaranda pardo.)
Louro Preto (another Brazilian wood).
Narra (also called amboyna; from the Philippines).
Ovangkol (a dark African wood about midway between rosewood and mahogany. Often appears in print with slightly different spellings.)
Tulipwood (another type of jacaranda known as jacaranda rosa; also used for marimbas.)

Mahogany

The best guitar mahogany is "Honduras" mahogany. As with many other names, this is an industry term and the wood may come from Latin American regions other than Honduras proper—even from Brazil. (It's sometimes called American mahogany.) Like rosewood, it's open-grained and hence treated with a filler before final staining and finishing. Philippine mahogany, sometimes used on cheap instruments, is a lighter, more porous, tonally inferior wood. European mahogany, while beautiful for furniture, isn't suitable for guitars.

Mahogany is softer and lighter than rosewood, and doesn't have nearly as good a reputation as rosewood does—except among those many guitarists who, like Doc Watson and Leo Kottke, prefer its warmth, balance, and sweetness to the brilliance of rosewood. In some ways, you could say that a mahogany guitar is to a rosewood one as a chamber-music violin or recorder is to a solo one. Or as a Guarnerius violin is to a Stradivarius. Big rosewood guitars are notoriously difficult to mike and to record because of their boominess; many studio guitarists prefer mahogany instruments for this reason.

Generally, mahogany is less projective, which is to say, less loud. That doesn't mean that a mahogany guitar may not be the guitar for you. And that doesn't mean that some mahogany instruments may not be very loud indeed.

There's a saying that "It's no shame to be poor, but it might as well be." The same could be said about being mahogany. Its bad reputation probably started because (as just about everyone agrees) it just doesn't work anywhere near as well as rosewood for classical guitars. The Martin company also comes in for a share of the blame. Martin's sonic values have always been very rosewood-oriented, and as a rule Martin, and the makers it has influenced, reserve their best spruce and greatest degree of attention for rosewood bodies. (In spite of this you'll find some mahogany Martins out there that will knock your socks off—especially among the older ones. And there are a number of makers, Don Gallagher and Harry Fleishman among them, who customarily give mahogany first-class treatment.)

Mahogany is sometimes used for tops on mahogany-bodied guitars (in the old days, before laminates, it was used especially on economy models). It produces a warm, balanced tone with a smaller voice than spruce's, which can nonetheless be very satisfying. As a rule, mahogany-topped guitars don't put out enough sound for professional use. However, you'll sometimes come across prewar mahogany-topped Martins and Gibsons that can overwhelm many modern guitars.

Mahogany is the standard wood for guitar necks because of its superior strength and stability under the kind of stress the strings produce. Straight-grained quarter-sawn Honduras is best. A neck that's not quartersawn is simply not going to hold up well over the long run. Grain structure running the length of the neck is the sign of a quarter-sawn neck blank.

Mahogany may also be used for back bracing, for the flat brace on the top above the soundhole, and for linings, end blocks, and heel blocks.

Maple

Maple is a strong, stiff, projective wood for back and sides, as loud as rosewood, with more cutting sound. If you're familiar with electric guitars, you'll know what it means to say that maple is to rosewood as a Telecaster is to a Les Paul. Maple doesn't bring out the bottom or low tones as much as rosewood does, which makes it less successful in small-bodied guitars than in larger ones where the body size helps reinforce the bottom.

Antonio Torres used maple on some of his instruments, and it's sometimes used for flamenco guitar bodies (though cypress is standard). The Gibson, Guild, and Santa Cruz companies in particular have made some very successful maple guitars, and in recent years Martin has turned to maple as well. (Although C. F. Martin himself did some work in maple, the Martin factory hadn't touched the stuff for well over a century.)

Maple comes in several patterns, named flame, curly, and birdseye according to the figure, which work well on guitars and have been used on the backs and sides of the world's greatest violins, cellos, and basses for over three hundred years. They sound and look good.

Maple is the wood of choice for mandolin and f-hole guitar bodies, which are inspired by the design of the bowed instruments. When these instruments are built to the highest standard, their backs must be tuned to the the tops by careful carving and shaping. Because of its hardness and pliability, maple surpasses all other tonewoods for this sort of carving.

Maple's density makes it a good choice for bridge plates. It's also often used for necks on guitars with maple and other light-colored bodies, for the sake of appearance. Because maple is not quite as stable for necks as mahogany, it's often laminated with cross-grained ebony or rosewood strips, which add strength and look good as well.

Maple on fine guitars may be either American rock maple or European flame maple. Japanese maple is similar to American maple. Red and silver maple are softer and are not generally used as solid woods but may be used as veneers.

Koa

Koa is a Hawaiian wood that came into fashion—especially on ukuleles and Hawaiian guitars—during the Hawaiian music craze of the twenties. It projects fewer lows than rosewood and fewer highs than mahogany, offering a compressed, woody midrange sound. Koa fell from favor after its Hawaiian novelty value faded at the end of the twenties, but its visual beauty, combined with the increasing rarity of other woods, explains why it was revived by Martin and other makers during the eighties. At its best, koa's figure is extremely beautiful: like deep flame maple with a tropical complexion. However, koa has recently been restricted by the Hawaiian government, so it may go the way of Brazilian rosewood.

Sometimes koa is also used as a top wood on koa-bodied guitars, in which case its midrange tendencies are even stronger. Koa-topped guitars have a voice all their own: soft, warm, sweet, sometimes with a slight abrasive edge, but not particularly crisp, clear, or well-separated. Maybe something like a mahogany top as heard through a mist.

Ebony

Ebony is an extremely dense wood, better even than rosewood for fingerboards. Most experienced players easily discern the firmer feel of an ebony fingerboard. You'll also find that, after years of playing, a rosewood fingerboard will show considerable signs of wear where ebony will not. However, ebony is a brittle wood and over time it cracks

A koa Custom H model by the Santa Cruz Guitar Co. *Photo courtesy Santa Cruz Guitar Co.*

more readily than rosewood. Filling cracks in ebony fingerboards with a mixture of epoxy and ebony dust is a common repair job.

Ebony's density also makes it a superior sound transmitter for steel-string guitar bridges. However, classical luthiers prefer rosewood for its sweetness with nylon strings.

The best ebonies are the almost jet-black woods from Ceylon and Gabon (West Africa), but many guitar makers use the more variegated Indian and Macassar woods dyed black for the sake of appearance. In any case, little ebony of any kind is totally black, so almost all is dyed. All ebonies are sufficiently hard, though the Ceylon and Gabon woods are somewhat harder and less porous. Ebony isn't very grainy in any case, but the less grain you can see, the better.

Other Woods

Ash is used for linings, and occasionally for bodies, with tonal characteristics resembling maple's. The few ash-bodied guitars I've played (not enough to make a safe generalization) have been extremely quick and vivacious, and quite enjoyable to play, though not profound. (Yes, guitarists sometimes sound like wine-tasters when they get to talking about instruments.) Quilted ash is a very beautiful wood, with a flame-like figure as deep as that of the finest maple. Ash is also used often in laminate cores.

Basswood may be used for linings.

Birch and sycamore are occasionally used as maple substitutes, especially as veneer facings.

Cherry, as both solid and laminate, is sometimes used for back and sides.

Cypress is used on the back and sides of nylon-string flamenco guitars to give these instruments their distinctive sharp cutting edge and piercing strummed sound. It is not used for steel-string guitars. I imagine it would sound tinny and jangly with steel strings.

Nato is a Pacific wood used as a substitute for mahogany on necks of less expensive guitars. Sometimes it's also used for bodies. It's less stable than mahogany, but a nato neck with adequate truss-rod reinforcement should be dependable enough for a reasonable price.

Pear and walnut may be used for bindings and are hard enough that they are sometimes used for fingerboards, where they are usually "ebonized": dyed and treated with epoxy resin or some other hardening filler to impersonate ebony. They are also occasionally used for backs and sides; pear sounds similar to mahogany and walnut somewhat closer to rosewood. Walnut is also sometimes used for bridges.

Pine, willow, or poplar are sometimes used for the heel block, end block, and linings—especially on less expensive instruments.

White holly, boxwood, and other ornamental woods are used for bindings, as are various plastics and "ivoroid" cellulose nitrate or cellulose acetate.

Finish

A beautiful piece of wood requires a beautiful finish to bring out its

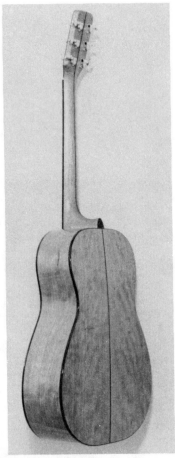

An unusual light cherry body on a Blue Lion guitar. *Photo courtesy Blue Lion Instruments.*

deep, gemlike inner glow. But finish is more than cosmetic: it also does duty to inhibit moisture absorption by the wood and to protect the surface.

Stain and Filler Preparation

Guitar woods are customarily stained before finishing and, in the case of relatively porous woods like rosewood and mahogany, a filler may be rubbed in as well. These are standard cosmetic practices shared with furniture makers and other woodworkers. Once the stain is dry, the instrument is ready to be finished. (Of course, if the instrument is going to have color lacquer applied, then it won't be stained.) On cheap guitars, the stain may be mixed in with the finish and sprayed on in one step. Cheapie guitars—usually minor-brand Korean products—are typically sealed with a heavy layer of polyester finish, which is excellent on boat hulls but doesn't much help guitar acoustics. Often the bridge will be glued directly over this finish, which makes for a weak joint. (In fine guitar making, the bridge is glued to bare wood before the entire top is finished.) Polyester finish grows crystalline and brittle with time, and eventually the bridge comes loose. Therefore, the cheap manufacturer may use bolts to hold the bridge down, with detriment to the sound.

Nitrocellulose and Acrylic Lacquers

The standard guitar finish is sprayed-on nitrocellulose lacquer. (This may not be the case much longer in mass-production domestic guitars, since OSHA doesn't much like the stuff. A lacquer spray booth is a dangerously flammable environment.) Makers are now beginning to use, or at least to experiment with, acrylic lacquer, which is also used on cars. Many feel it works as well on guitars as nitrocellulose does, and it's more suitable for color finishes.

A good lacquer job may consist of 6 to 12 thin coats, each finely sanded before the next is applied. A cheap lacquer job might be one heavy-handed pass through the spray booth, or maybe even past the spray robot. A good lacquer job leaves a thin, hard finish that allows the wood to vibrate freely, and possibly even enhances its sound qualities. A cheap lacquer job acts like a blanket, deadening the guitar, and is more easily subject to finish checking (small cracks in the finish due to sudden temperature change).

Compare cheap guitars with fine ones and you'll learn to see the difference in finish quality. However, even fine guitars from the best modern makers are (to my taste at least) these days too heavily finished. However, popular taste demands a slick appearance and makers are afraid of losing sales.

For the few who do prefer a less glossy look, some makers offer good-looking low-gloss or matte finishes. Remember, though, that a low-gloss finish isn't necessarily a lighter or finer one; it just has a different surface quality.

Sunburst Finishes

There's another form of ornamental finish, used on tops and sometimes backs, called "sunburst." In this design, a more dramatic version of the shading used on some fine violin tops, the center of the top is rich golden-orange hue, fading gradually to dark brown, black, or burgundy around the edges. For most devotees, the classic Gibson sunburst represents the high point of this art.

Charles Sawtelle's sunburst Martin dreadnought is also sunstruck in this photograph. *Photo by Larry Sandberg.*

Sunbursting is a difficult, time-consuming technique. It involves applying several layers of gradually darkening lacquer with an extremely delicate touch on the spray gun, and a goodly amount of extra rubbing and sanding in between. Some manufacturers may reserve their less visually-appealing spruce for sunbursting.

By tradition, incidentally, sunbursts are visually associated with flat-top guitars used by country and old-time bluegrass musicians, with f-hole guitars used by swing and mainstream jazz musicians, and (with a more orange-to-red graduation) with some of the Gibson Les Paul solid-bodies that really scream heavy metal. New-age guitarists seem to prefer natural wood, basic white, or basic black. As for sunbursting classical guitars, why, it's simply not done!

French Polish and Spot Finishes

Oddly, the resin- and gum-based varnishes used in violin finishing don't seem to suit the acoustic properties of guitars. (A quick though over-simplified explanation of the difference between lacquer and varnish is this: you rub a varnish into the wood, whereas you spray a lacquer on top of the wood, where it dries in a thin layer through the evaporation of volatile solvents.)

An exception is a difficult form of shellac varnishing known as French polish, which, after many painstaking rubbing and sanding steps, leaves an extremely subtle gloss. It's used on some fine violins and classical guitars, and a few luthiers offer it as a custom finish on steel-string guitars. Those repairpeople who have mastered French polishing also find it useful for spot-finishing damaged areas.

Tung oil is also sometimes used for spot finishing and restoration work, preferable on necks and headstocks rather than on tonewood. A vegetable oil in its pure form, it usually comes mixed with mineral spirits or petroleum distillates in commercial finishing preparations.

Glues

The traditional animal-hide glues are now being supplanted by synthetic white glues that are more stable under humid conditions. But though their tolerance is higher, like the animal glues they still loosen in excessive heat—the heat of a car trunk in summer, or of a guitar case under the hot sun. You wouldn't want it otherwise. The main joints in the guitar should be able to be loosened with a simple application of heat, so repair work, adjustments, and restorations can be made. Permanent glues are not the answer. The answer is not to leave your guitar in the trunk on a summer's day.

However, materials like epoxy resins and cyanoacrylate ("magic" or "super") glue are used by some repairpeople for specialized jobs. Epoxy is typically mixed with rosewood or ebony dust to build up pitted fingerboards, and sometimes it's used to seat frets—a practice strongly debated within the trade. Cyanoacrylate, which is so runny that its penetrating powers exceed those of any other glue, is used for hairline cracks and crevices and other spot applications where a possible need to separate the joint in the future is not an issue. This too is a hotly debated practice.

Of the white glues, most makers and repairpeople favor aliphatic resin—the standard woodworkers' glue of which Tite-Bond™ is the best-known brand. Sometimes polyvinyl resin glue is used (Elmer's™ is the best-known brand.) Polyvinyl resin is not as strong for manufacturing, but since it's less tacky (more runny), it's better for infiltrating tiny cracks and small spaces in repair work. Inferior white glues used on inexpensive guitars loosen more easily in hot, humid conditions.

Resorcinol glues are the standard for holding together construction-grade plywood and presumably they're used for guitar plywood too, but because the guitar industry is so secretive about its laminates, we don't know.

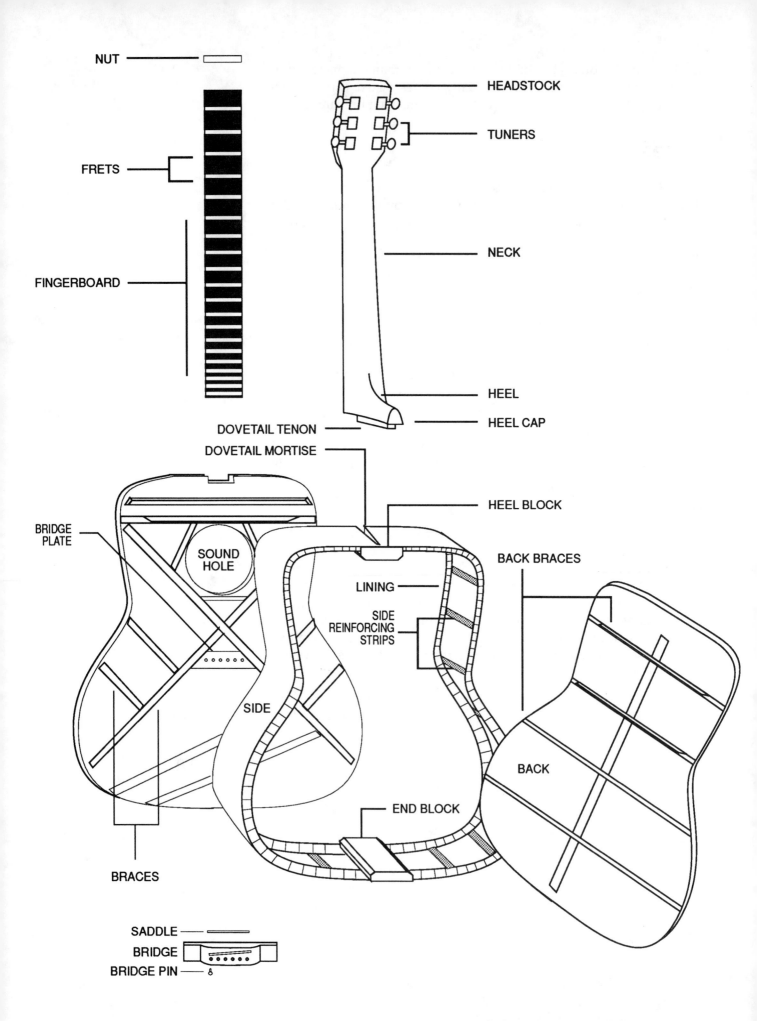

NUT

HEADSTOCK

TUNERS

FRETS

NECK

FINGERBOARD

HEEL

HEEL CAP

DOVETAIL TENON

DOVETAIL MORTISE

HEEL BLOCK

BRIDGE PLATE

BACK BRACES

SOUND HOLE

LINING

SIDE REINFORCING STRIPS

SIDE

BACK

END BLOCK

BRACES

SADDLE

BRIDGE

BRIDGE PIN

5

How Your
Guitar Works, 1:
Where the Action Is

Action and Setup

Action Strictly Defined

The term *action* refers to the distance of the string above the fingerboard. Action depends on:

- Nut and saddle height
- Neck straightness
- Neck set (the angle at which the neck joins the body)

Luthiers use the fret where the neck joins the body (usually the fourteenth or twelfth, depending on the model) as the standard reference point for measuring action. Normal string clearances at that fret for a steel-string acoustic guitar should be around 5/32 -inch for the sixth (low E) string and and 3/32 -inch for the first (high E) string.

These figures are based on the assumption that the neck itself is unwarped and properly set and adjusted. And they're starting points, subject to small adjustments for string gauge, playing style, and personal taste. When action is too high, the guitar becomes uncomfortable to play. When action is too low, strings buzz and lose volume and tone quality. Classical guitar action is usually a bit higher; electric guitar action a bit lower.

Action Loosely Defined

People also use the word *action* in a looser sense to mean the amount of *perceived* effort it takes to fret the strings. In this subjective sense, some other factors come into play:

- String gauge (insofar as heavier strings feel stiffer)
- Fret condition (worn-down frets require more finger pressure)
- Your technique, expectations, level of experience, and raw strength. A guitar that seems stiff to someone who plays an hour a week may seem wimpy to someone who plays six hours a day.
- Scale (string length; see the *Scale* section in this chapter). Strings feel stiffer when the scale is longer.

Setup

The Mechanics of Setup

The sum total of nut, saddle, and truss rod adjustments that determine the action of the guitar is called *setup*. A beautifully set up guitar brings out the best in the player and gives the greatest pleasure.

Setup also depends on the choice of strings. Changing between, say, extra light and medium strings affects the amount of tension on the neck (hence the need to readjust the truss rod) and may also pull up the neck a tiny bit.

Setup and Style

Some guitarists, especially beginners, have the idea that action should be so low as to be virtually imperceptible. The customer who asks to "make my action as low as possible without buzzing" is a standard joke among repairpeople; noted repairperson Matt Umanov used to post a sign in his New York shop saying "Will everyone who wants their action as low as possible without buzzing please leave." But many experienced players actually prefer to feel the strings assert themselves a little. The instrument feels crisper to play. Beginners have their hands full just trying to get their notes to start in the right place, but a good player is also in perfect control of when and how the note ends. Getting it to end definitively is easier when the strings snap cleanly back off the frets. Wimpy action doesn't give you as much control.

The kind of action you want is a matter of personal taste, coupled with the demands of your particular style. The permutations of personal taste and stylistic demands are almost endless. Let's look at just a few scenarios and their rationales.

- **String bending,** characteristic of blues, rock, and many contemporary styles, is something you'd think would be more easily accomplished with low action. After all, the fingers are using enough energy just getting the strings to bend; having to cope with high action in addition seems like too much extra to ask. But if you put such a deep bend on a string that it moves up into another string's space, you'll find that with high action you can get the bent string *under* the string whose turf is being invaded, which makes bending a lot easier. Therefore, lots of blues players favor the unlikely combination of light strings and high action. This kind of setup is a little more common on electric than acoustic guitars, though—especially at its most extreme.
- **Acoustic jazz** players tend to prefer an action similar to the one a mainstream jazz soloist would have on an archtop guitar: fairly low, very even up and down the fingerboard, and typically set up for medium rather than light strings. The problem is that, on

an archtop guitar, the neck is mounted on a different angle that makes it intrinsically easier to achieve this kind of setup. Luthiers gnash their teeth when asked to get this kind of a feel out of a flattop, because it goes against the nature of the instrument. The action is always on the edge of buzzing, frets have to be dressed with finicky attention, and the tolerances are so close that when a warm front blows through the next day the buzzing starts all over again. The fact that acoustic jazz guitarists tend to play with more of a heavy bluegrass touch than a light jazz touch doesn't make things any easier. Here's an idea: if you want a guitar that feels like an archtop, then consider getting an archtop.

- **New-age and Celtic fingerpicking** players usually ask for a setup similar to the one for acoustic jazz, but with lighter strings. The same teeth-gnashing problems and solutions exist. Some makes, models, and given instruments come out of the factory better disposed to this kind of setup than others, and these are the ones you should look for if you're into new-age and acoustic-jazz styles. Otherwise you'll be living in a perpetual world of neck resets, setups, and fret dressing, your guitar will spend more time in the shop than in your hands, you'll never be a happy person, and one day you'll wake up to discover that your spouse and best friend have just drifted away, possibly with each other.

- **Ragtime** guitarists and other players of complicated fingerpicking styles for the most part like the ideal of a low-action guitar similar to the one new-age guitarists favor. But because many of them also play blues and similar styles requiring a more aggressive touch, they usually wind up having to go with a somewhat stiffer action.

- **Bluegrass** and other aggressive flatpicking styles require a higher action in order to avoid string buzzing. The reason is not just because the string is set into a wider arc of motion merely from being struck more forcefully. It's also because good players learn that the most effective way to punch out a strongly punctuated note is to dig *into* the string, bringing the pick to rest against the next string. The direction of this pick motion causes the string to move more perpendicularly to the fingerboard, even further increasing the possibility of buzzing.

- **Slide guitar** requires an action high enough to keep the weight of the slide from pressing the strings against the fingerboard. Of course, if you play solos with the slide exclusively, the action can be as high as you like. But if you play the style of slide guitar where you wear a slide on your pinky for some notes, but use the rest of your fingers for playing regular notes and chords, you'll have to accept an action that's too high to be really comfortable. For this reason, most serious slide players keep a second guitar with regular action for regular playing.

- **Beginners** and most casual players, especially when they're using relatively inexpensive guitars, are for the most part best off with a relatively low, comfortable action and light-gauge strings until they reach a point in their development where other stylistic decisions might come into play.

The Neck

The neck extends the strings out from the body of the guitar. At the end of the neck are the geared pegs to tune the strings. Along the top of the neck is the *fingerboard*, a strip of dark hardwood in which the *frets* are seated. Where the neck butts the shoulders of the guitar body, it broadens out into a larger section called the *heel*.

Neck Materials and Construction

The necks of most steel-string guitars are made of mahogany—ideally quartersawn Honduras mahogany for maximum strength and stability. On less expensive instruments, nato, a mahogany-like wood from the South Pacific, has become a standard substitute.

On guitars with maple or other light-colored bodies, maple necks are often used. Because maple isn't quite as stable as mahogany, maple necks on better guitars are often cut lengthwise into halves or thirds and interleaved with strips of rosewood, ebony, or another dark hardwood. The darker sections are glued together with the grain in different directions for strength and warp resistance—the same principle that adds strength to plywood and corrugated cardboard. Dark woods are chosen for visual contrast; a well-made laminated neck is pleasing to look at.

Laminated necks are not inferior. Far from it; some very fine, sturdy necks are made this way. As a rule, though, they're pretty heavy—heavy

---

QUARTERSAWN AND LAMINATED NECKS

In a neck made of quartersawn wood the grain structure is perpendicular to the force of string tension, which helps resist warping.

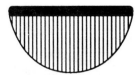

The grain structure of slab-cut wood is on a plane parallel to the force of string tension, which is more conducive to warping.

A neck with cross-laminations of ebony or other strong hardwood also presents a structure which resists warping due to string tension.

enough to upset the balance of the guitar in your lap. Therefore they feel best on large-bodied guitars where the body balances out the neck weight.

On many 19th-century instruments and classical guitars to the present day, cedar may be used for the neck. It works fine with nylon strings but doesn't hold up to the greater tension of steel strings as well as mahogany does. Most cedar necks have a *grafted* construction in which the headstock and heel sections of the neck *blank* (the rough-shaped piece of wood from which the neck is carved) are made of separate sections of wood glued together. It's hard to find cedar lumber large enough for a one-piece blank.

Stability of the neck wood is extremely important. Playability depends on keeping the strings a precise height above the fingerboard, so if the neck warps, the instrument becomes difficult or impossible to finger. Although a fine piece of mahogany holds up amazingly well against the 150 or more pounds of string tension on most guitars, it needs all the help it can get. Therefore almost all contemporary steel-string guitar necks are built with a metal reinforcing rod, or *truss rod* (see below).

Neck Shape and Contour

The contour of the neck may be more or less rounded around the back. Most guitarists find slender necks easier to play, and call them *fast*—though other elements such as action, fingerboard width, and the type and condition of the frets also contribute to how fast a neck feels. There are also those who don't mind a stout, clubby neck, or even prefer one. Clubby necks are stronger—there's more wood to them, after all. But now that metal truss rods are standard fixtures there's less need to rely on wood alone for strength, so necks have gotten more slender in recent years in response to the public's preference for them.

Back in the 19th century, a fair number of guitars were made with the backs of the neck more triangular than rounded in shape. If your hand position is one where you play a lot with the ball of your thumb resting on the backside of the neck, as classical guitarists do, such necks can be treacherous. But if you mostly loop your thumb around over the top of the fingerboard, a neck like this is even easier to play than a rounded one. (There's less distance for the thumb to reach around—after all, the shortest distance between two points is a straight line.) In recent years the triangular neck has been rediscovered, and is making a comeback on some top-of-the-line and custom models.

Relief

Function
It may come as a big surprise to learn that a guitar neck is not supposed to be perfectly straight. But it's true. Guitar necks should be a little warped, just like a sense of humor.

If you lay a straightedge against a guitar fingerboard, you might notice that it dips a little around the fifth to seventh frets. If you have a good eye, you may even be able to spot it by sighting down the neck. Guitar makers build this dip into their instruments to make the upper

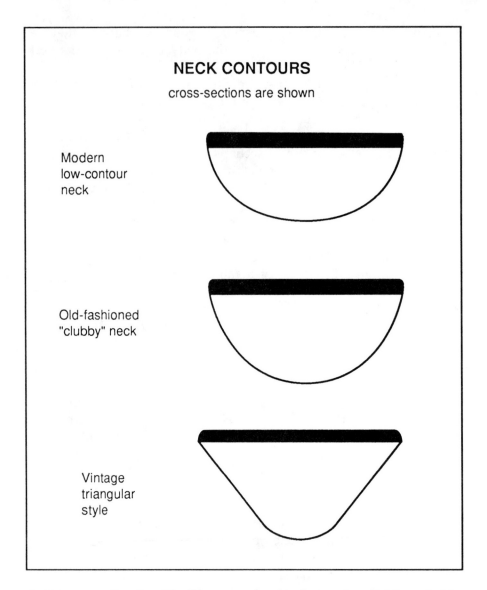

NECK CONTOURS

cross-sections are shown

Modern
low-contour
neck

Old-fashioned
"clubby" neck

Vintage
triangular
style

frets more easily playable. The name for this feature is *relief*. It probably comes from the fact that if you've just taken home your new $800 guitar and noticed that the neck isn't perfectly straight, you should be relieved to know that that's the way it's supposed to be.

The line between deliberate relief and unwanted warping is a thin one, measured in 64ths of an inch. String height above the crown of the sixth fret (for steel-string guitars with light-to-medium gauge strings) should be in the ball park of $\frac{1}{32}$ inch under the treble strings, and $\frac{3}{64}$ inch under the bass strings for a player with a moderate touch. Heavier strings and/or a heavier touch require higher relief. Short-scale guitars (see *Scale* later in this chapter) require less relief than long-scale guitars.

Adjusting Relief

Your dealer or repairperson can make fine adjustments to relief by tightening or loosening the adjustable truss rod, as discussed in the section that follows. On instruments made before the days of the adjustable truss rod, or on the very few instruments currently made without them, the repairperson has to treat relief adjustments as if they were warp symptoms, by bending the neck under heat or by removing the frets and planing the fingerboard.

Some luthiers and repairpeople reject the concept of relief, and prefer a straight fingerboard. I suspect that luthiers of this school are used to working mainly on solidbody and archtop guitars, where the neck angle is set further back than on flattops and relief is less important.

The Truss Rod

Simple Reinforcing Rods

After the beginning of this century, guitar makers found that their traditional necks, designed for gut strings, warped under the much

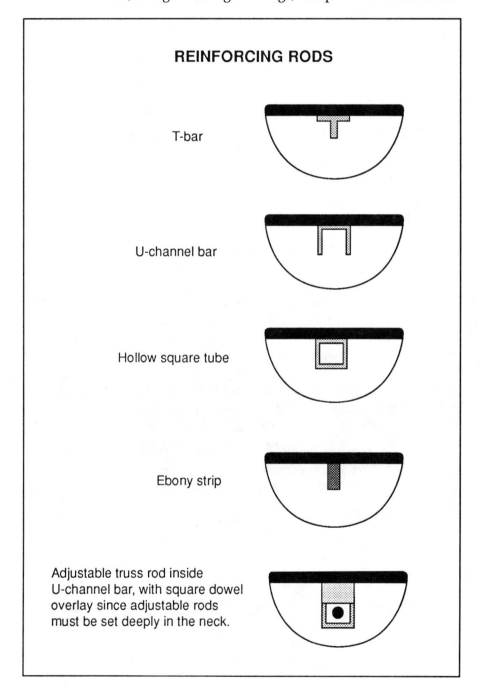

REINFORCING RODS

T-bar

U-channel bar

Hollow square tube

Ebony strip

Adjustable truss rod inside
U-channel bar, with square dowel
overlay since adjustable rods
must be set deeply in the neck.

greater pressure of the newly fashionable steel strings. Even giving up cedar for stronger Honduras mahogany wasn't good enough, so manufacturers like Martin started cutting a hidden groove in the neck before the fingerboard was glued on top, and laying in a long strip of ebony to add strength. Ebony lasted a few years, and then the makers discovered that a steel reinforcing rod was even better. (On most American instruments made during the steel-starved World War II years, though, the rods were either left out completely or ebony was again used.)

At first the rods were mostly T-shaped, but later on lighter hollow rectangular and U-shaped rods became standard—at least on good guitars. Cheapie guitars sometimes carried a "metal-reinforced neck" decal than meant little more than that some scrap metal, perhaps even a used hacksaw blade, was embedded in the neck.

Modern Truss Rod Design

During the 1920s, the Gibson company patented an improved reinforcing rod called the *truss rod* or *tension rod*. Instead of merely introducing stiffening support to the neck, it created compression.

The original Gibson design had a slight adjustable arch to it, which created tension to counteract the tension of the strings. One end of the rod was embedded in the heel so it couldn't rotate, while the other end of the rod had a hex nut that stuck out of a hole in the headstock, underneath a small cover plate that could be removed by loosening a few screws. Turning the hex nut increased or reduced the tension of the rod. A few unscrupulous cheapie manufacturers of past years built guitars with false truss rod covers that had nothing underneath, to convey the impression that their instruments were outfitted with the adjustable rods.

Now that the Gibson patent is expired, the adjustable truss rod is in standard use by almost every manufacturer. Even Martin, which had argued (not without justice) for years that well-made necks don't require adjustable rods, finally swallowed its pride and went over to them in the mid-eighties when they introduced a thinner neck contour.

Truss-rod design has improved over the years. Today's rods have turned around. Now their stable end is mounted into the headstock, while the adjusting end (usually in the form of a slot screw or hex socket)

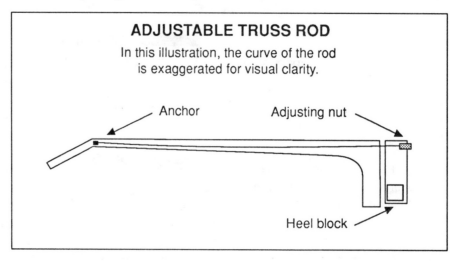

ADJUSTABLE TRUSS ROD

In this illustration, the curve of the rod is exaggerated for visual clarity.

Anchor   Adjusting nut

Heel block

BOW AND WARP

A warped neck.
This condition is also known as forward warp or forward bow.

A bowed neck.
This condition is also known as reverse warp, reverse bow, or backbow.

Cure

The way a repairperson cures moderate warp is to place the guitar in a *straightening jig,* which is a fancy way of saying that the neck gets clamped to a sturdy piece of pipe or straight lumber and left under infrared lamps for a couple of days. In more extreme cases, it may be necessary to remove the frets and plane the fingerboard to compensate for the warp.

In addition to warp and backbow, it's also possible for a neck to twist or *skew* around its long axis. This happens most often on 12-string guitars, where string tension on the bass side is disproportionately high. The treatment is fingerboard planing.

Joining the Neck to the Body

Neck Joints

The traditional way to join the guitar neck to the body is with a dovetail tenon in the heel. (You can't see the dovetail joint because the fingerboard covers it.) The tenon fits into a mortise cut into the *heel block* (also called *head block*), a solid block of wood mounted inside the body directly

Dovetail joint on guitar by Dennis Stevens. *Photo by Larry Sandberg.*

under the fingerboard. You can see the heel block by looking through the soundhole. It's the place where most manufacturers stamp the model and serial number.

Some instruments use other kinds of mortise joints or even necks that are bolted on through the heel block. On inexpensive instruments, substitution of a bolt-on neck for a dovetail joint is usually a sign of cost-cutting. However, not all guitar makers feel that the dovetail is ideal, so you'll also sometimes find well-made joints of other kinds on fine or experimental instruments from reputable makers—or even well-designed bolt-on necks.

Bolt-on necks, incidentally, are standard on solidbody electric guitars, while a combination one-piece heel and heel block, with a groove into which the guitar's shoulders are mounted, is the standard rig for classical guitars. The dovetail joint is standard on archtops, though.

Neck Set

If you sight down the neck, or lay the guitar flat on a tabletop and look at it sideways, you'll notice that the neck angles up a little from the plane of the top so that the base of the nut may be around ⅛ higher than the top. In other words, as you look down the neck from the nut toward the bridge, an imaginary line parallel to the top and extending from the base of the nut would hit the bridge about ⅛ inch above the soundboard.

The angle of the neck in relation to the body is called the *set* of the neck. A good set requires careful manufacturing tolerances in the neck joint. In the informal shopping survey I made in preparation for this book, what most disappointed me about guitars in the lower price brackets was the quality control of the neck sets. Not that many were really awful; it's just that too few were really right on, so too few guitars were as comfortable as they should have been.

Classical guitar neck set approximates that of a steel-string flattop, but on archtops the bridge is very high and the neck is set to angle down from the body rather than up. On solidbody electrics, necks are usually set parallel to the body or slightly downwards.

Resetting the Neck

Because of the way the neck angles up, action rises as you go further up the fingerboard. Action at the twelfth fret is roughly twice as high as it is at the first fret. (For the sixth string, that would be in the neighborhood of $5/32$ inch at the twelfth fret versus $1/16$ inch at the first.) A much greater discrepancy means that something is wrong. Another bad sign as you sight down the neck is a sharp angling up of the fingerboard just at the point where it leaves the body (though this usually means a problem with body distortion rather than neck warping).

Bad neck set can come from a cracked heel, loose neck joint, top warping due to string tension, imperfect manufacture, or the pulling up of the entire neck, including heel, by string tension. Surgery for it is completely different from surgery for warping or action problems. You can't cure bad neck set with a straightening jig or tension rod or by adjusting nut and saddle height. The only answer is to *reset* the neck, a fairly expensive job.

A neck reset involves loosening the end of the fingerboard from the top and loosening the heel from its dovetail joint in the heel block—a painstaking process involving delicate prying work with a spatula and hot water. Then the heel is shaved or shimmed to the proper angle and glued back.

When the neck needs to be tipped back rather than forward (which is usually the case), and only a little, it's sometimes possible to remove the back (a relatively easy operation) and then shim back the heel block a little from underneath. This is called a *heel block reset* or *head block reset*. And sometimes it's possible to plane or replace the fingerboard to compensate for the bad neck angle—also an easier and less expensive solution than a neck reset, though only a symptomatic one. Even so, these are all surgical operations well beyond the scope of mere adjustment.

On an inexpensive guitar, a neck reset might cost more than the value of the instrument. Sometimes a repairperson can buy you time and a smidgeon of comfort, and save you money, with a quick-and-dirty job of cutting down a saddle or some other setup adjustment. But it's not really a cure, and the instrument still won't really feel right.

Fingerboard and Frets

Fingerboard Materials

The *fingerboard* (also called the *fretboard*) is the flat section of wood lying across the top of the neck, into which the frets are seated. The portion of the fingerboard that lies over the body of the guitar is called the *spatula*.

Ebony is the fingerboard wood of choice because it offers a hard, positive feel to the fingers and resists wear better than the slightly softer second choice, rosewood. Ebony is brittle and hence more prone than rosewood to cracking over the years, but experienced players prefer it anyway. It's also much more expensive, so you'll only find it on top-of-the-line instruments. Lots of people are very happy with their rosewood fingerboards. You have to play a *lot* before you begin to notice the difference between the feel of ebony and rosewood. Don't kid yourself that you do—it could cost you a couple of hundred bucks you could be spending on your children instead.

Other hardwoods or even veneered plywood are used on inexpensive instruments. Walnut is marginally acceptable at a low price. Some woods may be "ebonized"—dyed black and hardened with epoxy resin to simulate ebony. You're better off with rosewood.

Position Markers, Inlay, and Binding

Most steel-string guitar fingerboards have some sort of dot or ornamental shape called a *position marker* inlaid in back of frets 5, 7, 9, 12, and perhaps also 3, 15, 17, and 19, in order to help the eye see where the fingers are. Sometimes *side dots* are also inlaid along the top edge of the fingerboard for the same reason. (By tradition, serious classical guitars don't have dots or markers, because serious classical guitarists are supposed to know where their fingers are without having to look.)

Some fingerboards, especially on fancy guitars, also have a strip of plastic or ivoroid cellulose nitrate *binding* along the edge. It's supposed to make the edges of the fingerboard feel smoother where the thumb rubs along the top, and the base of the index finger rubs along the bottom. (By tradition, classical guitar fingerboards are never bound, since in the correct classical hand position no part of the hand ever touches the edge of the fingerboard.)

I've always liked the way bound fingerboards look. As to the way they feel: half my guitars have bound fingerboards and half don't, and I never really noticed much difference one way or the other. In fact, until this moment when I had to put something down in writing, I never thought about it. If the frets are properly smoothed off at the edge of the fingerboard to begin with, there should be no need in the first place for a binding to cover them. I suspect that the reason you sometimes see makers of otherwise cheaply made instruments go to the expense of adding a fingerboard binding is that they expect the inferior wood of their fingerboards to shrink, exposing jagged fret edges.

12- and 14-Fret Necks

On almost all flattop guitars these days, the body begins at the fourteenth fret. On classical guitars and on steel-string guitars through the twenties, the body began at the twelfth fret. The modern 14-fret fingerboard was first offered to the public in 1930 by the Martin company on a new series of guitars called the OM (Orchestra Model). It had been developed over the preceding year at the suggestion of Perry Bechtel, a leading banjoist who, like most other banjo players at that time of changing musical tastes, was making the transition to the guitar. Bechtel pointed out that banjo players would be more used to a somewhat narrower neck, with two extra frets. (Banjo players were used to having a lot more frets accessible to them than the guitar offers.) Martin leapt at the idea, and the general public and Martin's competitors, as well as the banjoists, quickly embraced it. Few steel-string guitars today have 12-fret necks, though classical guitars still do.

The guitar designers created access to those extra two frets by shor-

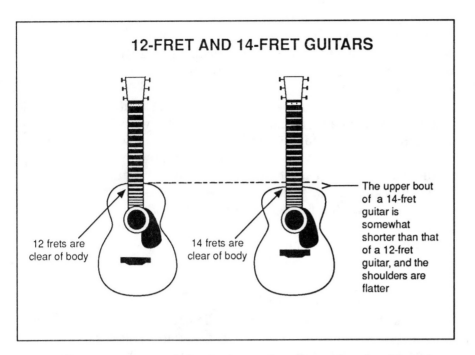

12-FRET AND 14-FRET GUITARS

12 frets are clear of body

14 frets are clear of body

The upper bout of a 14-fret guitar is somewhat shorter than that of a 12-fret guitar, and the shoulders are flatter

tening the upper part of the body, and making the shoulders less rounded. The total number of frets remained at 20 (varying to 19 or 21 on some steel-string models, while classical guitars generally have 18 or 19.) A few harmless eccentrics, myself included, fancy they hear greater richness of tone coming out of 12-fret bodies, but everyone else laughs at us. In any case, it seems perfectly clear that they would rather have easy access to those two extra frets, at whatever cost.

Fingerboard Width

Fingerboards vary in width from model to model. The standard for measuring width is at the nut, but on most guitars the fingerboard widens out a bit toward the spatula, to a degree that varies from model to model.

Today, $1^{11}\!/_{16}$ inches (the width of the nut on the standard Martin dreadnought model) is the fingerboard width most commonly offered by all manufacturers, and the one most people seem to find comfortable. (Add $\frac{1}{8}$ to $\frac{1}{4}$ inch on most 12-string guitars to compensate for the extra strings.) Small differences, even of $\frac{1}{16}$ inch, can be readily felt by experienced players. On 12-fret guitars, fingerboards are traditionally a bit wider, with $1\frac{7}{8}$ inches being a pretty standard figure. This is closer to classical guitar dimensions, where the standard width is 2 inches.

Most people find fingerboards wider than $1\frac{3}{4}$ inches uncomfortable for the fretting hand, especially if they mostly use the thumb-around-the-neck hand position typical of most vernacular styles rather than the thumb-on-the-back-of-the-neck style of classical playing. But suiting the fretting hand isn't what wide fingerboards are about. They're about increasing the distance between the strings for the benefit of the *picking* hand, so the picking fingers have plenty of room for a broad stroke that originates in the first knuckle joint. This is the usual classical guitar stroke. It gives you the most control and the fullest tone, but most steel-string fingerpickers prefer to move from the second knuckle instead. Because this stroke takes up less space, those who use it find wider fingerboards to be of no benefit. If you're among the small number of guitarists who like to have the extra picking space, though, you'll find a wider fingerboard well worth the trouble—if you can find one. Since so few people care for them, few are made.

Almost all flatpickers find wide fingerboards quite uncomfortable under the pick, because nothing but unnecessary work is accomplished by asking the flatpick to travel the extra distance between the strings.

For most guitarists, $1^{11}/_{16}$ inches seems to be the magic compromise figure that does the greatest good for the greatest number of people in both flatpicking and fingerpicking styles. If you like your fingerboard a tad narrower, you'll find a good number of models around to accommodate you, but if you like it wider, you'll have to search harder—possibly among used and vintage instruments as well as new ones—and will probably wind up spending more for your tastes.

Fingerboard Shape and Contour

Most steel-string guitars have a *contoured* fingerboard, which has a slight elliptical curve rather than a perfectly flat surface across its breadth. The degree of contour may vary somewhat from maker to maker or even from model to model. Most people find a contoured fingerboard more comfortable for the fingerings and hand positions typical of steel-string styles. Fewer steel-string guitarists like flat fingerboards, but they're found on most nylon-string guitars because they're more suitable for classical playing.

Whether you prefer a flat or contoured fingerboard, and the degree of contour you prefer, is entirely a matter of personal taste. If you're looking for a high-quality guitar with a flat fingerboard, though, I recommend you check out the appropriate Taylor models.

Replacing and Repairing Fingerboards

In time, fingerboards become pitted with wear and hard playing. Ebony outlasts rosewood, but unless you put in hours a day every day, even your rosewood fingerboard will probably outlast you. Pits and cracks can be repaired, up to a point, with rosewood or ebony dust mixed with epoxy resin. After 10 to 30 years of hard playing you might need to have a fingerboard replaced. It's not a cheap job—mostly because of the time spent on the new frets that have to go in as well—but it's a routine one.

Keep your fretting hand fingernails trimmed short and you'll save on fingerboard wear. They shouldn't be in the least bit long anyway, since they inhibit correct hand position if they are. But if good form won't motivate you, then maybe economy will.

Frets

Fret Design

The *frets* are the metal bars that run across the guitar's neck, against which you press the strings. Frets give the notes a clear sound and make sure they're in tune.

Good frets are made of *nickel silver*. This is a metal-industry name for

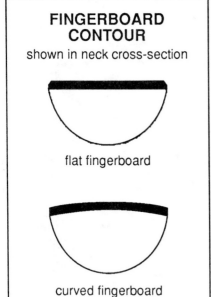

FINGERBOARD CONTOUR

shown in neck cross-section

flat fingerboard

curved fingerboard

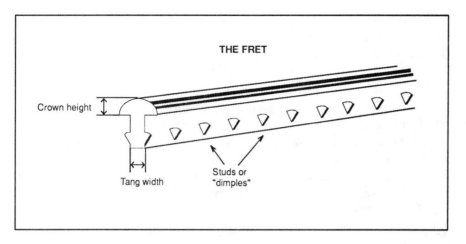

THE FRET

Crown height

Tang width

Studs or "dimples"

a hard nickel/steel alloy (sometimes also called *German silver*) that, in spite of its name, has no actual silver content. Cheaper guitars may use a softer metal, such as brass, that quickly wears down.

Fretwire has two components:

- The *bead* or *crown*, which is the part you actually see on your fingerboard.
- The *tang*, which is the metal tongue that actually holds the fret into the fingerboard. Tangs have *studs* or *dimples*, little protrusions that help grip the wood.

The tang fits into fine slots that the guitar maker saws at appropriate intervals in the fingerboard. The maker cuts the fretwire somewhat longer than the width of the fingerboard and then hammers them in. Once the fret is seated, the protruding ends are nipped off. Some makers and repairpeople like to seat the fret with epoxy glue in the grooves to hold them firmly; others are opposed to this technique because it makes the guitar harder to refret when the time comes.

Manufacturers provide fretwire gauged in many combinations of crown height and width; here are some ball park examples. A medium crown width of .085 inch and height of .045 inch is common and most acoustic guitarists like it. You'll find larger (so-called "jumbo") frets (to .115 inch wide x .050 inch high), on many electric guitars and on some acoustic guitar models as well—especially those marketed for players who are used to an electric guitar feel. Which you prefer is a matter of taste. Martins and modern Gibsons have medium frets and older Gibsons low jumbo frets; old small guitars have small frets (.078 x .045); some makers may vary fret gauge from model to model.

There are also very low "speed frets" (.110 inch x .035 inch) that are found on some electric guitars but not usually on acoustics. I mention them because you might hear about them and be attracted by their name, but most guitarists find them uncomfortably low. However, repairpeople sometimes use them in quick-and-dirty jobs to replace single frets on instruments where all the other frets have been worn low.

In addition to having different possible combinations of crown height and width, fretwire also comes in different combinations of tang height and width independent of crown gauge. Sometimes, when a guitar is refretted, a thicker tang gauge is used because pulling out the old frets

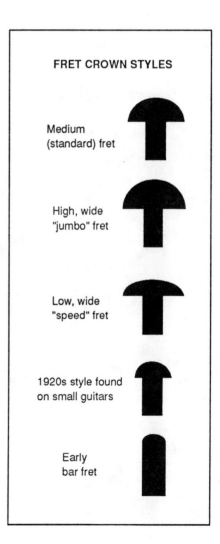

FRET CROWN STYLES

Medium (standard) fret

High, wide "jumbo" fret

Low, wide "speed" fret

1920s style found on small guitars

Early bar fret

will have enlarged the slots. A wider tang gauge can also have the effect of bending the neck into a reverse warp because the wider tangs expand the fingerboard. This technique can be used deliberately to undo a warped neck.

Because the crown forms a T-shape with the tang, this kind of fretwire was known as the *T-fret* when it came into general use during the 1930s. Until then, guitars were fretted with *bar frets* made of rectangular wire. T-frets are far more comfortable to play, more stable, and easier to install. Some collectors prefer to have older instruments refretted with bar frets to maintain historical accuracy, but this makes little sense from a playing point of view. Unfortunately, replacing bar frets with T-frets involves refilling the original fret slots, a process so tedious (as well as cosmetically unsatisfactory) that it's usually more cost-effective to replace the entire fingerboard.

Refretting

Frets become worn in time—especially under the unwound strings. They don't wear evenly, of course, but get flattened and grooved in the spots where you play the most. If you don't play much, you'll be able to get through the rest of your life without worrying about fret wear. But if you play a lot, then you'll probably find yourself asking a repairperson to dress your frets with file and sandpaper every few years.

When frets finally get too low, it's time to have them replaced. You waste finger strength pressing the string against the fingerboard, which does no good, rather than cleanly against the fret. And depressing a string against a too-low fret may bring its angle down enough that it buzzes against the next fret up the fingerboard. A temporary, dirty solution is to file down the next fret—although that can lead to a domino effect requiring adjustment of the *next* fret up the fingerboard, and so on. It's better to get them all replaced.

Fret Placement

In order for the guitar to play properly in tune, the frets have to be unerringly spaced to within microscopic tolerances, according to a mathematical proportion derived from the length of the vibrating portion of the string.

As recently as 25 years ago, it was easy to find inexpensive instruments with badly spaced frets. Thanks to today's computer designs, standardized assembly procedures, and improved quality control, you're not going to run into this problem on any instruments from the major manufacturers.

Nut

Functions

The *nut* lies across the end of the fingerboard and holds the strings as they cross over from the headstock. Its six equidistant grooves hold the strings in position relative to each other. It shares with the bridge saddle, the other bearing point of the strings, the duty of regulating the height of the strings above the fingerboard. It also helps transmit the vibrations of the open strings.

Materials

The nut should be dense and hard—dense to transmit sound effectively and hard to resist string wear. The traditional material for nut and saddle on fine instruments was elephant ivory, which, of course, is now embargoed in an attempt to save the elephant from extinction. Some luthiers have stocks of pre-embargo ivory (or at least that's what they say), which should properly be reserved for restoring historical instruments.

The standard material used these days by makers of fine handmade instruments is bone, preferably a dense one like beef thigh bone. It sounds fine.

Synthetic materials are used on less expensive guitars and some better ones as well. Some ceramics, epoxy resin products (like Micarta™), and graphite materials work adequately. Cheap plastics neither sound nor hold up as well, and some very poorly made guitars use hollow molded pieces that not only do the worst possible job of transmitting sound, but eventually collapse. Some older guitars used dark hardwood nuts, which look nice but give a softer quality to the open string tone. Most folks who own these older instruments have kept the original nuts on to preserve the historical sound of the instrument, or perhaps because it just doesn't seem worth the trouble to have a new nut cut.

It's easy to get new nuts cut if you need them. Suppliers sell blanks approximating the commonly used sizes and shapes, and it's small work for a repairperson to cut or grind them to final size, groove them, and mount them.

If you have an instrument with an adequate synthetic nut and are happy with the way it sounds, leave it in until the strings wear it down; then get it replaced with bone. If you want to try bone sooner, go ahead—it's not that expensive to have the job done. If your instrument is good enough to be responsive to such a change, you may hear some difference or improvement. If it's not a sensitive instrument, the change won't make much difference. The best way to get a mediocre guitar to sound better is to sell it for cash toward a better one, not to replace the nut.

If you want to match a new nut or saddle to an old guitar with bindings and other finishes that have yellowed with age, you can give a piece of bone or ivory, and perhaps some plastics, an aged appearance by letting it sit a few hours in a cup of tea.

Nut Height and Grooves

The ideal height of the string above the fingerboard as it comes off the nut is .007 to .009 inch measured between the string and first fret, with the string depressed at the fourth fret. In other words, not very high.

You might be able to measure this miniscule distance with a feeler gauge, but you can barely see it. The chances are that your guitar has a first string somewhere between .010 and .012 inch in diameter (see chapter 8 for more details.) Perhaps you can use this as a standard of comparison for your eye to estimate if the nut is obviously too high. You might also try getting a guitar first string of known gauge and slipping it under the string. It's not exact, but it can tell you at least if the nut is *way* too high.

Telling whether the nut is cut too low is easier. With each string in turn depressed at the fourth fret, try plucking them in the area between the nut and fourth fret. If you produce a ping that has some tone to it, you'll know that the nut isn't too low (though it may be too high.) But if all you hear are buzzes or dead thuds, then it's too low.

Many factories ship their instruments with the nut grooves a bit too high. It's always possible that the instrument's action might settle a little in transit, and the makers want to eliminate any chance of the strings buzzing when a prospective customer energetically strikes an open chord. Nothing kills sales faster. Dealers should make fine adjustments before the instrument gets out on the sale floor, but few bother—especially on cheaper instruments. It would not be out of line to discuss with a dealer whether or not the nut should be adjusted—at no charge.

If you're handy and don't mind experimenting, you might want to try adjusting the nut grooves yourself. Do it slowly, testing in stages. If you mess up, you can always go to a repairperson (be prepared for a scornful lecture and don't mention my name). Ideally, the right implement for the job on the wound-string grooves is a specialized woodworking tool called a round-edge joint file. Ideally you need a set of them, each one a couple of thousandths of an inch wider than the string diameter. In the real world, many guitarists adjust their own grooves with small triangular, rat-tail, or half-round files from the hardware store, and the music critics don't seem to notice. The grooves for the first and second strings should also be cut with a specialized tool: a knife-cut needle file or hobbyist's razor saw. It's a good idea to dress out the groove with a folded-over piece of fine emery paper when you're done filing. Rough edges in the nut groove lead to broken strings, or strings that catch in the grooves and hinder smooth, even tuning.

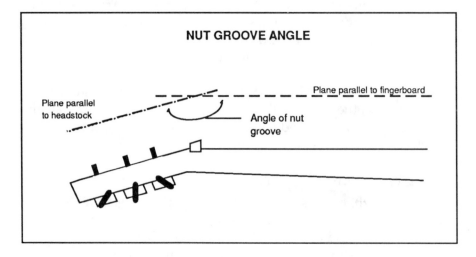

Grooves should be cut into the nut on an angle parallel to the plane of the headstock. If you groove a nut parallel to the plane of the fingerboard, you'll wind up breaking a lot of strings on the sharp edge where the string drops off the nut on its way to the tuners, and you'll run a risk of buzzing, foggy tone, and dubious intonation.

Ideally, the string should not ride deeply in the nut—not deeper than about the full diameter of the unwound strings and half the diameter of the wound ones. If the grooves are any deeper, the strings may bind, making them harder to tune and easier to break. In real life, this rule is often violated because players often do their own quick touchups with a file. It seems you can get away with sloppy work up to a point. In a perfect world, if the right height would require the grooves to be too deeply cut, the repairperson would instead remove the nut (a sharp blow does the trick) and lower it by grinding down the bottom.

A nut that's too low can be shimmed up without noticeable degradation of tone with hardwood veneer secured with aliphatic resin glue. In a perfect world, though, you'd have a new nut cut.

The function of the nut grooves is not only to hold the strings, but to space them evenly. Occasionally a factory turns out badly tooled nuts where the grooves are too widely spaced for the neck, so that those for the first and sixth strings are too close to the edges of the fingerboard. This makes you accidentally shove the string over the edge when you play—especially on the first string. Some instruments have nuts where the strings are a little too far from the edge than is necessary for most people. Most players of such instruments would be more comfortable if they replaced the factory nuts with nuts that had grooves cut further apart.

Scale

Scale is the length of the vibrating portion of the string—in other words, the distance from the point the string leaves the nut to the point at which it rests on the crest of the bridge saddle. You might think that all guitars were built to a standard scale, but that's not the case by a long shot. The guitar world is basically divided between long-scale and short-scale instruments, each of which has somewhat different playing qualities. From maker to maker there are minor variations within each of these two categories—luthiers and designers may feel than even a $\frac{1}{10}$ inch difference makes a difference to their design.

Scale is a function of neck length, not body size. It usually works out that larger guitars have a longer scale (a larger whole tends to have larger parts), but it doesn't necessarily have to be that way. Longer necks require the frets be spaced proportionally further apart, so each scale length has its own mathematically-derived system for fret placement. In addition to meaning "vibrating string length," the word *scale* also has the secondary meaning of the actual template that a luthier uses for positioning the frets for a given scale length.

Long and Short Scales

Long-scale instruments have a scale of about 25½ inches. (The usual range runs from the standard Martin dreadnought scale of 25.4 inches up to about 25.6 inches, favored by some luthiers but found less often

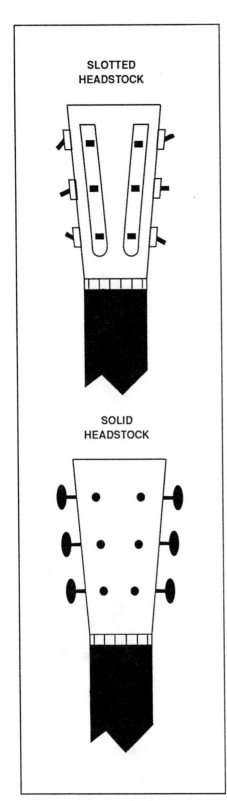

SLOTTED
HEADSTOCK

SOLID
HEADSTOCK

on factory guitars.) Almost all guitars made these days are long-scale instruments, even those with smaller bodies.

Short-scale instruments approximate 24.9 inches, which is the traditional scale for Martin smaller-bodied 12-fret guitars. However, most of the classic Martin short-scale models are now no longer in production or are available on special order only. You have to look pretty hard these days before you can find a new short-scale guitar from any maker—except, of course, for kid-size guitars, which are smaller overall.

Longer scale gives you greater string tension and also greater volume. It's the volume factor that is responsible for the dominance of the long scale in today's market. (I suspect it's because bumping up volume with a long scale is easier and cheaper than constructing a fine top and bracing to get the same results.) However, you can make the scale only so long before you get into the area of diminishing returns, since volume is also limited by the strength of your stroke and by the acoustic qualities of the body and of the strings themselves. While something around 25¾ inches seems the upper limit for steel strings, modern concert-quality classical guitars are often built to a 26-inch scale. These instruments have bodies considerably smaller than most of today's steel-string guitars, but they must produce enough volume to fill a concert hall.

The lower string tension of short-scale guitars makes them marginally softer to play and causes them to be more sensitive to vibrato and string bending.

You might think that long-scale guitars would be harder to play than short-scale ones because the frets are a bit further apart, but the extra stretch just doesn't seem to bother most people. And many even find the more closely spaced frets of a short-scale guitar more uncomfortable for executing cluttered chord shapes (like the basic beginner's A chord) where the fingers have to bunch up to cover several strings all at the same fret. But the real comparison test can only come if short-scale guitars are readily enough available that people can try them. As the market stands now, most people have never played a short-scale guitar and never will.

Headstock and Tuners

Headstock or Peghead

At the end of the neck is the flat section called the *headstock* or *peghead* (the terms are interchangeable) where the tuning machines are mounted. Most steel-string guitars have a *solid* headstock though which the pegs are mounted perpendicularly. A few, usually 12-fret models, have a classical-style *slotted headstock*, where the pegs are mounted in slots cut into the headstock. The extra neck width customary on 12-fret guitars makes the extra width of the slotted headstock more appropriate visually. However, aside from looks and tradition, there are no important structural advantages to either of the two headstock designs, nor will they affect your playing or handling of the instrument significantly.

Headstock size and shape may vary among makers. Most prefer a simple trapezoid, while others use a characteristic crest or other ornamental shape. The maker's name or logo usually appears on the headstock, either inlaid, painted, or as a decal. On fancy instruments, there may be ornamental inlay work on the headstock.

The top of the headstock is usually covered by a veneer of ornamental wood or other material—often the same wood of which the body is made. On cheap instruments a coat of paint may be sprayed on instead.

Most headstocks are carved, along with the neck, out of one neck blank. On some instruments, even good ones, mahogany blanks may be used which, for economy's sake, are not quite wide enough for the total width of the headstock. In this case, wing-like laminations of extra wood are glued on.

Laminated headstocks last the life of the guitar (or guitarist) without incident. The glue joint is about as strong as the wood, though some kinds of shearing trauma can break it. So can enlarging the peg hole for a larger brand of tuner. If these happen, it's easy enough to reglue the joint. I wouldn't let a laminated headstock affect a purchasing decision, or even think twice about it.

Handstop

You'll notice that the headstock of most guitars is bent back from the neck at about a 15-degree angle. This is done to create the tension that holds down the string where it crosses the nut. The point at which the headstock angles back from the neck is one of the weakest spots on the guitar, especially vulnerable if the instrument is dropped.

Some manufacturers, especially of banjos, used to carve their necks with an extra lip of wood at this point in order to create added strength. This is known as a *headstock reinforcement*, *handstop*, or *volute*. At this point, most handstops (if you find them at all) are vestigial, with greater ornamental than structural value. Martin still uses one.

Tuning Machines

The gadgets that you use to tune your strings are called tuners, machines, tuning machines, machine heads, heads, or tuning pegs. If you ever try to tune with a stripped or jammed gear on one in the middle of a performance, you'll probably come up with a few more names. Many early guitars had violin-style *friction pegs* (wooden pegs held in place merely by their own friction against their holes), but they are no longer used except on flamenco guitars. (In the traditional flamenco playing position, with the guitar almost upright in the lap, the instrument is difficult to balance if the headstock is weighted down with tuners.)

I'm not inclined to make too big a deal over tuning machines. Some are better than others in that they're smoother, made of more durable metal that won't strip out over the years, or have a greater (and therefore more sensitive) gear ratio. Some are fancier than others in that they have more ornate knobs, chasing, filigree, or gold plating. Manufacturers consistently offer better and/or fancier tuners on their models as price brackets go up. I suggest you take what you get without worrying too much about it.

Machines come in a variety of shapes. Some are individual; others

NECK BLANK WITH LAMINATED HEADSTOCK

(called *in-line*) are mounted three to a metal strip or *plate*, with one plate for each side of the headstock. Machines for slotted or straight headstocks are configured differently and are not interchangeable. But within each of these categories, almost all machines are interchangeable except for a few models (like the best Schallers and their imitators) that include a collar to help stabilize the shaft in the hole. These require a larger, countersunk hole to be drilled out.

Design is simple. Machines have a button that turns a worm-and-screw gear that turns the shaft or *barrel* on which the string is mounted. On straight-headstock models, the barrel is held in place on top of the peghead by a hex nut (possibly with a collar) and washer.

Here's what you need to know about tuners:

- Good tuners don't slip or have excessive play, are easy and pleasant to work, and turn evenly. If there are serious problems with any of these functions, your pleasure in your instrument will be impaired, and you'll find it more difficult to get and keep your instrument in tune. But you can probably live with minor tuner imperfections. You get used to them as you do a tricky clutch pedal. If you play in public or have to keep in tune with other people, though, having a good set of tuners becomes more worthwhile.

- Cheap tuners are constructed to imprecise tolerances and are made of inferior metal that wears out. Unless they're so awful even from the beginning that they aggravate, just use them until they begin to go. Then replace them with a better set. You don't need top-of-the-line tuners; just a set that works comfortably. Many dealers and repairpeople keep old tuners on hand and you may be able to get a decent set used. You can even put them on yourself if you're handy. If they require new screw-holes, *drill them out* first or you'll risk cracking the headstock. And be warned that the heads strip off the tiny screws easily.

- Tuners with a higher gear ratio are more sensitive, which makes fine tuning a little easier. However, lots of people manage to get through life without extremely high-ratio tuners.

- Unless your tuners have sealed ("self-lubricating") gears, *carefully* apply a little white grease to them maybe once a year. I find it easy to apply it on the end of a toothpick. (Use liquid oil only if you've semi-enclosed tuners that have a little oil hole in the case.) Keep on top of this; you should be able to tell when the gears feel stiff and dry. You can needlessly ruin a perfectly good set of tuners if you don't keep them lubricated. It's like not brushing your teeth. Decay occurs slowly over a number of years and you don't notice until it's too late.

6

How Your Guitar Works, 2: Body Language

The guitar's body is a semi-enclosed sound chamber that amplifies the sounds of the vibrating strings. The scientific name for such a body is *general resonator*; "general" because it covibrates with (and therefore amplifies) any frequency. (On the other hand, a *specific resonator* is a body that covibrates with only one frequency or a narrow range of frequencies; for example, your broken glove compartment latch that only rattles at the bottom of second gear.)

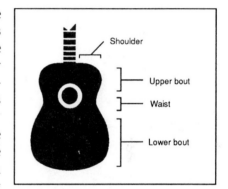

People use the word *body* in two senses: usually it means the entire chamber including top, back, and sides, but sometimes it just means the back and sides alone (for example, in talking about body woods, which are different from top woods). Context makes the sense clear. The body is also sometimes called the *soundbox* or just the *box*.

For the sake of description, luthiers have names for three separate areas of the body. The two curved portions are called *bouts*; the smaller is the *upper bout* and the larger is the *lower bout*. (Sometimes they're affectionately called the bust and hips.) The bouts are separated in the middle by the pinched-in *waist*, which helps you hold the guitar on your thigh. The area of the top in the upper bout below the bridge is called the *belly*, and the tops of the sides on either side of the neck are called the *shoulders*.

Wood type and quality are very important to the way the body works and sounds. You may wish to read the section on woods in chapter 4 if you haven't done so already.

The Top or Soundboard

The Soul of the Guitar

The *top* or *soundboard* (sometimes also called the *face* or *table*) is the voice and soul of the instrument. The quality and shaping of the top wood and of the bracing struts that support it from underneath determine sustain, volume, and presence. Only the best woods and the finest craftsmanship result in the perfect combination of rigidity and resilience that makes a guitar sound great.

The large area of the soundboard below the bridge is called the top's *belly*. On some guitars it may arch up just a bit from the tension of the strings, so don't be disturbed if it's not absolutely flat. (This is called *bellying*.) An arched belly is normal, but only when it arches a little. After you look at a few guitars you'll get a sense of how much arch is normal and how much is excessive. A severe paunch may indicate loose or broken braces.

"Playing In" a Top

Solid wood soundboards improve as the wood ages, but merely playing the instrument also helps to get the top to sound better by loosening it up. It's called *playing in* a guitar. Some instruments fresh out of the factory have inhibited, closed-in voices that begin to open up after only a few hours of playing. A year makes an even bigger difference, though of course this all depends on how many hours you put in during that year. It really takes 10 or 20 years for a top to mature completely, but this has to do with the chemical seasoning of the wood and finish as well as playing in.

Playing in and seasoning seem to work hand in hand. Many guitarists have observed that a well played instrument improves more in tone than a poorly played one, and even that the tone of a instrument passed on from a clumsy player to one with a fine touch also improves after a while.

Guitars also get lonely. It seems that a guitar left unplayed for too long loses some of its vivacity and usually has to be played back in for a few hours before it sounds congenial again.

The finer an instrument is, the more sensitive it is to these vagaries. Soundboards made poorly or of poor wood profit less from the benefits of aging and playing in, and are relatively oblivious to neglect.

Laminate and Solid Wood Tops

Laminate (plywood) tops don't age at all. Because of the aging qualities and overall acoustic advantages of solid wood, most makers now couple solid tops to plywood bodies on all but their low-end models. As you get into the better guitars, the difference becomes audible, though in poorer guitars the solid tops are more a sales point than a perceptible asset. Design and overall quality of joining is also important, so well-made plywood-topped instruments sound better than inferior solid-topped ones, and will continue to sound better because the inferior ones will not benefit to any significant extent by aging.

Top Materials and Building

Spruce is the standard soundboard wood. Some players and luthiers prefer cedar and redwood; they're slightly more brilliant to begin with but they stay about the same over the years rather that maturing as spruce does. Mahogany and koa, more often body woods, have warmer but smaller voices than spruce when used for tops.

Solid tops are furnished to the luthier or factory in halves (preferably bookmatched) by wood suppliers or the factory's own wood products division. The halves are glued together at their *center seam* by the maker. In mass-produced guitars, the tops are finished to uniform specifications with as much automated work as possible. In fine guitar making, tops are carved by hand and graduated in thickness from section to section. (Tops are also graduated a bit thicker on the bass-string side because of the greater string tension on that side.)

By instinct and training, luthiers determine graduation by tapping the top and listening to it, carving it until they get it in tune with itself by eliminating unwanted components of the sound. This is called *voicing* the guitar. You can teach yourself to hear an in-tune body. Tops and backs also should be in tune with each other. Go around and gently tap the sides and backs of different guitars. If you have a decent ear, you'll learn to hear how some are in better tune than others, and you can use this skill to help you judge a guitar.

The Soundhole

The soundhole is not there to "let the sound out." Having an orifice permits the top to vibrate more freely because it relieves air pressure inside the sound chamber. A sound chamber with an orifice is known among loudspeaker designers as a *ported enclosure*. Scientists call it a *Helmholtz resonator* after Hermann von Helmholtz, the 19th-century physicist who laid the foundations of modern acoustic science. One of Helmholtz's contributions was to demonstrate the existence of harmonics (see chapter 3) with a series of experiments involving ported enclosures.

Occasionally you'll see instruments with soundhole(s) located elsewhere in the soundboard than in the middle of the waist. These are called *offset soundholes*. Most often they're offset because the instrument is constructed with a nontraditional bracing pattern that requires the soundhole to be relocated, though some makers also believe that moving the soundhole so as to create the largest possible continuous vibrating surface helps bass response.

Soundhole Shape and Size

D-shaped, triangular, and elliptical soundholes are sometimes made for visual effect, but more often they too are the result of some modification in the traditional bracing pattern. For example, many cutaway guitars have elliptical soundholes because the bracing under the cutaway bout has had to be moved down a little toward the center of the guitar, and the hole has to be made less round to accommodate it. Merely making a round hole smaller overall would affect the tone. All other things being equal, a larger hole creates more of a treble balance; a smaller hole reinforces the lower notes.

The Pickguard

A sheet of protective material, usually black or tortoiseshell celluloid, is attached to the top beneath the soundhole of most steel-string guitars.

SOME PICKGUARD SHAPES

Standard (Martin-style) pickguard shape, here shown on a grand auditorium guitar

Traditional flamenco tap-plate, here shown on a classical-size guitar. Some steel-string makers favor this shape for ornamental wooden pickguards.

Sound-deadening oversize pickguard, shown on a dreadnought body.

This part of the top is prone to cumulative damage, so a pickguard makes sense. If you happen to acquire one of the few instruments now made without one and begin to notice damage, you can always have one added later. The small, thin pickguards usually found on today's guitars don't significantly detract from a guitar's tone and volume, and whatever difference they might make is amply repaid by the fact that you'll still have a top left after five years of digging picks and fingernails into it. However, heavy or oversize pickguards can make a perceptible difference in sound and don't really seem to offer any greater protection in return, so you should avoid them. Pickguard material should be no greater than .03 inch thick.

Pickguards on some early guitars were made of genuine tortoiseshell, which may have some marginal acoustical advantages over synthetics. But celluloid drove expensive tortoiseshell off the market decades ago, and now it's illegal and immoral to use. Sometimes on fancy instruments you'll see a thin hardwood pickguard, which is supposed to be less detrimental to tone. I haven't had enough experience with them to comment.

Although classical guitars have no pickguards, flamenco guitars are fitted with a plastic or wood "pickguard," traditionally more squared-off in shape than those on steel- string guitars, called the *tap-plate* or *golpeador* (Spanish for "striker"). Its job is to accept the percussive fingernail tapping that is part of flamenco. When classical guitarists are required to execute flamenco effects, they tap on the bridge. Archtop guitars are usually fitted with a large, heavy celluloid pickguard mounted on screwed-in struts and spacers so it floats above the surface of the instrument.

Bracing

The insides of the guitar's top and back are reinforced by a system of struts called the *braces*. Braces are usually of spruce for the top and mahogany for the back, though other woods may also be used. You'll find additional information on bracing in chapters 1 and 13.

Top Bracing

The top braces do more than just reinforce the top against the pressure of the strings. They also have an acoustic function, but it's hard to define exactly, because acoustic engineers don't fully understand how the braces work.

From looking at the braces, you'd think that they lead sound outward from the bridge into the soundboard. But that's not so. Scientists have used holography and oscilloscopes to study the way the top moves, as well as the low-tech approach of scattering graphite dust on the top and watching the way the particles dance when notes are plucked. They've discovered that the top vibrates in complex and surprising patterns that appear to be centered in various places depending on pitch. It's nothing at all like ripples moving outward from the bridge, nor are high and low vibrations confined to the high-string and low-string sides of the guitar. Take this and add in the many other interactions still not fully understood by the engineers—the effects of the density and flexibility or rigidity of the sides, the mass of the neck, the many variations on bracing pattern, the magic of the wood itself—and what you're left with is the mystery that makes luthiery an art rather than a science.

There are three major types of traditional bracing: transverse bracing, fan-bracing, and X-bracing. Throughout the history of the instrument there have also been, and continue to be, other experimental and transitional patterns, as well as new proprietary designs that manufacturers come up with from time to time.

Transverse Bracing

In the earliest days of the guitar, makers used just a few braces that ran transversely across the top—either straight across or at a slight offset. This style of bracing confers no great acoustic benefits and not a great deal of strength either. Transverse bracing was used until recently by some of the cheapie American companies, but when decent X-braced Japanese instruments took over the American market in the 1970s, they pretty much wiped out the American transverse-braced instruments.

Transverse bracing is also called *straight bracing*. Sometimes it's also called *cross-bracing* (because the struts go straight across the top), but this can be confusing because some people use *cross-bracing* to mean *X-bracing* (because the two main struts cross to form an X).

Fan Bracing

Guitar makers in the early 19th century had worked with three to five struts fanning out under the top's belly, but it was the great Spanish luthier Antonio Torres who, around the middle of the century, developed a system of seven main fans (plus other secondary braces) that is still the basis of classical guitar bracing design.

Fan bracing works well with nylon strings and their 70 pounds of tension, but it can't hold up against even the 125 pounds of extra-light steel strings, much less lights or mediums.

X-Bracing

X-bracing, the standard design for steel-string guitars, is named after the two main struts that cross each other to form an X just below the soundhole. There are also several secondary struts under the belly, as well as transverse struts and flat struts under the spatula and around the soundhole.

The X-brace was developed by C. F. Martin around the same time Torres was developing the fan brace, and was used increasingly in the Martin factory until, by the last decades of the 19th century, it became the sole bracing pattern of Martin guitars. It was developed decades before steel strings came into fashion, but it suited them perfectly when they arrived.

Voiced and Scalloped X-Bracing

An ordinary bracing strut is a long thin rectangle, sometimes with the top gently bevelled to a crest, with tapered-down ends. On early Martin guitars, the tops of the struts were shaved with a wood chisel into parabolic curves so that they resembled the shape of a suspension bridge. Shaving the struts made them lighter and let them flex more, so the top could move more freely. However, the tops also arched up

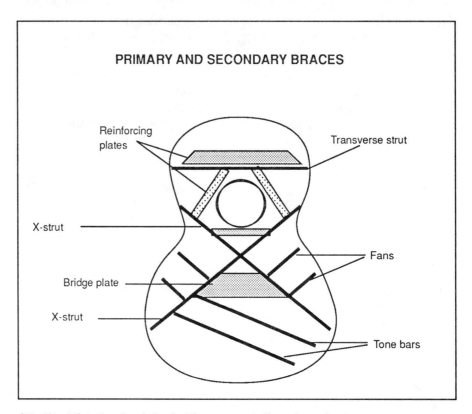

PRIMARY AND SECONDARY BRACES

Reinforcing plates

Transverse strut

X-strut

Fans

Bridge plate

X-strut

Tone bars

("bellied") in back of the bridge, especially when the instruments were strung with the medium-to-heavy strings more fashionable then than now. The tops were supposed to belly, at least a little, but the public perceived the bellying as a fault. Eventually Martin got tired of customer complaints and in 1944 discontinued shaved braces in order to create more support for the top and reduce bellying. Five years earlier, Martin had moved the crossing point of the X about an inch further away from the soundhole, possibly also for the same reason.

Scalloped bracing—along with the high-brace position—gives most early Martin guitars a distinctive sound, and its cachet derives from the very real difference it makes in most of those instruments. In the sixties and seventies it became fashionable—maybe in places it still is—for owners of modern Martins to have their struts shaved by a repairperson skilled in the job. Martin wasn't crazy about the idea, and (quite reasonably) refused to honor warrantees on custom-scalloped instruments. In any case, word was getting around that scalloped was better than unscalloped (or at least was *supposed* to be better, and was certainly hipper), and in the mid-seventies Martin reintroduced scalloped bracing on selected models. (The original high-brace position is now also again available on selected models.)

In a fine instrument, both the soundboard and the braces are *voiced* by the luthier—a sensitive process of listening to how the wood sounds when tapped and gently shaving with a sharp chisel to bring it perfectly into tune with itself. On mass-produced instruments, though, the braces may be preshaved, which cancels out much of the value of scalloping.

In contemporary guitar marketing, scalloped bracing may be at times nothing more than a buzzword. What's important, after all, is that the

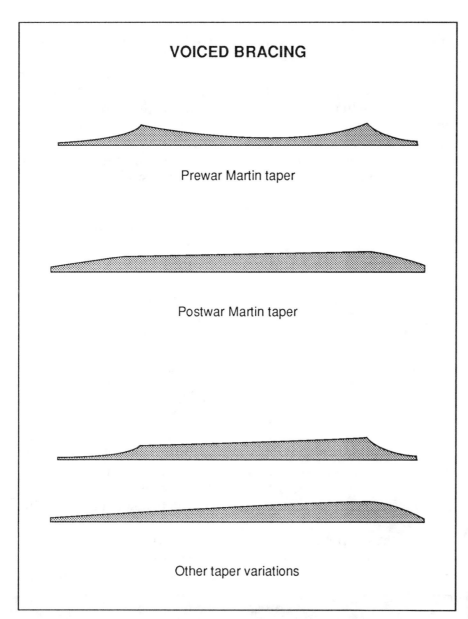

VOICED BRACING

Prewar Martin taper

Postwar Martin taper

Other taper variations

top should move, and if the top isn't good, then fooling with the braces is meaningless. So after you read the sales specs, use your ears.

If you read sales literature, you'll see some other terms that mean about the same thing as scalloping—maybe. *Shaved* and *parabolic* usually mean scalloped in the traditional manner, but not necessarily. *Tapered* usually means simply that the brace ends are tapered down. *Voiced* implies that the top and braces have been finely tuned by hand-shaving, whether the shaving is a scalloped shape or not.

Kasha and Other Bracing Systems

A physicist named Michael Kasha has influenced several contemporary luthiers by proposing radically new bracing theories based on the principle (which I'm somewhat oversimplifying here) that every desired harmonic component of the guitar's tone must find some section of the instrument in which to vibrate.

In Kasha-style bracing, the struts are arranged in a circular pattern

A guitar by Mark Wescott with the off-center soundhole and asymmetrical bridge often found on Kasha-braced guitars. *Photo by Mario Romo, courtesy Mark Wescott.*

around the bridge with the idea of evenly and effectively distributing vibrations to all areas of the guitar. The design also partitions the top into numerous small areas that reinforce vibrations of the various harmonics. Kasha-braced guitars are also usually distinguished on the outside by an off-center soundhole and a bridge that is wider on the bass side. The soundhole is positioned off-center both to accomodate the bracing and provide a larger unbroken surface area to vibrate. The bridge is wider on the bass side to more effectively support low-frequency vibrations; sometimes the bridge is even designed in two pieces to permit the bass and treble sides to transmit vibrations independently.

Many years ago I had the opportunity to play a couple of experimental Kasha-inspired guitars. My recollection is of power, extremely even balance, and a certain impersonality. A friend who has played several more recent Kasha-braced instruments describes them as "terrifyingly efficient" in their balance of volume and tonal qualities on all strings throughout the instrument's range, but he, too, was left somewhat cold in spite of the instruments' indisputable assets. Great guitars, like great personalities, often have foibles and weaknesses, and eliminating them would destroy an ingredient in their character. This is one of the reasons so many serious guitarists own more than one instrument.

Kasha instruments are produced by only a few luthiers, including Gila Eban, Richard Schneider, and Mark Wescott. Sociologically, they are cult instruments which have not achieved mainstream appeal or impact, though Gibson did carry on a short and superficial flirtation with Kasha principles for a while during the seventies. That almost no one has had a chance to try a Kasha-braced guitar, and that no major performer uses one, doesn't help. There seems to be more interest in Kasha instruments among classical guitarists than among steel-string players.

Some other current makers have come up with their own systems; Ovation, for example, uses several bracing patterns including an A-shape as well as a reworked version of the fan-brace for its Adamas

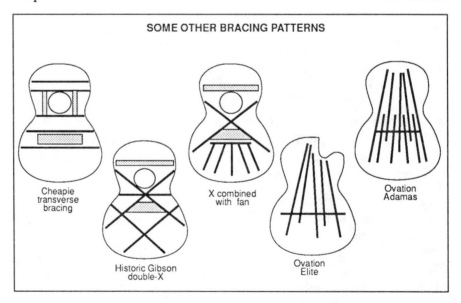

SOME OTHER BRACING PATTERNS

Cheapie transverse bracing

Historic Gibson double-X

X combined with fan

Ovation Elite

Ovation Adamas

series of graphite fiber-topped steel-string guitars. The response of the Adamas instruments is, to my ear, similar to that of Kasha-style instruments in some ways. In addition, many luthiers have their own variations on the traditional X-brace.

Damaged Braces

Top and back braces can come loose or split from climatic shrinking, or sometimes just from a blow that leaves no sign of external damage. Loose or split braces may cause buzzes and rattles, which can sometimes seem to be coming from the strings rather than from inside the guitar.

An experienced person may detect brace damage simply by tapping the guitar and listening. Sometimes damage can also be seen with an inspection mirror, or felt by reaching inside the guitar.

Brace repair may sometimes require taking off the back, though over the past 20 years special clamps and jacks have been designed to eliminate this as much as possible, thus making brace work cost-effective even on relatively inexpensive instruments.

Bridge

Function and Structure

The *bridge* helps to support the strings above the top and to provide an anchoring point for them. It also transmits the vibrations of the strings to the top of the guitar, so what it's made of affects the sound of the instrument.

The actual bearing point of the string is the *saddle,* a strip of bone or similar material that rests in a groove in the bridge. The bridge also works in partnership with the *bridge plate,* a wide, flat strut located directly under the bridge a little below the point where the X-braces cross.

The bridge should be glued directly to bare wood. On super-cheapie guitars the bridge may be glued over the finish, in which case it won't stay there long. Cheapie makers may bolt down the bridge in addition to gluing. Bolting doesn't work in the long run because the bridge pulls away from the wood anyway, even if the bolts keep it from actually coming off the guitar. In addition, the bolting system is acoustically inferior. Bolted bridges are as a rule acceptable only on very, very cheap guitars. Sometimes an otherwise fine guitar maker has a strange need to add bolt support to a bridge.

The Bridge Plate

It's not the bridge that actually holds the strings onto the guitar. Under the bridge is a flat brace of dense hardwood—maple and rosewood are best—that reinforces both strength and acoustic transmission. When you insert the ball at the end of the string through the pin hole in the bridge, it pulls up against the bridge plate. The purpose of the pin in the bridge hole is not to hold the string *down,* but simply to keep the ball jammed under the bridge plate.

When a soundboard begins to warp due to climate changes, one possible treatment is to straighten it in a press and then put in a larger bridge plate to help strengthen the area and more widely diffuse the string tension. Size and quality of the bridge plate somewhat effect the instrument's balance, volume, and sustain, and a cheap plywood plate may produce unwanted elements in the tone. Over time (say, two to four decade's worth; less for a plate of inferior wood) the string ball ends chew up the plate and it will need to be replaced. If on an older guitar the strings are not deeply enough seated in the bridge holes so that the winding from the ball end rides up, it's a sign that the plate may need to be replaced.

Bridge Woods

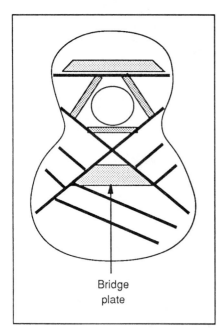

Bridge plate

On most steel-string guitars, bridge and fingerboard are made of the same wood for the sake of appearance—though on cheap instruments they may only *seem* to be made of the same wood. Ebony is the wood of choice, but it's expensive and you'll only find it on top-of-the-line models. Rosewood is a bit softer and marginally less brilliant in tone than ebony. On a few top-grade guitars, the maker may use a rosewood bridge because ebony is not as well-suited for the particular instrument. Ebony is considered too harsh-sounding for classical guitars in general and rosewood is preferred for those instruments.

On less expensive instruments, "ebonized" walnut or other hardwoods may be used. They're not as good as rosewood but they're acceptable if the price is fair.

Martin and some other makers used ivory bridges on a few models through the 19th century and into the beginning of the 20th. They sound like ebony, perhaps brighter, and are very beautiful.

At the other extreme are the plastic and extruded nylon bridges that some manufacturers—even Gibson, at a low point—tried on cheap models around 15 years ago. I think that no one is using them anymore. I certainly hope not. Avoid them; they're no good at all.

Bridge Shapes

The usual guitar bridge shape is the *belly bridge*, so called because it resembles a rectangle with a paunch. (This has nothing to do with the part of the top called the *belly*.) The paunch is there to provide greater surface area for gluing and for diffusing string tension and vibrations. On Martin's and almost everybody else's bridges, the belly points toward the end of the body. By tradition, Gibson mounts its bridges with the belly pointing toward the soundhole. Belly bridges came into fashion in the early thirties, probably as a way of dealing with the heavier gauges of steel strings then becoming popular.

Most bridges in the days before the belly bridge were simple rectangles, but there were ornate variations. The classic Martin *pyramid bridge* was rectangular with a small pyramid carved on each foot. Some Larson Brothers bridges gracefully tapered into a long triangle at each end. Gibson still uses the ornate mustache bridge, so called because its feet are shaped like the elaborate waxed mustachios of a Gay Nineties dandy, on its J-200 model. Today you'll still find ornamentally-carved bridges on some custom models, as well as some bridges flared out on the bass side by those luthiers who subscribe to a theory that this increases acoustic efficiency. On flashy models, there may also be inlay work in the bridge feet. (These are not to be confused with the "ornamental" inlay dots that cover bolt holes on cheapie bridges.)

All these bridges are varieties of *pin bridge*, designed with holes through which the string ends are seated and then held in place against the bridge plate with a pin. C. F. Martin was committed to the pin bridge from the beginning of his career and it seems likely that he was impelled to develop his X-brace design at least in part to accommodate the pin holes, since fan bracing leaves no room for them. Like the X-brace itself, the pin bridge was invented in the days of gut strings but made great sense for steel strings once they came along.

By contrast, classical guitars have a *loop bridge* in which small holes are drilled though a raised section of the bridge in back of the saddle. The strings are then looped through these holes, so that, unlike steel-string guitars, it is the bridge rather than the bridge plate that holds the strings. Put a set of steel strings on a classical guitar and the bridge won't stay mated to the body for long.

Archtop and Maccaferri guitars are constructed on the violin principle: a raised bridge holds the strings up off the top, but the strings run over the bridge and are mounted in a *tailpiece* bracket attached to the end of the guitar. You could also once find tailpieces used on cheap flattop guitars to save the maker the trouble of constructing an adequate bridge, but I don't think anyone's still building that poorly anymore.

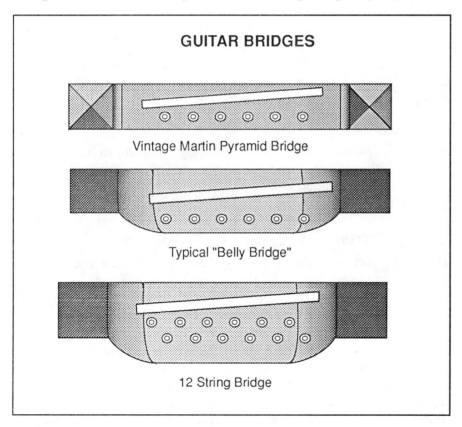

GUITAR BRIDGES

Vintage Martin Pyramid Bridge

Typical "Belly Bridge"

12 String Bridge

Saddle

Function, Structure, and Materials

The strings rest on the *saddle*, a strip of bone or other dense material seated in a groove in the bridge. The saddle may be shimmed up, or filed down, or replaced to help compensate for changes in action caused by humidity changes, warping, and the natural settling in of the guitar.

Saddles are made of the same materials as nuts: ivory on fine historical instruments, dense bone on today's better instruments, and synthetics on cheaper instruments. (Please take a look at the *Nut* section in chapter 5 for more information.) Some cheapies of earlier times, and perhaps of the present as well, used a piece of fretwire for a saddle, which made them sound tinny and strident.

The top of the saddle should be smoothly curved. A sharp edge along the top causes strings to break too easily where they cross it. Grooves should not be cut into flattop and classical guitar saddles, though they are customarily used on archtop and electric guitars. (Sometimes it may be necessary to groove the saddles on 12-string guitars in order to make sure that the pairs of strings lie correctly, but this should not have to be done if the bridge pins are positioned well.)

Adjustable Saddles

During the 1960s a few manufacturers came out with adjustable saddles that could be raised or lowered by screw mechanisms at either end. Adjustable saddles are not detrimental on electric guitars, and not detrimental enough to worry about on f-hole guitars. But on flattop guitars they're a disaster. They kill volume, dull the tone, and inevitably buzz and rattle. Fortunately, it's not a prohibitively big job for a repairperson to pull out the adjusting mechanism and replace it with a wooden plug and properly seated saddle, or else to simply replace the bridge. Some decent instruments from this period—many otherwise respectable Gibsons, for example—can be greatly improved with this operation. You will still find adjustable saddles on some misguided instruments. Try to avoid them or, if the guitar is otherwise satisfactory, get them replaced.

Compensation

The saddle, and hence the bridge, must be perfectly placed in order for the guitar to play in tune. (The quality of singing or playing in tune is called *intonation*.) Since the twelfth fret is the halfway point of the string, the saddle should be located as far from the twelfth fret as the twelfth fret is from the nut—*plus* an extra $1/16$ inch added in to make up for the distance your finger depresses the string to make contact with the fret.

But compensation doesn't end there. On steel-string guitars, there needs to be additional compensation because a physical property of strings causes their actual vibrating lengths to be slightly different from their measured lengths, depending on material and diameter, so that each string needs its own separate adjustment. The greatest difference of all is between the two unwound strings and the four wound strings.

Without compensating for this physical phenomenon, the guitar will not play in tune across the entire length of the fingerboard.

Compensation is accomplished by adjusting the shape and angle of the saddle within the bridge. Take a look at the way the saddle groove is cut into the bridge. On almost all modern guitars, the groove is cut on an angle so the end of the saddle under the low strings is about ³⁄₆₄ inch further back from the neck than the end under the high strings. This is called *offset*. An offset saddle provides sufficiently good intonation for most people's ears, but even more sensitive adjustments are possible in order to get closer to perfection.

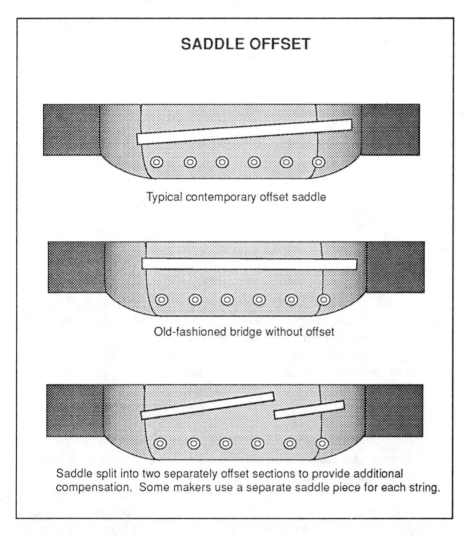

SADDLE OFFSET

Typical contemporary offset saddle

Old-fashioned bridge without offset

Saddle split into two separately offset sections to provide additional compensation. Some makers use a separate saddle piece for each string.

Because of the differences between wound and unwound strings, the most accurate degree of compensation is achieved by separately offsetting strings 1 and 2, and then starting a new offset for strings 3 through 6. Some instruments have two to six separate saddle pieces seated in a staggered offset arrangement, but even a single-piece saddle can be filed or ground into this shape. If your guitar has only offset, or is an older instrument with no offset at all, you can have your saddle compensated by an experienced repairperson if you care to. If you're playing a real cheapie, don't bother. Poorly made instruments usually don't sound in tune anyway. You're better off saving your money for a better guitar than putting it into upgrading an inferior one.

If you inhabit the world of pure mathematical truth, the amount of compensation on your guitar should ideally be adjusted to within at least 1/64 inch precisely to suit your individual action and string gauge setup. But in the real world, few if any people actually get a new saddle cut just because they change string gauge. There's a point at which you can't really hear much difference, and for most people that point is around 1/32 inch. In any case, experienced players usually fine tune while they're playing by bending the strings slightly, even on notes within a chord.

However, if you're one of those blues fanatics who prefer an unwound third string to make string bending easier, you're going to run into some pretty audible intonation problems, so you should consult with a repairperson if your saddle is not specially compensated for an unwound third.

Sometimes humidity changes may cause a guitar to shrink so severely over time that the entire instrument contracts enough for the change in intonation to be audible, which requires the crest of the saddle to be moved back a little by reshaping it. If the saddle isn't thick enough or the case is extreme, the only remedy is to replace the bridge with one in which the saddle slot is cut further back. (Regluing the entire bridge a smidgeon further back isn't such a good idea because it leaves an unsightly strip of unfinished wood, which would then have to be spot-finished, with necessarily imperfect results.)

There's a little test you can run to see how accurately the string intones. Lightly touch a string directly over the twelfth fret without depressing it; then pluck it and, at the moment of plucking, release the fretting finger. This will produce a clear, bell-like tone called a *harmonic*. (It may take you a few tries to get the hang of it.) Then fret and pluck the note at the twelfth fret and see if the fretted note is exactly the same in pitch as the harmonic. Do this with all the strings, one by one. Ideally the harmonic and fretted notes should be exactly the same. In real life, I've noticed that many respectable guitars are not quite perfect, but even allowing for this you should at least be able to tell if compensation is grossly off. It probably won't be. If it is, remember that the problem might be due to shrinkage, moisture expansion, or a pulled-up neck as well as faulty saddle placement.

Nylon strings don't require compensation. Electric guitars do, but many of them have massive saddles with adjusting mechanisms for each individual string. Such a mechanism would be sound-deadening on an acoustic guitar.

Back and Sides

The traditional woods for back and sides have been rosewood, mahogany, and maple. Each has its own distinctive sound qualities: rosewood brilliant, maple brightly astringent, and mahogany sweet. The characteristics of these and other less commonly-used woods are described in greater detail in chapter 4. For maximum projection, the back and sides of the guitar need to reflect sound rather than absorb it.

The wood must be stiff, yet must also have resilience and tone-coloring qualities as well.

Raw material for back and sides is supplied by wood merchants in precut *sets* consisting of the back pieces and two sides. In the best-quality sets, the back halves and side pieces are each bookmatched. (Three-piece backs, with two "halves" and one large center section, are becoming more common as the remaining tropical hardwood trees large enough to provide wood for a two-piece back become rarer.) Good-grade sets may be matched visually by the supplier, but in fine guitar making the back and sides should be acoustically matched as well. (As with tops, the luthier tells by tapping the wood.) Ideally the back and sides should both come from the same tree, but such sets are rare and expensive.

Nowadays most guitars have plywood back and sides, with veneers of mahogany, maple, rosewood, or some other hardwood. At this point in marketing history, the makers are not giving us any details about the structural quality or inside ply materials of the wood, but to guess from what the guitars actually sound like, plywood quality seems to improve in the higher price ranges and in the instruments of the better makers like Guild and Alvarez-Yairi. Some of the better plywood instruments actually sound like maple or mahogany or whatever they're "supposed" to be made of. But when you get down to instruments in the lower price ranges, especially under $500, the difference in woods is mostly cosmetic, and only minimally reflected in the sound of the instrument.

Because plywood can be readily steamed and pressed, a few makers offer instruments with slightly arched plywood backs said to "focus" the sound. Guild, in my opinion, has made this idea work very well.

Back Bracing and Side Reinforcement

Guitar backs are also braced with a combination of low, flat and high, thin struts. The purpose of back bracing is structural and I'm not aware of any theories of how back bracing affects sound, though I'm sure some people must have some.

On most good solid-wood instruments, the sides are given added strength and rigidity by strips of cloth soaked in glue. Sides, being made of bent wood and particularly subject to knocks and other close encounters with hard objects, are particularly vulnerable and prone to cracks and trauma.

Linings, Bindings, and Blocks

The back, sides, and top are less than ⅛ inch thick, which is not a lot of surface area for the glue joint where they meet at their edges. Therefore, the insides of the joints are supported at the sides by additional ribbons of wood called *linings*, which are notched (the woodworking term is *kerfed*) in order to make them easier to bend to the shape of the sides. Cedar or other woods are used for linings.

On the outside of the guitar, the joints are reinforced by thin strips of *binding* material, usually celluloid plastic, but sometimes an ornamental wood. Bindings may be simple or have decorative patterns. The struc-

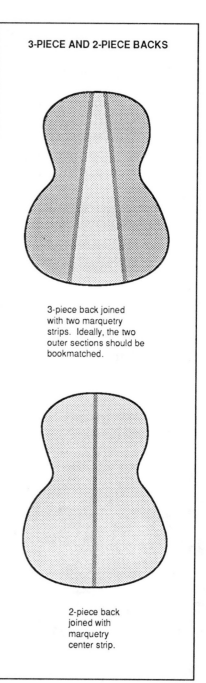

3-PIECE AND 2-PIECE BACKS

3-piece back joined with two marquetry strips. Ideally, the two outer sections should be bookmatched.

2-piece back joined with marquetry center strip.

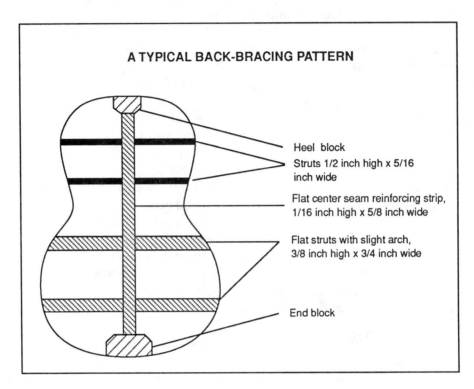

A TYPICAL BACK-BRACING PATTERN

Heel block

Struts 1/2 inch high x 5/16 inch wide

Flat center seam reinforcing strip, 1/16 inch high x 5/8 inch wide

Flat struts with slight arch, 3/8 inch high x 3/4 inch wide

End block

tural value of bindings is small, however, and their decorative value is incidental. Their most important job is to seal the edges of the back and sides against moisture penetration, because wood sucks up atmospheric humidity mostly through the edge grain. On very cheap guitars, the "bindings" may be painted on.

The sides themselves are somewhat fragile, so many manufacturers reinforce them by gluing on strips of cloth every few inches to help keep cracks from spreading. This is not necessary on plywood.

Additional reinforcement is given to the two sides where they join at the top and bottom by the *heel block* (or *head block*) and *end block*, respectively. The heel block also provides the location for the mortise of the dovetail joint that joins the neck to the body, and may also provide support for a strap button. The other end of the strap is attached to the *end pin* mounted in the end block.

Size and Shape

This section describes the major guitar sizes and shapes, and explains their nomenclature. You'll find additional information on how size and shape affect you as a player in chapter 7.

APPROXIMATE STANDARD GUITAR SIZES

Body length is for 14-fret models (except classical)
12-fret guitars usually have slightly longer bodies.

Size Nomenclature	Martin Size Prefix	Body length (in.)	Upper bout width (in.)	Lower bout width (in.)	Max. depth (in.)
Concert	0	18⅜	10	13½	4¼
Grand Concert	00	18⅞	10⅞	14⁵⁄₁₆	4⅛
Classical		19⅛	11	14½	4⅛+
Auditorium	000	19⅜	11¼	15	4⅛
Grand Auditorium	J	20⅛	11¹¹⁄₁₆	16	4⅛
Jumbo	J-M	20⅛+	11¹¹⁄₁₆+	16+	4⅞
Dreadnought	D	20	11½	15⅝	4⅞

The preceding table gives an approximation of the standard guitar sizes, along with the standard industry designations ("grand concert," "dreadnought," and so on). Of course, actual sizes and proportions may vary somewhat from maker to maker, and there are various oddball sizes as well. Instruments in the jumbo range are especially subject to variation from maker to maker. Many concert or auditorium-size "electro-acoustic" models with built-in pickups are designed primarily for amplified use, so they're built with shallow bodies (about 3 inches deep), closer to the feeling of a solidbody electric guitar body.

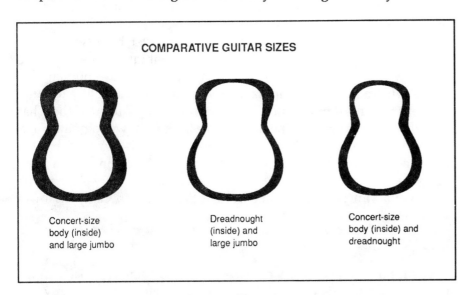

COMPARATIVE GUITAR SIZES

Concert-size body (inside) and large jumbo

Dreadnought (inside) and large jumbo

Concert-size body (inside) and dreadnought

For reference, I've also included Martin size designations in the table, though they're dealt with more thoroughly in chapter 13. The Martin company uses a series of prefixes (pronounced "double-oh," etc.) to designate the size of its models, and these prefixes are also in general use among guitarists to describe the approximate sizes of other brands as well. Thus, someone describing a small guitar about the size of the first one in the table might call it a concert size or "single-oh" guitar, even if it wasn't made by Martin. I suggest you also take a look at the section on Martin sizes and shapes in chapter 13.

In addition to the standard models listed here, there are also a small number of ¾- and ⅞-size models made for kids, which are smaller overall including neck and fingerboard dimensions.

Three of the basic size/shape configurations: a) a 12-fret concert model (Martin O) b) a 14-fret grand auditorium model (Martin OOO) c) a dreadnought model (Martin D) *Photo courtesy Martin Guitar Co.*

BASIC GUITAR SHAPES

The 12-fret, 14-fret, and dreadnought silhouettes are the three basic guitar shapes in common use. Each of these shapes may come in smaller or larger sizes.

12-FRET GRAND CONCERT GUITAR	14-FRET AUDITORIUM GUITAR	STANDARD DREADNOUGHT GUITAR
Note the round shoulders. A classical guitar is almost the same size and shape, though a bit broader in the upper bout.	Note the broader upper bout and flatter shoulders.	Note the narrower waist and more oblong proportions.

The concert size was standard around the time of the Civil War, but over the years public taste has more and more shifted toward the bass-heavy sound that comes from a larger-bodied guitar. All things being equal, larger guitars are also louder. However, because loudness also comes from the soundboard's ability to vibrate, some old small guitars with extremely vibrant tops are amazingly loud—loud enough to overwhelm most contemporary dreadnoughts. The ability to build such instruments is now almost lost; certainly the will to build them has been. It's easier to get loudness from size than from wood quality and painstaking care. In any case, contemporary taste is mostly for bassy instruments and the public perceives bigger as better in general, and makers are not going to make what no one wants to buy. As a result, small guitars are hard to find at every quality level, especially the lower ones.

Shape

You'll find some oddities of shape now and then, especially in the work of experimentally-minded luthiers, but there are really only two basic guitar shapes in general use today: the dreadnought and the ordinary, nondreadnought shape that has no particular name. Each of these in turn has two main variations. Among dreadnoughts, most follow the square-shouldered Martin design, but a few follow the rounder-shouldered design of instruments like the classic Gibson J-50. Among nondreadnought guitars, most are 14-fret square-shouldered models, but 12-fret guitars have rounder shoulders and slightly larger upper bouts.

The dreadnought shape, which quickly became popular after Martin introduced it as a standard production model in the early thirties, is extremely broad-waisted in order to maximize cubic volume, and therefore maximize bass frequencies and overall acoustic volume. (See the section on dreadnoughts in chapter 13, Part II for more detail.) Dreadnoughts are also large, deep guitars overall. There's no particular reason why the broad waist can't be used on smaller instruments as well, and it's been done, but it's usually used only with large instruments to begin with.

Body depth is important in bringing out bass notes. Traditionally dreadnoughts have been deeper and most smaller-bodied guitars shallower, but in recent years guitar makers have experimented with deepening smaller-than-dreadnought body sizes. Lowden has made interesting grand auditorium guitars almost as deep as an acoustic bass. Martin offers its jumbo models in two body depths. And several contemporary makers and luthiers now offer instruments inspired by Gibson's Nick Lucas model of the 1920s—until recently an obscure instrument with a cult following—which is approximately grand concert breadth but with some extra depth of body that gives extra depth of sound in the low end.

The basic body shape variables are these:

- Smaller + shallower
- Larger + shallower
- Smaller + deeper
- Larger + deeper

Each combination of these variables affects the qualities of low and high notes, and the relationship between them, differently.

Cutaway Guitars

Some guitars also have a *cutaway* upper bout in which a large area is simply removed in order to permit easy access to the upper frets. Pointy cutaways are called *Florentine* cutaways; rounded ones are called *Venetian*. The difference is cosmetic. *Double cutaways*, in which portions

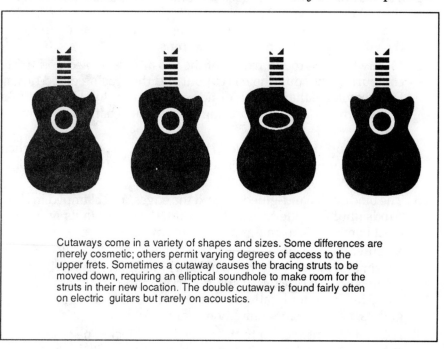

Cutaways come in a variety of shapes and sizes. Some differences are merely cosmetic; others permit varying degrees of access to the upper frets. Sometimes a cutaway causes the bracing struts to be moved down, requiring an elliptical soundhole to make room for the struts in their new location. The double cutaway is found fairly often on electric guitars but rarely on acoustics.

Standard
body

Cutaway
body

are removed from both sides of the bout, are often found on electric guitars but hardly ever on acoustics. Taking out some of the bout degrades tone and volume to a certain extent—too great an extent with a double cutaway.

Putting the Guitar Together

Procedures vary from maker to maker, but here are the major steps Martin takes in putting together one of its guitars. (All operations, major and minor, add up to over 300 steps, according to Martin.) The other high-quality makers, like Santa Cruz and Taylor, probably work in a similar way. Note that preassembly milling operations (the cutting to shape of the various pieces of wood) are not included here.

Martin, of course, works more slowly and carefully than a midrange mass marketer, and with less automation. Instruments are set aside to stabilize between major operations, so the steps below take place over a period of three to four months. Mass produced instruments are made far more quickly, using more operations that are automated or done by machinery rather than by hand, and the finishing would be simpler. (For example, there would be fewer lacquer coats, all neck and body joints would be uniform rather than unique, final shaping of necks and braces would be done by machine, and so on.)

1. Side and back pieces are selected and visually matched. Back halves are assembled and braced. The sides are soaked in water and bent to shape by hand over hot cylindrical shaping irons, then checked against molding jigs. (On cheaper makers' guitars, especially those made of plywood, the wood is steam-pressed rather than worked by hand.)
2. The end block and heel block are glued into place to support the sides as they are joined together. Linings are glued into place, using ordinary wooden clothespins as clamps. At this point, the edges of the guitar look like a row of clothespins.
3. Meanwhile, the rough halves of the top are assembled and finely contoured. The soundhole is cut out and the bracing glued down. Fine shaving of the braces is done once they are glued in place. (On cheaper maker's guitars, bracing is precut and handwork is minimal.)
4. Now, the top and back are glued to the sides. The body, sandwiched between softwood boards, is left for several hours in a clamping jig resembling a press until the glue sets.
5. The binding is hand-glued around the edges, and clamped in cloth bands until the glue sets. At this point, the guitar in its wrapping of ribbon looks like an Egyptian mummy.
6. Meanwhile, the neck blanks (mahogany billets milled to approximate shape by electric bandsaw) are finely shaped by hand, using carving tools, files, rasps, sandpaper, and an almost-obsolete woodworking tool called a draw knife. (On cheaper makers' guitars, necks are more highly machined.)
7. A dovetail joint is cut into the body's heel block. The tenon at the end of the neck heel is individually shaped to fit the heel block

mortise, and the neck and joint are fitted together (but not glued). The set of the neck angle is then checked against a measuring jig. (This is all handwork, so a Martin neck fits only the guitar for which it is made. On mass-produced guitars, the joint is machined to uniform specs.) From now on, the neck and body, though not yet married, travel together through the assembly process.

8. The truss rod is mounted into a groove cut into the neck below where the fingerboard will be mounted. Then the fingerboard (with fret slots already cut) is glued on top, and the frets are mounted and finished. The entire neck/fingerboard is given a final trim and inspected; then the frets are hammered into their slots.

9. Neck and body are scraped and sanded smooth and, where applicable, wood filler is rubbed into the pores before the wood is stained—the first step in the finishing process. Then the still-separate neck and body are sprayed with seven to 10 coats of lacquer finish. Each coat, when dry, is finely sanded, so that the final thickness of the finish is .007 inch. When the finish is dry, the bodies and necks are buffed with a wax compound.

10. Neck and bridge are glued into place and left for the glue to set. The self-adhesive pickguard is mounted. Then saddle and tuning hardware are mounted and the instrument is strung up and ready for final visual and playing inspection and adjustments before shipping.

A cutaway guitar by the Santa Cruz Guitar Co. *Photo courtesy Santa Cruz Guitar Co.*

7

Suiting Yourself

Making a Good Marriage with Your Guitar

Chapters 5 and 6 are called *How Your Guitar Works*, but it's really you who does the work. The guitar just sits there until you come along. When you do, it will be with a flatpick, fingerpicks, bare fingers, or some combination of these. You're going to use them to pluck the strings somewhere more or less over the soundhole, or maybe down closer to the bridge. You will have put some strings on it that are relatively light or heavy. Your style of playing is going to be relatively loud or soft. It may involve strumming chords, or picking out individual notes, or some combination of both. You may need to be heard in a kitchen, a living room, or auditorium, or barroom. You may be a soloist, vocal accompanist, or part of a band. And exactly which notes you play, and how you want them to sound, will be a function of the style of music you play: bluegrass, blues, folk, pop, or whatever.

These are your choices to make as you will, but your guitar also has a will of its own. Depending on its size and its shape and its wood and its bracing pattern, your guitar may be better or worse suited to express your own will, and a mismatch will lead to a frustrating battle of wills—a battle which your guitar will win, since it's more intransigent that you are. This chapter offers some suggestions to help match your will to your guitar's. As you learn more about guitars, you'll discover that they have personalities all their own. Some have an all-around competence: they do what they're told, but they have no fire or spiritual brilliance of their own. Great guitars have character. Like great historical and artistic figures, they may have flawed as well as brilliant sides. You learn to live with, and within, the instrument's weak and strong points. It makes life more interesting. Players who like instruments like this are usually the ones who keep two or three around. Players who prefer all-around competence can get what they need from only one instrument.

The Ideal Guitar Does Not Exist

The guitar is a bundle of compromises that would put even the U. S. Congress to shame. It sounds better the more lightly it's built, but if you build it too lightly, it warps or pulls apart. The body wood on a good instrument is only around 3/32 inch thick, which is barely enough to hold it together. It sounds better with lots of mass in the neck and headstock, but if a maker actually puts extra mass there (and, yes, it's been done with lead weights!), then it won't balance comfortably in your lap. Unlike a violin or archtop guitar, where string pressure compresses the instrument together, the flattop guitar is built with explosive string tension that wants to tear it apart—and someday it will.

Even if the ideal guitar did exist, it might not be ideal for you. The highest ideals of guitar making are qualities like balance, separation, and dynamic range. These are the qualities that a virtuoso soloist demands, yet they may not satisfy other needs. It's not so much that a fine solo guitar would be overkill for strumming rhythm in a country band as that it would flat out be the wrong tool for the job. So you have to know who you are, or at least who you want to be, in order to find the guitar that's ideal *for you*.

In each of the following sections we'll take a look at the guitar from many perspectives, one at a time. For example, you'll learn in *Suiting Your Style* why a dreadnought shape might be exactly the shape you need for the style of music you want to play, and you'll learn in *Suiting Your Body* why a dreadnought shape may be a poor choice in terms of your comfort in handling the instrument. Balancing out these pros and cons is entirely up to you.

The ideal guitar may not exist, but neither does the ideal guitarist, so it all balances out in the end.

Guitars Differ Differently

Never forget that guitars of the same model are not always identical in sound and quality. Dreadnought sound differs from jumbo guitar sound in typical ways; the Martin sound differs from the Santa Cruz and Gibson sounds in typical ways; rosewood sound differs from maple sound in typical ways. But not all rosewood Martin dreadnoughts or maple Gibson J-200s, even of the same period, sound exactly the same either.

Everything boils down to the individual instrument. Fine guitars have more distinct personalities than inexpensive mass-produced ones, but these too have their differences. Even among fine models from fine manufacturers you have to watch out for the occasional dog, but for the most part you'll be listening for fine points of balance and tone quality between individual instruments—differences in the realm of taste and suitability. Among lower-end mass-produced instruments there's more sameness, but even so it pays to be on the lookout for differences here as well. But at this level, don't look so much for fine points as for gross differences: is this guitar dead or alive; is it comfortable to fret the strings or not; do the high strings sound full or tinny?

Suiting Your Body

Size and Shape

Your Body and the Guitar's

Most people just assume that the popular dreadnought shape is the one to get, since bigger is supposed to be better. Many wind up being happy with their dreadnoughts, but others find that the dreadnought shape is just too large to be comfortable. You may find that the instrument isn't comfortable if you're a small person overall, or have short arms—although some small people seem to be able to make themselves comfortable with large guitars anyway.

Even the larger jumbos, some of which may have broader lower bouts than a dreadnought, may be more comfortable because the waist is deeper so the instrument sits lower in the lap. Less broad and less deep jumbos may be more comfortable still.

Although the even smaller sizes are less popular these days and are harder to find, there's a lot to be said for them. Not only are they comfy for smaller people, but they're often downright congenial for just about every size person. They're much friendlier to hold and often give you a much more satisfying sense of listening to yourself; the big guitars seem to project their sound more outwards to the audience than to the ears of the player. There's much to be said for the friendliness of small guitars, especially if you're playing mostly for yourself.

Some people with large busts or broad middles are also uncomfortable with very large guitars, though for others it's just not an issue. Arm length may be the deciding factor. Using a strap even while seated may help an instrument of any size lie comfortably against a large person.

Cutaways

Do you need a cutaway? Probably not. Most acoustic guitarists find they can get all of the music they need and want out of the first fourteen frets. Twelve, in fact. Cutaways are special devices for specialized lead guitarists whose styles demand them. I suggest you keep away from them unless you *know* you're going to need one, or unless the guitar you're in love with just happens to have one anyway.

A cutaway may take away more than it gives you. Building a cutaway is a big job that can easily bring an instrument into a new price bracket, especially for beginners, the extra money is better spent on sound and playability instead.

There's an additional irony in the way cutaways give you a poor return for your dollar on beginner-quality instruments. Inexpensive guitars are the ones most likely to suffer from weak-sounding high notes and stiff action on the highest frets, so when you get a cutaway on such a guitar, all you're getting for the extra money you're shelling out is access to the least satisfying, least congenial area of the fingerboard.

The sound of the highest frets also tends to be weak on large-bodied guitars, even better-quality ones. If you know for sure that you'll need a cutaway because you play lots of high notes, then I'd recommend looking at smaller guitars or electro-acoustic models.

a

b

Contemporary variations on the traditional Martin dreadnought design from the Santa Cruz Guitar Company: a) the Tony Rice model with oversize soundhole and other internal features, based on the Martin dreadnought once owned by Clarence White; b) cutaway dreadnought with a somewhat wide fingerboard. *Photo courtesy Santa Cruz Guitar Co.*

Left-Handed Guitars

A Special Note For Left-handed Guitarists

If you're a lefty, you've got three choices . . . and the choice is entirely up to you. I don't think this is a decision that anyone can make for you, though you should certainly get as much advice as you can from your teacher and other left-handed guitarists.

1. You can play the guitar the way righties do. Among the better-known left-handed people who play this way are Artie Traum, Dave van Ronk, Christine Lavin, and Nils Lofgren. I'm sure that there are even more closet lefties who play like this, and that a good many of them feel they have a definite advantage over right-handed guitarists, since in most styles it's the fretting hand that does most of the hard work.

2. You can play a left-handed guitar. This is a guitar on which it's possible to reverse the order of the strings so that the low strings are still on top (toward the ceiling) when you hold it with the neck pointing right. You need a special lefty guitar to do this because guitars are braced more strongly on the bass side to compensate for the extra tension of the heavier bass strings. Left-handed guitars also have the pickguard mounted on the opposite side of the soundhole. When you purchase a left-handed guitar, it's important to confirm that the instrument is actually braced in reverse, rather than just having the superficial pickguard change.

3. The final possibility, one that hardly anyone would recommend, is to play a regular guitar upside-down. That is to say, hold a regular guitar lefthanded (with the neck pointed right), but *don't* restring it. This means that not just the guitar but everything else too will be turned upside-down so as far as your picking-hand work goes, you're in a completely different universe from the overwhelming majority of guitarists, and you will have to develop a set of unique accommodations to the instrument. You'll find it more difficult to learn from and share with other guitarists, and, while you may be able to develop some original stylings, you may also find it difficult or impossible to play some of the things that guitarists are normally expected to be able to play. Most of the people who play this way are self-taught musicians who grew up in primitive or isolated environments. Elizabeth Cotton, the wonderful guitarist who wrote the fingerpicking standard *Freight Train*, was one.

Whichever course you choose, be prepared to stick with it. Once you learn to play one way, you'll find it nearly impossible to switch.

Among the companies that have marketed left-handed guitars in recent years are Santa Cruz, Takamine, Ovation, Gibson, Martin, Taylor, and Washburn. La-Si-Do offers some inexpensive models, including a fairly inexpensive 12-string.

There are at least two retailers that specialize in left-handed instruments:

Gauche Guitars (1844 Union St., San Francisco, CA 94123) handles fine left-handed guitars.

Shane Musical Instruments (7010 Brookfield Plaza, Springfield, VA 22150) stocks left-handed musical instruments of all kinds.

Guitars for Kids

You're not going to help your kids learn to play by putting a grown-up size guitar into their hands. They need a ½-, ¾-, or ⅞-size guitar not only with a body small enough to hold comfortably, but with a fingerboard width and scale suitable for small hands. There are few such steel-string instruments currently available. As a result, most people wind up getting low-grade Korean nylon-string instruments which, for most kids, work well enough. Nylon-string instruments have the added advantage of being easier on the fingers. Nylon strings will do for basic music lessons and school events. If your kid is serious or talented enough to need real steel strings to achieve a certain sound, then you're going to have to look harder. Goya makes an otherwise nice kid-size dreadnought that unfortunately has so much weight at the headstock end that it's hard to imagine a kid being able to balance it properly, but substituting lighter tuners might help. If only the best is good enough for your children, Martin makes a small-bodied mahogany guitar (model 5-18) on special order and many luthiers would also enjoy the challenge of a kid-size instrument (Linda Manzer of Toronto offers one as a standard model). There are probably a few other cheaper models that have escaped my attention, and it may also be possible to find a used small instrument from another maker. Decades ago Gibson made a nice one, but no one who owns one ever wants to part with it. Most people who own the little old Gibsons and Martins realize what little treasures they have, and they save them for the next generation.

Suiting Your Eye

Ornamentation

Most forms of guitar ornamentation have functional origins. Bindings seal the edges of the top joints. Headstock inlays are a form of manufacturer's logo. Fingerboard inlays provide visual clues to help the fingers navigate up and down the frets.

I've never seen an absolutely plain guitar, though I suppose it would be possible to build one. I'd just as soon have a simple looking guitar that glowed with the inner light of its wood and nothing else. It's too bad the Shakers didn't—couldn't have—made guitars. However, some makers reserve their best woods for the top-of-the-line instruments that wind up getting a lot of inlay work, so as a result I've had to compromise on owning at least one ornate guitar just because it sounds so good, and so might you.

But ornamentation can be very pleasing to those who enjoy it and admire the skills of fine woodworking and inlay carving. In particular, the craft of cutting and engraving mother-of-pearl and abalone has its own set of aesthetic conventions going back hundreds of years. (If you really want to get into this, though, you'd better give up on guitars and get into fancy banjos instead, where the legacy is much richer.)

An ornate 12-fret dreadnought custom-made by the Santa Cruz Guitar Co. for the noted instrument collector Harry West. Note the extensive abalone purfling, mother-of-pearl vine fingerboard inlay, "flowerpot" headstock inlay, and even the abalone inlays on the bridge pins. *Photo courtesy Santa Cruz Guitar Co.*

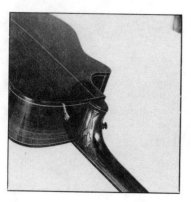

Fancy heel carving on a guitar by Harry Fleishman. *Photo courtesy Harry Fleishman.*

Some luthiers also enjoy woodcarving as well as inlay work. Since carving up the body is unwise from a structural and acoustic point of view, the neck heel and the headstock are basically the only areas where ornamental carving can be indulged in. The headstock shape, whether ornate or simple, is one area where many luthiers seek to establish a characteristic design. Ornate neck heels are, by tradition, more commonly associated with banjos than guitars, but from time to time—and almost always as the result of a custom request—a luthier will ornament the heel area with relief carving.

If you have all the money in the world, you can even commission custom inlay work from a luthier or one of the high-quality factories. If you're on a limited budget, though, it makes much more sense to make sound and playing features your first priority.

Let's look at some more typical forms of ornamentation.

Headstock and Neck Inlay

Both abalone and mother-of-pearl are used on fine guitars, and plastic imitations thereof on cheaper ones. Folks generally call mother-of-pearl "MOP" or "pearl" for short, and sometimes the term includes abalone shell as well. A "pearl Martin" is one of the 40-series Martins richly decorated with abalone purfling and MOP inlays.

Pearl or pearloid plastic is typically used for position markers and decorative headstock inlay, which can be quite extravagant. (Conventional patterns include the leafy designs called "flowerpots," gryphons, eagles, nubile masthead-like figures in various stages of undress, snakes, lizards, and whatever else turns you on.) Some makers treat the headstock inlay as a standard logo; others vary it from instrument to instrument.

The position markers are usually pearl, pearloid plastic, or some other light-colored material such as a white hardwood, for maximum contrast with the dark fingerboard. Simple circles are usual, though small diamond-shaped inlays of the sort used on many early Martins are also common. Sometimes the twelfth fret gets an especially large inlay, and some instruments use giant blocks of abalone or other material instead of small markers.

Headstock inlay on a guitar by Harry Fleishman. *Photo courtesy Harry Fleishman.*

Another convention, though not as common on guitars as on banjos, is the ornate leafy vine or "tree-of-life" inlay running up and down the entire fingerboard. And a final possibility is to have your own name inlaid across the fingerboard. It does wonders for getting your guitar back if it's stolen, but (unless you're a celebrity) it may make your guitar pretty hard to sell. Still, it won't get you into as much trouble as having "Fifi" with a heart and arrow tattooed on your left arm.

The most garish fingerboards and head plates ever made are those of the iridescent pearloid plastic known affectionately as "mother-of-toilet-seat" (sometimes abbreviated MOT in descriptive catalogs). It was also used even more extravagantly on banjos than on guitars, likely enough inset with fake glass rubies and emeralds. Gibson was the worst culprit, particularly in the thirties—I guess people really needed something to cheer them up during the depression. This stuff really shines under the spotlights, folks, and if I'm not mistaken, the Gibson factory's custom shop will still do it for you it you want it done. And it goes just great with fezzes, plumes, and shiny cloaks and tunics.

Mary Flower and her Krimmel guitar with abalone rosette and mother-of-pearl position markers. *Photo by Selian Hebold.*

Binding, Purfling, and Rosettes

Various plastics and hardwoods may be used for the bindings, including the grainy-looking off-white nitrocellulose or cellulose acetate known as ivoroid. Many makers use plastic binding in a solid color on their least expensive models and with increasingly complicated alternating light and dark stripes on their more expensive models, as status symbols.

The extra strips of inlay inside the edges of the binding are called *purfling*. The most famous purfling designs are the inlaid abalone strips on 40-series Martin guitars and the legendary "herringbone" purfling pattern used by Martin on its better guitars from the 19th century until 1944. The prestige of "herringbone Martins" has nothing to do with the herringbone and everything to do with the scalloped bracing design that was also discontinued in 1944, but since it's a lot easier to put on herringbone purfling than it is to do labor-intensive handwork on braces, you'll see herringbone purfling on all sorts of guitars at all sorts of quality levels these days. (Even Martin has responded to the public's lust for herringbone by imitating itself: the herringbone purfling and the scalloped bracing as well are now once more available on some models.)

Sometimes, particularly around the soundhole and down the center of the back, you'll see ornate marquetry strips of multicolored dyed wood. These are actually thin sections cut from larger blocks of glued-together wood strips. The soundhole inlay, whether of marquetry or any other material, is called the *rosette*.

Finish

If you're a professional, or even a wannabe, then you have to think of suiting your audience's eyes as well as your own. The fashion these days among most stage musicians, especially those who front a band, is not so much inlay as colored finishes. For a while white was big, but at this writing black is in. If you decide you want an instrument with a colored finish, remember that you'll probably be sacrificing sound to get it. Most colored finishes are heavy enough to be acoustically detrimental; in addition, you may reasonably expect most makers to reserve their worst-looking wood, which is also likely to be their worst-sounding wood, for opaque finishing. If you're a strumming singer standing in front of a band, then looks may be as important as sound and a colored guitar may be a reasonable compromise. And when fashions change every few years, you can just take it down to an auto body shop for a new color job.

Suiting Your Style

The sound qualities that make one sort of guitar more suitable for one style than another become more pronounced as the qualities of the wood and craftsmanship get better. The most inexpensive instruments are less distinctive, so the following generalizations are less applicable in lower price brackets. And remember, they *are* generalizations.

General Playing; Casual Styles

For all-around playing and self-accompanying country and other contemporary songs, most players do well with an auditorium- or jumbo-sized guitar, or with a well-balanced dreadnought. The jumbos are particularly good for strumming chords, dreadnoughts for strumming chords with articulated bass notes and bass runs, and auditorium or smaller sizes for fingerpicking. Smaller jumbos and grand auditorium guitars make reasonably good compromises for people who both flatpick and fingerpick. However, it's also possible to find individual dreadnoughts that are well enough balanced for fingerpicking, even though this isn't what dreadnoughts are really all about.

Most casual players who are going to play a variety of songs and styles around the house wind up walking out of the music store with a dreadnought. But if this is your goal, I urge you to consider the advantages of smaller guitars for comfort, a more balanced sound, and overall congeniality. Guitars in the jumbo and, to a lesser extent, the

Tony Rice prefers a dreadnought for his bluegrass-derived new acoustic playing style. *Photo by Mark Farris, courtesy Rounder Records.*

auditorium-size range are fairly easy to come by in a number of styles and price brackets. Smaller guitars are harder to find new, but since they're less popular you can sometimes find some very reasonable deals on used ones if you're lucky. In any case, your best bet for versatility is a well-balanced instrument rather than a boomy, bass-heavy one.

Bluegrass and Old-Time Music

For punchy bluegrass playing, fiddle tunes, and old-time stringband music, a strong dreadnought is what most players prefer. You'll have to make your own decision whether you prefer a more balanced instrument or one that really booms in the bass, depending on how you play. For an authentic period sound in old-time stringband music, though, you'll want a smaller guitar.

Blues

You can play blues on anything, even a dreadnought, but the most authentic sounds come from instruments with strong, thick-sounding trebles. This usually means a smaller-bodied guitar, and perhaps mahogany rather than rosewood. Many accomplished country-blues stylists who use period instruments prefer Gibsons and minor-brand guitars of the thirties and forties. If you fingerpick more than flatpick, consider a slightly wider than usual fingerboard.

Contemporary Fingerpicking

Many exponents of complex picking styles such as ragtime, new-age music, and contemporary Celtic music prefer a clean, brilliant well-separated sound most likely to come from a guitar about auditorium size or smaller, with a somewhat wide fingerboard to help separate the strings so the picking hand has enough room to do its best.

Acoustic Jazz

For acoustic jazz and postbluegrass new-acoustic music, most players prefer extremely well-balanced dreadnought or jumbo guitars, perhaps with a cutaway for playing single-string solos high up the neck.

Suiting Your Suitcase: Travel Guitars

There are at this writing two companies that make small-bodied guitars with pretty much normal necks, designed to save space when you travel while allowing you the feel of a normal fingerboard so you can keep up your chops. Expect a surprisingly pleasing but small sound, with weak lows.

Outbound Instruments, Box 1052, Boulder, CO 80303
Vagabond, Box 845, Albany, NY 12201

Suiting Your Pocketbook

Here are a few suggestions about what to look for in each price range. Remember that street prices are often considerably lower than list prices.

The following advice is what I give to my own students, based on those instruments I've used or sampled over the years. Some of my students ignore my advice and wind up with instruments that satisfy them, and sometimes even me, anyway. There are many exceptions to these generalizations.

Under $150

If you have a lot a patience and the time to look around, and live in a population center with lots of guitars to browse among and lots of turnover in the newspaper classifieds, or else if you're just plain lucky, you may be able to find a quite decent used instrument at this price. Most of the new instruments available in this price range are not very good, so I'd strongly advise trying to find a used one if your budget can go no higher. If your community has a music store that stocks playable junkers at 50 bucks and up, then you're really in luck.

At this price, go for playability first, and settle for the best sound you can find among the playable instruments. Since larger (dreadnought and jumbo) guitars are currently in fashion, it's sometimes possible to pick up a decent smaller Japanese or Taiwanese guitar from the sixties or seventies at a fairly low price.

Most instruments in this price range will not hold up very well over the long run, and won't give you much satisfaction once you get beyond the basics of playing, so figure that you'll want to move on to a better guitar after a year or so, and start planning ahead now.

$150 to $250

Among new guitars, my favorites in this price range are the instruments from Goya and La-Si-Do (Minstrel and Seagull). It's also possible to find used instruments from the next highest list price bracket in this range. As with the cheaper guitars, it's unreasonable to expect that instruments in this range, or, for that matter, the next highest range as well, will hold up well over the long term.

Sometimes you can find decent-sounding used solid-wood guitars, like sixties Harmony Sovereigns, in this price range—though all too often they have acquired warped necks or other action problems over the years. There is also a tendency for some dealers to overprice such instruments.

$250 to $500

In my opinion, many of the new instruments at the bottom of this range are not much better than the Goya and La-Si-Do guitars mentioned above. Moving up in this range, I like products from Sigma, Simon and Patrick, Takamine, and Yamaha, and it should be possible to find a satisfactory solid-topped instrument among them.

Sometimes you can find decent used all-solid-wood guitars in this bracket, especially small-bodied models that are a little beat-up. Some of the lesser Gibsons from the fifties or later still sound better than contemporary laminate models in this price range, and if you're very lucky you might even come by a small mahogany-topped Martin at the very top of this range.

$500 to $800

At the beginning of this range, I'd suggest looking at new laminate instruments from Takamine, Washburn, and Yamaha. Toward the top of the range, add Alvarez-Yairi, Guild, Washburn, and Shenandoah, assuming a good discount. Also look for used top-of-the-line instruments from these makers.

As you get to the top of this bracket, you begin to find high-quality used smaller-than-dreadnought instruments from Gibson and Martin. If you're willing to accept a the idea of a smaller guitar, you can wind up with quite a good solid-wood instrument, for example a sixties Martin 00 model, for under $800.

$800 to $1200

In this price range you can get good-sounding new top-of-the-line laminate guitars from Alvarez-Yairi, Guild, Shenandoah, Takamine, Washburn, and Yamaha, many with high-quality built-in pickups and controls. (For pure acoustics, I prefer Guild and Shenandoah.) Street prices of solid-wood Guilds and Montana Gibsons also begin in this range.

But this is a tricky range, because it's also possible to get very good used solid-wood guitars—especially from Gibson and Martin—at these prices if only you're willing to wait for one to come along. At the place and time of this writing, for example, a late-seventies Indian rosewood Martin D-28 goes for around $950 in the classifieds, and perhaps for a bit more than that in a shop.

Over $1200

As you get above $1200, look at all-solid-wood instruments from Martin, Santa Cruz, and Taylor. Some instruments from these makers, of course, go much higher. If your budget goes that high as well, you should also look at guitars from small-production makers (like Schoenberg) and private luthiers.

If you can afford an instrument in this price range, then you should also consider the used instrument market very seriously. Fine prewar Martin dreadnoughts go for many thousands of dollars these days, but excellent smaller-bodied models can be had for a good deal less.

8

Strings

String Basics

Your guitar has six strings, numbered 1 to 6 starting with the one closest to the floor as you hold the guitar. In other words, the thinnest string, the one highest in pitch, is the first string.

The convention in numbering strings is to start with the highest, but the convention in giving the note names of the strings is to start with the lowest. (I don't know why this is the case. If you think it's done deliberately to confuse you, maybe you're right. I can't think of any other reason.) In standard tuning, the guitar strings are tuned EADGBE in the order low to high; 6 to 1. Therefore, you can call the second lowest string either the A string or the fifth string, as you please. The sixth and first strings are distinguished as "low E" and "high E."

One end of the string has a loop wound around a little metal grommetty kind of widget called a *ball*, even though it isn't. It's more like a barrel, if anything, and its function is to hold the string in place underneath the bridge. Therefore, guitar strings are reasonably enough called *ball-end* strings—reasonable, that is, if you accept that the thing that's not a ball is a ball. There are also strings called *loop-end* that are for banjos and mandolins. Loop-end strings, strangely enough, actually have loops on the end.

Strings come in different materials and in different sets of gauges (diameters). The kind of strings most people have on their acoustic guitars, and want to have on their guitars, and that you'll most likely find on your own first guitar when you bring it home, have first and second strings of plain stainless steel wires, and third to sixth strings with a core of steel wire overwound with fine brass wire. Therefore they're called the *wound* strings. (The technical name for them is *roundwound*.) The lower strings are wound because they need to have more mass in order to vibrate slowly enough to produce their lower pitches. If you made strings with that much mass out of a solid piece of wire, they would be so thick that they would loose their elasticity and not be able to vibrate properly. Winding becomes necessary on steel guitar strings once the string diameter gets larger than about .021 inch.

From Catgut to Stainless Steel

People loosely use the term "catgut" to refer to musical instrument strings, but Morris and Garfield have nothing to worry about. Instrument strings in the old days, like violin strings in the present day, were typically made of sheepgut. No one is even sure where the term "catgut" came from. Historians suggest derivations from words like *kit* (an ancient form of mini-violin) and *catlin* (a term in ship-rigging, the technology of which influenced early string makers). Others speculate that Catigny, the French town that was an early center of the string industry guilds, had something to do with it. (Gut instrument strings were originally made by the same craft guilds that made strings for tennis and badminton racquets. Perhaps this explains why the words "Stop that racquet!" are so often applied to beginning players of string instruments.) Technology for making wire strings has existed since the late middle ages, when it was discovered that it is possible to reduce the diameter of superheated high-carbon iron rods by drawing them through a series of thinner and thinner holes in a die.

Metal wire was used in early days on the harpsichord and some lute- and mandolin-family instruments like the *chitarra battente* and cittern, but gut was used for the lightly-built guitar. During the 19th century, however, gut-string technology improved and manufacturers were able to produce more powerful strings with greater tension than before. (It seems possible that the development of the X-brace by the C. F. Martin Company during this period was a response to this emerging string technology; see chapter 13.) In the end, the gut-string manufacturers undid themselves, for as guitars grew larger and stronger, they became able to tolerate metal strings.

Guitarists may have begun to use steel strings as early as the 1880s. Some early modern guitars, like those Orville Gibson made around the turn of the century, seem to have been heavily made just for this purpose. Martin didn't start uniformly bracing its guitars for steel strings until the late twenties, although their guitars had tended to become more robust over the preceding few decades. Classical guitarists continued to use gut strings until the late forties, when Albert Augustine introduced nylon strings made with new technologies developed by DuPont during World War II. Steel strings just don't give classical guitarists what they need in the way of tone and handling.

Today's steel strings are still made by drawing metal through a series of ever-decreasing holes in dies. Wire for the unwound first and second strings is drawn through circular dies, but wire which will be used as a core for the wound strings is now usually drawn through hexagonal dies, the better to create a gripping surface for the winding. (Such strings are called *hex-wound* or *hex-core*.) Then the core is placed in a lathe-like machine that rotates it while a wrapping of even finer wire is wound tightly around it.

Picking Your Strings

Now that you know enough about strings to get confused, you're entitled (by the standards of contemporary society) to call yourself an expert. But before you start giving advice to others, you'd better figure out what kind of strings you want for yourself.

The only way to decide what sort of string you want to use is by experimenting. The information in the rest of this chapter should help you make some informed decisions about the range of your experiments. In short, your decision will be based on the following factors:

- **String gauge**. This is the diameter of the string, the main factor in determining how hard you have to press down.
- **Kind or material**. What the string is made out of, and its design, play an important part in how it sounds and, to a lesser extent, in how it feels under your fingers.
- **Your guitar**. Personal taste aside, some instruments just work better with some kinds or gauges of strings than others.
- **Brand**. This is the least important factor, since most manufacturers sell similar products.

If you absolutely need to have someone give you a starting point, here it is. Unless your guitar is delicate enough to require extra-light or compound strings, start off with light gauge 80/20 bronze, and then cycle through other kinds for a couple of years until you settle on what you like. If you're new at the guitar, it will be a while before you can hear or play well enough to tell the difference, anyway. You'll also discover that a fresh set of strings—no matter which kind or brand—almost always sounds better than the ancient grungy set you just took off, so you'll have to teach your ear to compensate for that as well.

Figure it could take a couple of years before your ear learns to sort out what you like best. And once you have decided, don't be afraid to change your mind every so often. You're allowed to. It's called "artistic growth."

What Are Strings Made Of?

The strings that we loosely call *steel strings* fall into two main groups: bronze-wound strings for acoustic guitars, and nickel-wound strings for electric guitars. There are also compromise kinds called *compound* strings that are halfway between nylon and bronze and *copper-coated steel* that are halfway between bronze and nickel. Other kinds of strings, like the *nylon* strings used on classical guitars, aren't suited for nonclassical music as a rule.

Bronze-wound Strings

The strings most people use on acoustic flattop guitars are generally called "bronze" in the music industry, even though most are actually brass. (Bronze is an alloy of copper and tin, while brass is an alloy of copper and zinc.) Some brands label their strings according to the alloy.

"80/20" strings are 80 percent copper and 20 percent zinc, and "60/40" strings are 60 percent copper and 40 percent zinc. "Phosphor bronze" strings are true bronze (90 percent copper and 10 percent tin) with an added fraction of phosphorous that is said to lengthen the life of the string.

How you hear strings is a matter of taste, so to speak, but there's a pretty good consensus that phosphor bronze strings sound softest and warmest, 80/20s are somewhere in the middle, and 60/40s are the brightest and coolest. (Most brands with the word "bright" in them are 60/40s.) In the case of brands that don't tell you the alloy, you'll just have to use your ears to tell you whether you like them or not, without being prejudiced by metallurgical data.

Copper-coated Steel Strings

These are designed for acoustic guitars with magnetic pickups. The copper (around 30 percent of the string mass) lends warmth and authority to the acoustic tone, while the remaining 70 percent steel is enough to activate magnetic pickups. But they're compromise strings. The acoustic sound doesn't suit most people as well as the sound of bronze strings, nor the electric sound as well as the sound of nickel-wound strings (see below). Nonetheless, because you can't have bronze and nickel-wound strings on your guitar at the same time, you might like copper-coated steel best after all.

Nickel-wound Strings

These are for electric guitars. They're pretty much the same as acoustic guitar strings except that the windings are made of a nickel-iron alloy or nickel-plated steel. This is because the magnetic pickups used on true electric guitars are designed to pick up the vibrations of the magnetic field of the string, so you have to use strings that have magnetic properties. If you have a magnetic pickup on your acoustic guitar, you'll have to use nickel or copper-plated strings (above) to get the pickup to work properly. (See this book's section on pickups for more information.) Most guitarists feel that nickel strings are not as resonant as bronze when used on an unamplified acoustic guitar, though every so often you'll run across someone who prefers them.

Nickel-wound strings last somewhat longer than bronze before they fray or go really dead, which over a period of years will save you some money. Because they're made of harder metal they'll also wear down your frets faster, which over a period of years will cost you some money.

Compound ("Silk and Steel") Strings

In compound strings, the first and second strings are regular steel, usually equivalent to those in a regular light-gauge set. The difference comes in the lower strings, which are wound over a much thinner metal core than usual. Additional microfilaments of nylon (formerly silk) floss are added to the core to give the string enough mass to function, with minimal tension of the string. The result is a moderate-tension, easy-to-play string, usually with a sweet, warm tone and soft volume. The bass strings usually have a little less separation than those in a bronze set, though this also depends on the guitar. Don't expect to actually find any silk in a set of strings labelled "silk and steel."

Compound strings are sometimes good for a beginner's first set, because they're gentler on fingertips that haven't grown calluses yet. They can sound excellent on 12-strings, where they produce a pleasingly airy sound in addition to having the advantage, especially crucial on 12-strings, of lower string tension on the bridge. They are the string of choice for delicately built guitars, early Martins, and similar instruments, but they still exert far too much force to use safely on classical guitars.

Gauges of compound strings may vary significantly from brand to brand, just as they do with regular strings. Most brands of compound strings actually exert a tad more string tension than extra-light roundwounds. But even so, many players prefer the touch and sound of compound strings to extra-lights on small or fragile guitars. It depends entirely on the guitar and on personal taste. Using a set of extra-lights, but replacing the first and second strings (usually .010 and .014) with .012 and .016, is also an alternative worth trying.

Flatwound and Groundwound Strings

Winding and Squeaking

There are several ways of treating the windings of both bronze and nickel-wound strings to make them feel smoother and cut down on string squeaking. The best way to cut down on squeaking, though, is to learn to run your fingers more lightly along the strings. The correct way to navigate on the fingerboard is to maintain some contact with a string to guide your fingers, which means that a certain amount of squeaking comes with the turf.

Music stores also carry a spray-on lubricant called Finger-Ease™. I've never felt a need even to try it, but I know people who have used it for years without harming their fingerboards. Check to make sure it also won't hurt the ozone layer.

Flatwound Strings

Flatwound strings are wound with flat wire ribbon. They have an extremely well-centered but dull sound that's not very popular among acoustic guitarists, though the few who do like them swear by them. The flatwound concept works somewhat better with electric guitar strings and very well on the electric bass and members of the violin family, so they're more popular on those instruments.

By nature, flatwound strings are a bit less flexible than regular strings. Few brands market guitar flatwounds and few retailers bother to carry them.

Groundwound Strings

There's also a compromise string variously called *groundwound, half round, polished,* or *flat polished,* where the outside of a regular round winding is polished down to created a smoother, almost flat surface. Like flatwounds, they're more popular among bass players than guitarists. Most guitarists find them a sonic no-man's-land that offers

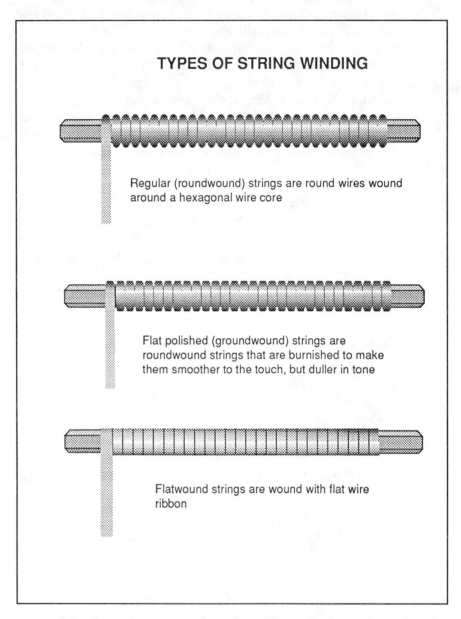

TYPES OF STRING WINDING

Regular (roundwound) strings are round wires wound around a hexagonal wire core

Flat polished (groundwound) strings are roundwound strings that are burnished to make them smoother to the touch, but duller in tone

Flatwound strings are wound with flat wire ribbon

none of the clear advantages of regular or flatwound strings, and all the disadvantages.

Remember that regularly wound guitar strings are called *roundwound* to distinguish them from all these other types. But in normal talk, when you just say "strings" everyone assumes that you mean roundwounds. Do not confuse roundwounds with groundwounds, ground round, or tofu.

Nylon Strings

In a nylon string set, the first through third strings are nylon monofilament (like fishing line), while the lowest three are a multifilament nylon floss core wound with copper, silver-plated copper, bronze, or another metal. Nylon strings are intended for classical guitars, which are built much more lightly than folk guitars. Nylons don't put out enough energy to drive the top of a folk guitar effectively, and almost always sound so weak on a guitar intended for steel strings that it's not worth putting them on, even as an experiment. However, many 19th-century Martins and similar guitars were originally built for gut strings and are too delicate to accept even compound strings, so you must put nylons on them.

Classical guitar bridges don't have pins. Instead of seating the end of the string under the bridge plate, you run a nylon string through a hole in the bridge parallel to the soundboard, and then wrap it around itself. Once the string is tightened, tension holds the wrap securely in place. A few string makers offer ball-end nylon strings for those who are too wimpy to learn to wrap the string properly. Using them is considered uncool by the cool people who wrap their strings. They also don't last long, since they tend to break off at the ball. Because of differences in pliability and friction, most players prefer to wrap the unwound strings around themselves two or three times, but the wound strings need only one wrap.

Like steel strings, nylons are available (though in a more limited variety) in different gauges and winding materials. An oddity in the nylon-string world is the metal-wound third string. They're hard to find and most dealers will deny they exist. (Among the few companies that make them is the French firm Savarez, which catalogs them as item number 527R. Savarez strings are widely available in this country.) Wound third strings are good for giving some vitality to poorly made classical guitars, which tend to have particularly weak-sounding third strings. They also work well on old Martins that have to be strung with nylon, because they make the guitar play a little more like a steel-string instrument. And they also break readily. Buy twice as many as you think you'll need.

People still refer to nylon strings colloquially as "gut," even though almost half a century has passed since nylon drove gut off the market. When I was a kid, I once found a set of real gut guitar strings and tried them out. Don't bother.

String Gauge and Tension

Gauging String Gauge

Although many players approach string gauge with an attitude bordering on mysticism, there's no mystery about it. It's cut and dried and strictly quantitative: gauge is the diameter of the string as measured in thousandths of an inch. The "heavier" the gauge, the thicker the string is, the more tension it exerts. You also have to work harder to depress a heavier-gauge string against the fret. As a rule, heavier-gauge strings generate more energy and therefore drive the top more strongly. (In other words, they're louder.)

As a beginner, you may not believe that differences of one or two thousandths of an inch make much of a difference, but (on the high strings, at least) experienced players can detect such differences instantly, and find them very important in determining their sound and style. If you manage to sample a variety of string gauges over the next year or two, you'll learn to tell the differences yourself, without even trying.

The string industry sells guitar strings in sets usually named ultra-light, superlight, extra-light, light, medium, and heavy. The exact gauges of each string within a set usually vary slightly from brand to brand. For example, one brand's "light" set might offer a slightly lighter-gauge third string than most other brands', so that brand might appeal to you if you play a lot of blues and want a third string that's easier to bend.

Let's take a look at the properties of some of the string gauge sets.

Ultralight, Superlight

These are generally used only by electric guitarists who like to do a lot of string-bending. They don't put out energy to drive the top of an acoustic guitar past a thin whisper. However, sometimes someone will use them on an acoustic guitar for a special effect.

Extra-light Gauge

Extra-lights are good for delicately built guitars and for some blues and contemporary styles that require a lot of string-bending and vibrato. (The lighter the string, the more responsive it is to these techniques.) They're a bit too light for most of the student-grade instruments on the market these days, but if you're just starting to play you might want to use extra-lights for around a month, until you build up some calluses, and then move to lights.

Compound strings

Compound or silk and steel strings (see preceding section) have roughly the same degree of tension as a set of extra-lights, but sound and feel a bit softer overall.

Light Gauge

Light gauge strings are probably the best strings for you, and certainly the best starting point unless you have a delicate instrument that absolutely must have lighter strings. For most people's playing, they offer the best compromise between tone production, easy of playing, sensitivity to bending and vibrato, and feel under a flatpick, fingerpicks, or bare fingers.

Medium Gauge

Mediums are for people who play hard with flatpick or fingerpicks, don't need to bend strings much, and have sturdy instruments that can withstand their tension and effectively diffuse the amount of energy they put out. If you play a lot, you *can* learn to bend medium strings, but most people find it too hard and painful.

Some instruments, including as strange bedfellows both cheaply made plywood-topped guitars and exquisitely delicate guitars, actually lose rather that gain volume when they are strung with mediums instead of lights.

The stiff feel of medium strings goes very well with a stiff flatpick, because the strings let the pick come off quickly to help with fast playing. A lighter string gives under the pick, distracting its motion.

Medium strings are generally favored by bluegrassers and heavy strummers who use robust dreadnought and jumbo-size guitars. They take some getting used to, but for some styles and guitars they do the job much better than lights.

Heavy Gauge

Most flattop guitars can't tolerate the tension of heavies; in fact, using them voids the warranty on most new instruments. They're good for big-band acoustic archtop rhythm guitars, which are built like the pyramids and require a huge amount of energy to get the top moving. Some resophonic guitar players also use them, though most prefer mediums.

The tool that's used to gauge string—or the breadth of any small object—is called a *micrometer*. Many guitar stores and repair shops keep one around, even though a good steel model, with accuracy to a thousandth of an inch, is pricey. (The less costly plastic models made for other crafts are only accurate to a hundredth of an inch—not a fine enough tolerance for measuring guitar strings.) If you get hold of one of these gadgets and go around measuring guitar strings, you'll sometimes find that a string is not exactly the diameter it says on the package. So if from time to time a string feels heavier or lighter than you think it should, it may not be fantasy.

Typical String Gauge and Tension

Because exact gauges vary slightly from brand to brand, the table below gives the gauges of a mythical "average" set, and the approximate total string tension of that set assuming it's strung on a normal long-scale guitar (25.4 inches). On a short-scale guitar (24.9 inches), tension would be a tad lower.

In comparison to the tension figures below, tension on nylon-string guitars is usually in the neighborhood of 75 pounds. Tension on 12-string guitars ranges from about 205 to 250 pounds, depending on gauge and scale.

TYPICAL STRING SETS
in thousands of an inch; exact specifications vary slightly according to manufacturer.

Set	first	second	third	fourth	fifth	sixth	approx. tension (lbs.)
Electric Ultralight	.009	.012	.016	.024	.032	.042	105
Compound	.011	.014	.023	.028	.038	.047	130
Extra light	.010	.014	.022	.030	.039	.048	125
Light	.012	.016	.025	.032	.044	.053	150
Medium	.013	.017	.026	.035	.046	.056	175
Heavy	.014	.018	.027	.038	.048	.059	200

Making Up Your Own String Set

Not all manufacturers gauge their prepackaged sets exactly alike. If from among them all you still can't find a set you like, or if you just want to experiment a little, you'll find that most dealers also sell strings individually, so you can mix and match to make up your own custom set. (Because buying strings one at a time is more expensive than buying sets, it may cheaper to just buy a whole set and then discard and replace one or two strings. Sometimes dealers will give you a little back in trade for the discards.)

As a rule, electric guitarists are more into making up custom sets than acoustic guitarists. Among the super-light strings used by electric lead guitarists, small differences in gauge feel much more pronounced than they do among acoustic guitar sets. (The lighter the gauge, the larger the percentage difference a thousandth of an inch makes.) Many electric guitarists, and some acoustic players as well, get extremely finicky about string gauge—often with good reason, even though they appear silly about it sometimes. But it's also a great area for one-upmanship and prima donna affectation, if you're into that.

However, prepackaged gauged sets generally make sense. If you start mixing in grossly disproportionate custom strings, they will no longer feel and sound balanced with each other. On most guitars, if you mix (say) an extra-light fourth string into an otherwise light gauge set, you'll probably find that (1) you get disoriented whenever you pick the fourth string because it gives much more than the others do; (2) its tone color is out of place; and (3) it's not as loud as the others. On many electric guitars you can adjust the pickups for relative loudness on each individual string, so the last problem can be easily solved. Not so on acoustics.

Nonetheless, each guitar and each player's touch is unique, and sometimes accommodations have to be made. One very common need is for a slightly lighter third string, to make easier the bluesy sounds you get when you "bend" the string by pushing up on it. Some people even go so far as to use an unwound third, which is great for bending, but requires that you recompensate your saddle. (And even with a recut saddle, it's still very difficult to keep an unwound third playing in tune. Unwound thirds are more commonly used on electric guitars, many of which have adjustable saddles.)

Individual strings are also handy for people who need to replace only one string, or who find, as many do, that they like to replace the unwound strings more frequently than the wounds. (They seem to die faster, and to feel dirty faster.)

Strings and Setup

Ideally, a guitar's action is set up for a given string gauge. For example, a guitar set up with low action would buzz more with hard playing when strung with light strings than when strung with mediums. But the choice of light gauge strings in the first place suggests that the player doesn't intend to do much loud playing. If volume is your priority, then a big guitar with medium strings is the usual way to get it.

String Brands

String makers start with raw drawn wire obtained from the same vendors that supply wire for pianos, electrical and communications cable, fencing, baling, construction, and so on. The guitar string companies wind the strings, add anticorrosive chemicals, wrap in the metal ball ends that hold the strings under the bridge, cut the strings to length, package them, and ship them out. Because the manufacturers are not the original makers of the actual wire, they are known in the music industry not as string makers, but as "string winders." If you call them that you'll sound either hip or incomprehensible, depending on whom you're talking to. But then, that's what talking hip is all about.

There are relatively few string winding companies. As a rule, they market their own brands and also supply strings to other packagers who sell them under different brand names. Sometimes the original winder is named in small print on the package, sometimes not. Most brands offer a similar variety of string types (brass, bronze, compound, etc.), and differ from each other mostly in the gauge specifications within each set. Some brands with widely differing list prices ultimately come from the same string winder.

I don't see much point in recommending any specific brand. Try them yourself and make up your own mind—no one else can do it for you. Unless you're in a small town where your retailer has no competition, you should be paying something like 50 percent to at most 80 percent of manufacturer's list price for your strings. Many retailers offer good string discounts to help increase their walk-in trade. Others happily discount orders of a half-dozen or a dozen sets. Strings will keep for a long time, and a little tarnish won't hurt them.

When you go string shopping, you'll notice that some brands market string sets according to style: "blues" strings, "bluegrass" strings, etc. Some are created to meet the specifications of a famous player who endorsed the set. All this means is that the individual gauges of the strings making up the set have been customized to meet somebody's set of expectations about what is ideal for that particular style.

Bad Vibes, Heavy Metal Fatigue, and Other Tough Breaks in the Life of a String

What happens when strings get old? It's not a pretty picture.

- The winding wears and breaks at the point where the string contacts the frets. Unwound strings become thinner where they rub against the frets. The string's molecular structure changes under tension, and metal fatigue sets in.
- The string becomes corroded with perspiration acid, tarnished by airborne impurities, and rusted from ambient humidity.
- Dirt, finger oils, and dead skin tissue coat the string.
- All the above factors result in uneven mass throughout the string length, causing "dead frets" (not the fret's fault) and erratic intonation. You can help matters significantly by making sure your hands are clean before you play, and giving your strings and guitar neck a quick wipedown with a clean rag when you're done.

Why do strings break? Sometimes they just wear out or get struck too hard. But if you find that you keep breaking the same string in the same place, look carefully at the guitar where the string breaks. Often the problem is caused by a nut or bridge saddle that is improperly shaped, or a nut that is improperly grooved, or a bridge pin hole on an older guitar that has worn away, causing the string to cross the bridge at too sharp an angle. If you suspect that any of these string bearing points are a cause of excessive string breakage, check with your repairperson. A minor adjustment or replacement could cure the problem.

When to Replace Strings

Unless you're replacing a single broken string on a newish set, don't replace your strings one at a time. Trust me: you'll be happier that way. Otherwise your strings will all be out of sound balance with each other and you'll go crazy trying to remember which string you replaced when. (Unless, of course, you keep such data on your computer log, in which case you're crazy to begin with.)

How often should you change strings? It depends on how much you play, on how hard you play, on how abusive your body chemistry is on strings, on the kind of strings you use, and on your personal taste. Some people get weeks and months out of a set of strings. Some deposit a heavy layer of sweat and dead skin tissue on a set of strings within minutes. Still others have a knack for causing strings to tarnish without affecting their sound. Though most people prefer the sound of strings that have been played in for several hours, some professionals have a signature sound that depends on the jangly brightness of brand new strings. They pay for their sins by having to change them before every performance.

Generally speaking, change strings when any of these happens:

- They won't stay in tune, or sound out of tune when you play.
- They sound obviously dull, or you find yourself playing harder and harder in order to draw a lively sound from them. (This only means that they sound unobviously dull).
- They've been on for a while and one of them breaks.
- They feel dirty. (Sometimes a quick wipedown will get you through a few more days or weeks. I like to use a rag moistened in rubbing alcohol, being careful not to drip any onto the fingerboard or body.)
- The windings fray or develop obvious worn spots.

9

Pickups and Amplification

Amplified versus Natural Sound

As you know from chapter 3 on guitar sound, each musical instrument has its own unique blend of vibrations. Pre-electric instrument-building traditions are all designed to produce an instrument whose vibrations mix together in the air a few inches or feet in front of the performer, reaching the audience as a tasty acoustical stew of tones and overtones blended together from the various resonating surfaces and chambers of the instrument. When you introduce a pickup or even a very closely placed microphone, you skew these factors and the instrument sounds different. If you're a grouchy old guy like me who grew up in ancient times when the sound of amplified or recorded music was considered the exception rather than the norm, you may hear amplified or recorded sound as untrue. If you're younger (or just more open-minded), then you may perceive electronically altered sound as normal, or even as a whole new world of possibilities. Whatever the case, it's certainly true that few people have ever had the opportunity to listen to a fine guitarist playing a fine acoustic guitar in an intimate setting, with no amplification. Even so-called "live" performances in small halls and coffeehouse-type venues are amplified.

The great value of pickups is that they free performers from the microphone, offering advantages in terms of posture and stage movement as well as clarity of sound in the audio mix with voices and other instruments. But many professionals who use add-on or built-in pickups and electronics regard them as necessary (or convenient) evils in performing situations, but don't much care for them privately. It's just more satisfying to listen to your own guitar purring softly on your lap. The performer you see on stage with an electro-acoustic laminate guitar is very likely to regard that instrument as a tool for the road, to be discarded for a new one every few years, and to own a fine all-wood guitar to play at home and in the studio.

So, it's important to recognize that you can't put a pickup inside an acoustic guitar, run it through an amplifier or recording console, and still have it sound like an acoustic guitar in a living room. Oh, the manufacturers say their equipment does it, but it doesn't. The proof comes once a year when they announce a new pickup design that *really* sounds like an acoustic guitar this time. At best, it may sound like a well-miked guitar. Don't kid yourself. Pickups have a sound of their own. Once you accept this, you'll be in a better position to judge which pickup you prefer, and enjoy it for what it is.

Should You Buy a Guitar with a Pickup?

You have to make your own decision, but here's what I'd do.

If I knew I'd be playing with amplification most of the time, I wouldn't spend a lot of money on a fine all-wood guitar and then have a transducer added. I'd look for a well-made laminate or synthetic-bodied guitar with solid top, built-in tone and volume controls, and probably a built-in preamp as well. Since the guitar would be amplified, I wouldn't worry much about its unamplified volume, but good sustain would be very important to me.

If my interest were in playing quietly at home by myself or with a few friends who also play acoustic instruments, I'd put my money into the best-sounding acoustic guitar I could afford, instead of spending it on a pickup, interface, and the amplification equipment I'd need to make them work. Why? Because as soon as you start plugging in, you ruin the intimacy and fellowship of playing acoustic music. Unless you know that you're going to be playing with electric guitars, drums, pianos, or other loud instruments, forget amplification. I think you'll be happier, and I know your family and neighbors will be.

Finally, if it were the sound of a true electric guitar I wanted—one with a solid or semi-hollow body and magnetic pickups—then that's what I'd get. Don't mess with acoustics if you really want an electric.

Pickup Interfaces

There's more to "picking up" than the pickup itself. Most players find that the sound of a bare pickup alone just isn't good enough. Pickups put out a fairly weak electrical signal, and when the amplifier is cranked up to boost it, the process adds noise of its own. Therefore, it's common to use a preamplifier ("preamp") between the pickup and the amplifier or console.

In addition, pickups often produce a sound that is imbalanced, tinny, or lifeless. Therefore it's also common to add an equalizer, tone control, or other sound-processing device between the pickup and the amplifier or console. (Equalizers are essentially glorified tone controls that let you boost or suppress selected frequency ranges.) An antifeedback device called a *notch filter* is also useful in professional environments.

Some guitars with built-in pickups also come with built-in volume and tone controls, and possibly a built-in equalizer and preamp as well. If you're adding a pickup to an ordinary guitar, you can get these gadgets assembled in a small box, called a *pickup interface*, that sits on the floor at your feet or, in some cases, may clamp onto your belt or hang from a strap over your shoulder as well. Many pickup manufacturers offer a matched interface box for their pickup, or you can buy one separately. You can try to get by without one, but they'll usually make you sound better and also put more control of the way you sound into your own hands, instead of leaving you at the mercy of whoever is operating the sound system.

Electro-acoustic Guitars

In some instruments, called *electro-acoustic* guitars, one or another combination of volume/tone control, equalizer, or preamp is usually built into the guitar along with the pickup. Most (not all) electro-acoustic guitars are designed on the assumption that they will be used with the pickups all the time, so they don't have as much unamplified volume, or as full an unamplified tone, as a true acoustic guitar. Adding a bunch of extra hardware inside the guitar body degrades the sound at least a little, so it's always a tradeoff. And many of these instruments are shallower than purely acoustic guitars, in order to make them more congenial to players used to the thin bodies of electric guitars.

When you go shopping for an electro-acoustic guitar, you'll find that some makers offer famous-name pickups, while others offer their own house-brand pickup (that may be originally made by one or another of the famous-brand factories anyway.) Don't necessarily be influenced by pickup brand name when you make your buying decision. It's the whole package you're buying, so listen to the whole sound.

Amplifiers and Sound Systems

True electric guitars with magnetic pickups (see below) feed into guitar amplifiers. Guitar amps are great for making you sound like Eddie van Halen (or kind of), but their circuitry is not designed for use with microphones, or in amplifying the human voice, and they don't sound particularly good when you use them this way. For microphones and voice, the best amplifier is the kind of sound system which people still call a "PA" (for *public address system*) or "voice amp," even though today's music-oriented systems are much more sophisticated than what a high-school principal uses to make a speech in the gym. For professional *sound reinforcement*, as concert-quality amplification is called, microphones and pickups for each performer are fed into a master console where they are equalized and mixed, just as they would be in a recording studio. Acoustic guitar pickups are designed primarily to feed into a voice amp console along with voice and instrument mikes, rather than into a guitar amp. Running a guitar pickup directly into the mixing console is called *direct input*, or DI for short.

Don't be surprised if your pickup doesn't seem to sound as good as what you hear coming over a professional sound reinforcement system at a stage show. A road guitarist in a major act may use much more than a small interface box between the guitar pickup and the sound system—hundreds or even thousands of dollars worth of sound-processing equipment, in fact. Then add a professional sound system worth more than you make in a year, operated by a professional technician, and it's no wonder that you don't sound like that in your living room.

Also remember that the usual professional setup many pros prefer is to have the acoustic guitar miked and DI'd at the same time, giving the sound technician two separate signals to work with. (As a variation on this, you'll also sometimes see a guitar player working with a combination of mike feeding into the sound console, and pickup running into an onstage guitar amplifier used as a stage monitor, and which might also be miked. Doc Watson often works like this.) Neither of these setups are exactly the kind of thing anyone is likely to run in the living room.

Transducers

Introduction to Transduction

Transducer is the technical term for any kind of gizmo that converts one kind of energy (like sound) into another (like electricity). The ordinary microphone that you say "testing, testing" into is a kind of transducer too, and so is the dilithium chamber on the Starship Enterprise (I *think*). In the more down-to-earth realm of guitars, there are three main types of transducers: contact pickups; magnetic pickups; and mini-microphones. All are mounted inside the body or soundhole of the guitar, and these days almost all are provided with a wire that leads to a connecting jack built into the end pin.

You can buy a guitar with a built-in pickup, or add one to the acoustic guitar you already own. (Depending on the kind and brand of pickup you get, it might be a job for a repair shop or it might be something you can do yourself. If you're adding a pickup to a guitar you already own, you'll probably have to have the end-pin hole reamed out to accommodate the larger-sized jack.) Then you plug a connecting cable into the end-pin jack, run it to your amp or sound system, crank it up, and *get down.*

Contact Pickups

Contact pickups are transducers mounted in direct contact with the guitar's wood. They work by sensing the wood's vibrations.

In *dynamic* transducers, the vibrations set in motion a diaphragm that moves a coil inside a magnetic field to create the electrical signal. In *piezoelectric* transducers, a crystal does the same job. Piezo pickups (as they're called for short) have a much wider frequency sensitivity and, if properly engineered and mounted, minimize the annoying bass boominess that is typical of dynamic pickups. For these reasons, piezos have just about wiped dynamic pickups out of the marketplace. Pronunciation, by the way, is *pie'-zo,* as in apple, cherry, or coconut cream.

Pickups, Preamps, and Impedance

With most piezo pickups, you'll find you get better sound if you use a preamplifier. Make sure you get one with an impedance level precisely suited to that particular brand of pickup. Impedance is the level of electrical resistance that the circuitry of the preamp or amp offers to the signal from the pickup, measured in units called *ohms*. Like economics, impedance is a theoretical area that remains a mystery to most people. It's confusing because the specified impedances of two devices don't necessarily have to be the same in order for them to work together. Far from it, in fact. Think of it as something like marriage.

The exact figures (in ohms) that are required to match two pieces of equipment may vary individually from one piece to another, so study the manufacturer's specs carefully and test the system before purchase. A system in which all the elements do not balance will produce disappointing sound, usually by killing the low notes and making the high notes tinny.

Most contact pickups are mounted on, in, or near the bridge, where the vibrations are strongest. Some brands are actually available in the form of bridge saddles. You'll have to experiment to see which brand of pickup, and where it's placed, gives you the sound you like best. Some do-it-yourself pickups come with putty for semi-permanent mounting; you can move the pickup around to experiment. However, bear in mind that the putty could have a muting effect on tone.

If you're having a repairperson install the pickup, you may delegate the responsibility for where to mount it. Most repairpeople have strong, mutually exclusive, opinions about where best to mount pickups, and their taste may differ from yours as well as from each others'. Some favor installing two pickups on either side of the bridge for better balance and control of tone.

For after market add-on pickups, you'll do well to begin by looking at products from FRAP, Barcus-Berry, L.R. Baggs, and Fishman, among others. Fishman is the hip pickup at this writing, though that could change by the time this book gets into print because competition in this market is intense and new models come out frequently.

Mini-microphones

Another way to amplify your guitar is to mount a small microphone somewhere in the soundhole of your guitar. Mikes differ from contact pickups in that they sense not the movement of the guitar's wood, but rather the sound pressure levels of the surrounding air as it is set in motion by the vibrating wood. Mikes potentially give you the most natural sound, but also offer you the greatest sensitivity to feedback, which is a hassle to be avoided. As with contact pickups, you'll have to experiment to see exactly where you want to place the device to get the sound you want.

Some mini-mikes clip right onto the edge of the soundhole. (It may be because they're specifically designed for this purpose, or because they were originally intended to clip onto a newscaster's lapel.) If not, you can rig some sort of mount yourself out of duct tape and baling wire, or have a experienced repairperson construct a wooden mounting bracket for you. Most miniature microphones get to be miniature because some of their components are left out of the pickup unit; instead they may be included in a small box that sits at your feet or clips onto your belt.

Various models are available from different manufactures, and you'll have to experiment to see which you like best. Here are some characteristics to evaluate.

Directionality

Mikes may be designed either to pick up sounds from all over (*omnidirectional*), or in a narrow (*cardioid*) or *unidirectional* pattern. Since omnidirectional models are the least fussy, they require the least fuss in finding a mounting place. But the other models may let you focus on specific sounds and achieve more specialized effects. You'll have to experiment to see which suits you best.

Power

Some mikes draw their power from the console; others from batteries. Mikes which draw console power usually deliver better sound than battery-powered mikes. (Battery-powered mikes tend to be the less expensive, subprofessional models, and they may be just fine for you.)

The microphone market is so volatile that I wouldn't care to recommend particular model numbers. However, I'll happily point you to Radio Shack for a real cheapie if you want to experiment at a safe cost, to Fender products in the lower-range, and to the Audio-Technica, Electro-Voice, Sennheiser, and Sony companies for well-regarded high-end equipment.

Magnetic Pickups

Magnetic pickups are the kind of pickups used on electric guitars. The energy that they pick up and convert into an electrical signal is not sound vibration, as it is with the other types of transducer, but rather the oscillation of the magnetic field of the vibrating string. Therefore you have to use strings with magnetic properties, designed specifically for electric guitars. (Sorry, a vibrant personality and good haircut are not enough.) For more information, read about copper-plated steel and nickel-wound steel strings in chapter 8.

Built-in magnetic pickups are often placed just above the soundhole at the end of the fingerboard. Aftermarket magnetic pickups usually clip across the soundhole. It's the easiest place to mount them and it puts them close to the strings, where they must be. When you start shopping, look at products from D'Armond, DiMarzio, Seymour Duncan, and Dean Markley, among others.

10

Used and Vintage Guitars

Looking for Mr. Goodfret

Lots of professional musicians own used instruments. It's easier for them to come by a good used instrument than it is for you. Pros hang around music stores and other musicians and know what's available. They know what to look for and how to evaluate an instrument without having to do research and make comparisons the way you do. They buy instruments from each other. And because they already have what they need, they can afford to sit tight until something they like comes along at a good price.

For you, it's harder. You can wait forever before what you want appears in the classifieds, you may (correctly) feel insecure about your ability to spot anything wrong with an instrument, and you won't have the advantage of immediate sound and feel comparisons the way you do when you work your way through a dozen guitars in a guitar store. If you make the rounds of thrift stores, flea markets, and garage sales the prospects are even more dismal. Sometimes you can luck out, but not often. What you usually find is unplayable junk on which ignorant sellers have put too high a price because someone told them that old guitars are valuable. Even pawnshops, which were once good hunting grounds, have turned sour. Most pawnbrokers know that good old guitars can be valuable but wouldn't recognize a good guitar if they saw one, so they overprice everything out of fear. Some also stock junky new instruments to sell to people who think they're getting a good deal just because they're buying from a pawnshop. They're not.

Finally, be suspicious of good instruments being sold at an absurdly low price. They could be hot. It happens all the time. Use your head and don't get greedy.

But buying a used instrument is a great way to save money. If the classifieds don't help, try to get one from a dealer or other reputable trader (some teachers and working musicians deal instruments on the side). Some dealers don't like to sell used instruments, because profit margins are higher on new goods. But some always have a few used instruments around that they've taken in on trade, and a few even enjoy the public service of keeping around a bunch of beat-up, adequately playable junkers for quick turnover at low prices. Some of them are off-brands that aren't worth buying new, but if you can find a playable used model for 50 bucks to get you through the first six months of testing your commitment, they make sense at that price. You're still not getting a very good guitar, but at least you're getting what you pay for.

Looking for a used guitar in a higher price range makes sense when you want features that have been discontinued. For example, small-bodied Martins, Gibsons, and Guilds are no longer in standard production, but you can find good used models from the sixties. At this writing Martin no longer routinely specs quartersawn back and sides for models other than dreadnoughts, but quartersawn models may be available from earlier years. Brazilian rosewood Martins and most solid-wood-bodied Guilds have also been discontinued, but you can find them used. But if you're dealing with a knowledgeble seller, then be prepared to pay more than bargain rates, or even more than the cost of new instruments with Indian rosewood or plywood bodies.

Getting a used guitar makes even more sense when you're looking for a good-quality instrument if you just want to save a few bucks. At this writing, the list price of a new Martin D-28 is $1790. A good mail-order discount would be around $1075 (40 percent off). You'll also have to pay shipping and insurance costs, but perhaps not a sales tax. But if you want to sample the instrument before buying you'll probably find that, unless you live in a high-population area with strong competition, your local discounts are less, and you'll have to pay sales tax. By comparison, a private person selling an Indian rosewood D-28 a couple of years old would at this writing probably ask around $850 to $950 in a metropolitan market (maybe more where dealer prices are higher and stock harder to come by), and sales tax won't rear its ugly head. As an extra bonus, the instrument will already be played in for you. And you won't have to worry about putting the first scratch on yourself. (For more on mail-order, see chapter 11.)

Vintage Guitars

Old and Vintage Guitars

Decent guitars may reach their stride at age 20, but they still don't get any respect until they're 50 or 60. The so-called "vintage" acoustic guitar market consists mostly of instruments from before World War II. (Some other models from more recent years are also allowed into this category, depending on a combination of rarity, value, and fad. For solid body electric guitars, on the other hand, "vintage" doesn't even begin until the 1940s.)

The demand for "vintage" instruments originated in the early 1960s, when folk music revivalists were learning to copy earlier musical styles and wanted period instruments to play on. They soon discovered that the old instruments sounded great and could be bought cheaply. After all, there were no vintage guitars in those days—just used ones.

Eventually cults developed and there emerged wizards and

loremasters who could recite all the brand names under which the old Larson Brothers workshop marketed their instruments and could date a Martin at 20 paces just from the squareness of the headstock (the corners of the old Martin headstocks got more rounded over the years as the template wore down). Guitars were no longer tools for creative musicianship. They were degraded to the status of collectibles, as if they were nothing more than doggie figurines, bubble gum cards, or Van Gogh paintings.

The Nature of a Collectors' Market

When you get into a collectors' market, you're playing a whole new game. Prices become based on quantified standards like rarity of a particular feature, or a given year's production run.

It bears remembering that being old doesn't automatically make a guitar great. The instrument has to have been great from the moment it came out of the factory. It's arguable that a higher proportion of the top-line instruments that came out of the factories in the vintage days were great guitars than they were in later decades. But that still doesn't mean that the vintage crop doesn't have its share of mediocre-sounding instruments and outright dogs.

Some vintage dealers evade the issue of sound quality by dismissing it as subjective. *Of course* tastes and preferences in sound are subjective. But that doesn't mean that there are no standards. It doesn't mean that a panel of good guitarists won't generally agree that a dog is a dog, and be able to hear its snarl 50 feet away.

Sometimes this works to players' advantage. Instruments most valued as collectibles are those in original mint condition. Cracks, dings, refinish jobs, or nonoriginal frets may bring price down, regardless of sound quality. As a result, it's still sometimes possible for players to get their hands on superb-sounding vintage instruments at relatively low prices compared to new instruments. (Prewar Martin dreadnoughts are the great exception, because demand is so very high.)

The Nature of Collectors

"The first thing we do, let's kill all the lawyers," cried a revolutionary rabble-rouser in one of Shakespeare's histories. Some musicians feel the same way about guitar collectors. As with lawyers, the argument has its merits. At their best, collectors are informed experts, and sometimes tasteful musicians as well, who preserve important artifacts of Americana and of musical history. At their worst, they are boorish ignoramuses who, as another English poet once put it, know the price of everything and the value of nothing.

Can you detect new frets and fingerboard or a contemporary refinishing job? Do you know in what year Martin went from bar frets to T-frets, or altered its X-bracing pattern? Was the original bridge plate maple or rosewood? Has someone carved a new ebony bridge to replace an ivory original? When did Martin change from the pyramid bridge to a belly bridge? Can you spot a Prairie State that's been altered from an archtop to a flattop? Do you know the date of each modification in the Gibson script headstock inlay? Even more important, can you trust the person who's pricing and selling the guitar to tell you these things, or to recognize them in the first place? One of the greatest dangers is run-of-the-mill music store dealers who do not customarily deal in old instruments and, when they do, price them even higher than the specialized vintage dealers do. As I write, someone is trying to sell in my local paper's classifieds a 1945 Martin D-28 advertised with "prewar specs" for $5200. This is one of the classic "herringbone" dreadnoughts, so-called because of the herringbone-pattern ornamental edge binding that Martin used on its 28-series instruments until 1946. But though Martin kept using the pretty binding until 1946, they quit using their scalloped bracing in 1944, and they altered their original X- brace placement in 1939. These are the qualities that give the (older) herringbone dreadnoughts their sought-after sound. Is the seller putting you on, or is he or she just ignorant? In any case, you could be in trouble if you don't know better.

On the other hand, if it's worth $5200 to you to be seen in the parking lot at bluegrass festivals playing an old Martin with herringbone binding, then go ahead and buy it. It may sound great, anyway. But with a little looking, might you dig up an equally great-sounding instrument for half the price? Very likely. Maybe for a third the price, with luck and perseverance.

Vintage Guitars as Investments

Vintage instruments generally maintain their value at resale *if you buy at a good price* to begin with. You will also do well if you purchase just before one of the occasional surges that occur in the overall market or among certain classes of instruments. Such a surge took place, for example, while this book was in preparation. However, if you pay a top-dollar collectors' price from one of the pricier dealers, you'll find that you generally have to undercut that price to move the instrument quickly, so you might take a loss if you can't afford to wait.

If you spend much time listening to vintage instrument dealers, you'll hear talk of buying guitars as investments. The vintage market got a big ego boost around 1970, when Sotheby Parke-Bernet and Christie's, high-class auction houses specializing in fine art, antiques, and other artifacts used by the wealthy to store their wealth, added vintage guitars and banjos to their catalogs. But guitars and banjos never really took off in that upscale environment, and have now settled into making nothing more than cameo appearances in the seasonal violin and rare instrument auctions.

Dealers sometimes cite statistics that purport to demonstrate that a vintage instrument collection is a good hedge against inflation. Some are based on dubious premises. Figures based on the original prices of the instruments or on pre-vintage-craze prices of 30 years ago are irrelevant if the price you're going to pay *now* is top-dollar dealer's price. Other projections are based on turnover, which means you'd be dealing rather than collecting—a completely different activity.

By all means, put your money into vintage instruments if you love them. But don't do it if you're motivated by money alone, because you can make better money in other ways. If demand continues as it does, you'll probably stay on top of inflation anyway—especially if you know enough to buy the right models at the right prices. But when it comes to trends in musical taste, only the hardiest of prognosticators would venture to guess where the fickle finger of fate will point next. If the next craze turns out to be the return of the big bands, then you'll wish that you were sitting on a garage full of Paris Selmer wind instruments instead of all those useless old Martin, Gibson, Vega, Stahl, and Prairie State guitars that no one will want any more than they did in 1956.

Why Some People Think Old and Vintage Guitars Are Better

Vintage aficionados argue that the best older and vintage guitars are made of better woods than most modern guitars, and constructed more skillfully. In a few cases, like that of prewar Martins, the older instruments have certain design characteristics that are only available today on a limited number of models, if at all. Some sizes and shapes are hard or impossible to come by today, unless you commission a custom instrument from a luthier.

Add to these considerations the magic acoustical qualities of aging. It may have to do with the polymerization of wood resins and lacquers, their crystallization and molecular alignment along lines of vibration, and the continued evaporation of elements of the wood sap and finish long after the instrument is completed. It's never been fully explained, even in the case of Stradivarius and Guarnerius violins, the most-studied instruments in history. But to the ears of some, the sound of the best vintage instruments has a magic which cannot be duplicated.

Other ears are less sensitive to the magic of the vintage sound, or are just as happy if not happier with the sound of a fine modern instrument. But once you've played through your first couple of dozen old instruments it's impossible not to sense that they have greater character than modern instruments, and therein lies their greatest charm. It seems that in the old days specifications were not rigidly adhered to, there was greater respect for the eye and hand than for blueprints, molds, and templates, and the artisans and foremen had greater authority to make personal decisions. From instrument to instrument of the same model, neck width and depth, body and top wood thickness, fingerboard contour, color of finish, bracing dimensions, and other important aspects may differ considerably—much more so than on today's instruments. And so, of course, do the sounds of the instruments. Personalities run much deeper and are more distinct.

Why Some People Think New Guitars Are Better Anyway

Some feel that fine modern guitars are made better than older ones because the technology is better: quality control is more even, specs are standardized, the acoustic qualities of lacquers are tested scientifically, woods are hygrometer tested, factories are climate-controlled, and everything comes out the way it's supposed to be.

This is probably true of low-price and midprice guitars. For fine guitars, it's like arguing that Trump Tower is better made than Rheims Cathedral because architectural and engineering techniques have improved. But fortunately, there are also guitar makers today who are still trying to build the equivalent of Rheims Cathedral.

Private luthiers, as well as companies like Santa Cruz, Taylor, and Martin itself, have studied the great instruments of the past and learned from them. With a little bit of looking you can find superb-sounding modern instruments that have a lot of magic already in them, even fresh out of the factory. Some of them *already* sound better than some vintage instruments, even without the chance yet to age or be played in. The best of today's guitars are very impressive—more impressive, I think, than the general run of instruments of the fifties, sixties, and seventies.

There's also the very important matter of the instruments' playing feel. Today's market insists on low action and fast, low-contour necks that approach the ease of playing of an electric guitar, and most manufacturers are doing their best to oblige as well as possible. Older instruments were generally built with thicker, clubbier necks (especially in the days before the modern truss rod), and the standard of taste in those days accepted a stiffer action as well. You can find a certain number of vintage instruments that happen to feel fast anyway, and others can be made to feel faster with a good setup job and perhaps some minor surgery. But generally speaking, if like most people you prefer the feel of a modern guitar, then it's modern guitars you should be looking at.

PROS AND CONS OF BUYING A USED GUITAR

	Used	Vintage/Collectible	New
Price	Cheaper when bought at fair value. Do not pay vintage price for a merely used instrument.	Most expensive. But good deals are possible on styles not currently in vogue, or on instruments not in original condition.	More expensive. When comparing to used and vintage instruments, be sure to compare at discounted street price, not manufacturer's list.
Value	More likely to retain approximate current value if purchased at fair price from private person. May appreciate in long term if a good instrument.	Will maintain value or appreciate in long term if purchased at reasonable price. May be quickly sellable only at loss if you paid top dollar.	Immediate or short term depreciation likely. However, a fine instrument is likely to appreciate in the long term.
Condition	Whatever you get.	Whatever you get.	Brand spanking new, for a while.
Sound	Usually played in.	Usually played in.	Needs playing in.
Prestige	Yes, in hip circles, and then only if you have a hip instrument.	Yes, among those who know what it is or know how much you paid for it.	Yes, if you value newness and think used means tacky.
Structure	Depends on instrument and age. Modern plywood is probably more stable than the solid wood used on cheap instruments of the fifties and sixties.	Woods probably better and better aged. Glues and neck reinforcement probably inferior to modern instruments.	As a rule, most new low-and midrange instruments have better glue and neck reinforcement than instruments from the fifties and sixties.
Features	Small bodies, certain woods and ornaments, etc. are less commonly found among today's production models than among used instruments.	As for Used.	Modern truss rods, low-contour necks, and built-in electronics are only available on new or very recent used models.
Outlook	If after 5, 10, or 60 years of use the neck is still good and the body is relatively uncracked, the instrument will probably stay stable unless you change climate, strings, etc.	As for Used.	You don't know what's going to happen. Manufacturer's warrantee and reputation are your only security.
Warranty	Usually no, unless you negotiate individually for dealer warranty. Most mail-order dealers sell on approval.	As for Used.	Yes, from manufacturer.

Finally, new guitars look new and old guitars usually look kind of beat up. In some circles (bluegrass, for example, where folks are folks and heart is still more important than appearance for most of those folks), beat-up instruments are acceptable. In fact, the more beat-up, the better. But in most situations where you go before the public, you'll find that people are miffed or patently offended if instruments, outfits, and attitudes aren't bright and shiny.

Historic Guitars

Becoming an Expert

This is not a book about vintage guitars. They're worth a couple of books of their own, so I won't try to make you an expert.

If you want to learn more about vintage guitars, start with the books, magazines, and book and instrument dealer catalogs listed in the *Resources* section at the end of this book. Don't forget to see what your public library has. But that's only the barest of starts. You then have to make it your business to seek out places where there are vintage guitars and absorb everything you can about them. Get your hands on as many as possible. After a year or so, things will begin to fall into place, assuming that you can get around enough instruments. But remember that the real experts—and I'm not one of them—have about 30 years' head start on you. And they've got banjos, mandolins, electric guitars, and a few other instruments under their belts as well.

Great Names of the Past

For most people, vintage flattop guitars means vintage Martins and maybe a few Gibsons. Yet there were many more guitar manufacturers in the first heyday of the American guitar. Here are a few names from the past that you should know about. If you start hanging around with guitar buffs you'll hear these names often, sometimes spoken with reverence. You may even come across some of these instruments yourself. Some of these brands have died more than once, only to be revived over the years by new companies for different product lines, so don't be surprised if you still see them today—even on instruments imported from Asia. And remember that some of these makers are better than others, and some produced several lines and models in a variety of quality ranges.

Bacon & Day (mainly a banjo maker)
Bruno (C. Bruno & Son; a few were subcontracted by Martin)
Ditson (subcontracted by other makers, including Martin)
Harwood
Haynes
Kalamazoo (Gibson's economy line)
Larson Brothers (marketed under the brand names Prairie State, Euphonon, Stahl, and Maurer)
Lyon & Healy (also includes various subcontracted models)
Orpheum (mainly a banjo maker)
Regal (mostly cheapies, but their top-of-the-line Recording King was

good. The brand name has gone through many changes of style and ownership over the years.)

Stella (comment as for Regal, above)

Vega/Vegaphone (mainly a banjo maker)

Washburn (not the same as the present Washburn company)

Weymann (mainly a banjo maker)

Junk Chic

You might from time to time run into people who collect low-grade and obscure guitars. Twenties Oahu Hawaiian guitars with palm tree paint jobs, fifties Supro resophonic guitars that you can float in your bathtub, booming thirties Stella 12-strings, clean-sounding sixties Harmony Sovereigns (if you can find one with a straight neck): they're subject enough for a whole new book. Some are better than fine guitars for producing period sounds.

These instruments have a fascination all their own. Many are quite rare, if only because they weren't made well enough to survive long. (And, being cheaper, they were also more prone to being abused and discarded.) Some, like goat cheese, have strong and unmistakable characters. They provide incredible opportunities for one-upmanship. If you want to learn about Martin models, all you have to do is memorize a half-dozen books and articles and hang out on the scene for a while and you're three-quarters of the way toward being an expert. If you want to be an expert on old Regals, Stellas, and Kalamazoos, where are you going to even start?

An unusual Harmony cutaway guitar, probably from the sixties, offers solid but mediocre woods, good sound, and unstable construction. *Photo by Larry Sandberg.*

11

At the Point of Purchase

Dealing with Dealers

Finding a Good Dealer

A good retail business is run with the idea that it's possible to turn an honest profit by providing honest, professional service to the customer. Many, perhaps most, guitar stores are like this.

I wish there were some litmus test I could recommend to separate the good dealers from the bad ones, but there isn't one. A stock of both relatively inexpensive and high-quality new and used merchandise, an affiliated teaching staff, and a repair center (especially one authorized by major brands) are usually good signs, but not always. A sloppy-looking hole-in-the-wall could be the lair of a sleazoid, or merely the business place of an unkempt musician who loves guitars, manages to make a living with a high turnover of mostly used instruments at fair prices, and has never been able to raise the capital for major-brand franchises.

However, I would suggest that you keep away from stores that mostly stock cheap minor-brand Asian imports and whose stock of major brands and high-quality guitars is small or nonexistent. These are usually bad signs. I'd also keep away from mall stores and mass-market chain stores.

All other things being equal, you'll usually (though not always) get a better choice of merchandise and more knowledgeable service from a specialized guitar shop than from a band instrument dealer who also stocks a sideline of guitars.

Try to get a feel for the atmosphere of the establishment. Do they want to just sell people a piece of goods and move them out the door, or do they seem to want to cultivate repeat business from a loyal clientele? Does the dealer get uptight when you ask questions, or are you learning more about guitars each time you visit?

The best bet, of course, is to ask around. Local music teachers and professional musicians are often good sources.

Finally, a dealer should be willing to tune the instrument and play it for you, and to let you sit in a corner and try it out yourself. Twenty years of listening to beginners try out guitars has most dealers ready to climb the walls at the drop of a D chord, but they still owe you this courtesy. In return, you should treat the instrument carefully, watch out for zipper, belt buckle, and pick scratches, and play in an inoffensive manner.

Negotiating Setup

An honest dealer will not knowingly sell you a faulty instrument. But business ethics (which are, after all, to ethics as military music is to music) don't compel them to be scrupulous that every instrument is set up absolutely perfectly. Most of the student-level instruments I've seen in guitar shops (and in the hands of students, for that matter) could be improved by about 15 minutes' attention to nut and saddle by a competent technician.

Twenty-five years ago it was much easier than it is now to find a good guitar shop that would not put an instrument—*any* instrument—up on the wall until it had been set up and adjusted to be the best it could be. Because this required time and effort, these shops could not discount their instruments as highly as other shops that sold guitars right out of the box. The Crazy Eddie mentality has pretty much sacrificed service to discount in today's marketplace, so dealers now rarely pay that degree of attention to any but the most high-priced instruments—if even to them.

However, dealers who have a repair shop or skilled staff member will often be happy to make a small adjustment at no charge if it means making a sale. If a little more work is required (say, replacing a nut or saddle or fairly extensive shaping), even a nominal charge might not be out of line on a discounted instrument. Don't be afraid to say something like "I like the sound of this guitar, but can it be made more comfortable to play?" Most dealers will either oblige, or explain to you why they think that the guitar should be left the way it is.

Negotiating Approval or Warranty Terms

Some dealers will allow you to return an instrument *for credit* after a few days if it turns out you don't like it (and, of course, if you haven't damaged it in any way). This is a very reasonable stance and, if you're not certain you know what you're doing and need some time to get used to the instrument or seek advice, it's a good deal to look for or to ask for. But (except in the case of faulty merchandise) asking for a total refund would be out of line with normal business practices.

When you purchase a new instrument, you're usually protected by a manufacturer's warranty. In the case of a used instrument, you are protected by whatever warranty you can negotiate with the dealer and obtain in writing. In addition, most states and localities give you certain rights in addition to warranty terms; for example, grossly faulty merchandise is usually held to be "unmarketable," and you may be entitled to a full refund on your purchase price. Unfortunately, it may be necessary to aggressively research and insist on your rights, perhaps with the help a Better Business Bureau or legal advisor, before you can obtain them. Purchasing on credit card also may give you some additional protection against faulty merchandise.

Negotiating Trade-In

I'm strongly in favor of beginners starting off with a fairly inexpensive instrument and moving up later, when they have a better idea of what they want. Some dealers offer accommodating trade-in policies after six months or a year. Find out about them while you're still shopping around for your first guitar. In some cases they're just a way for the dealer to make money; other dealers have more reasonable terms. If you move up to a pricey instrument, I'd suggest you seriously consider hanging onto your original instrument as a knock-around guitar, if your budget allows.

Sales and Marketing Techniques

As you make the rounds of music stores, you'll see that each manufacturer's line has a fairly bewildering array of features that include woods, ornamentation, grades of tuning hardware, and structural features such as scalloped braces. These feature sets exist in the guitar business for the same purpose they exist in the bicycle, camera, and electronics equipment businesses: to establish marketing positions and provide the dealer with sales points to use with customers.

The marketing game is based on two key concepts: *price point* and *step-up feature*. Price points are increments which reflect the customer's budget: do you have two, three, or four hundred dollars to spend? Step-up features are distinguishing features within price ranges: for only $100 more, you can have scalloped bracing, Schaller tuners, and rosewood instead of mahogany. A manufacturer will usually try, if possible, to come up with at least one important (or important-seeming) feature to distinguish its guitar from its competitor's guitars *in a given price bracket*. For example, manufacturer X may be offering the only instruments with scalloped bracing at the $400 level.

The acoustic guitar is a pretty simple and conservative instrument, so by its very nature the manufacturers can't really get into the degree of technological competition that causes the rapid turnover of product lines and specifications that you find within, say, the camera market. Even so, you'll find that there are changes in product line from year to year as each maker strives to come up with competitive new features at each price point.

In my opinion, many of the step-up features offered on low-range and midrange guitars are fairly meaningless when considered in and of themselves. There *are* differences in tuning hardware but you can live with whatever you've got. The *sound* differences between mahogany, rosewood, and maple are far less pronounced and consistent in laminates than they are in solid woods, though appearance is another matter. Fine points of bracing only make a real difference when the rest of the instrument is well-enough made overall to respond to them. You're better off trying to develop a sense of what makes a given instrument sound and feel best to you when you hold it in your lap and play it, rather than trying to sort out catalog descriptions and feature sets.

The marketing techniques described here are true mostly of mass-market imported laminate guitars. In the case of fine instruments, there is more of assumption that sales are going to be made to expert buyers, and the differences between instruments more truly reflect genuine differences in quality and construction.

Discounts

Most factory guitars are sold to dealers at terms that permit discounting from list price. How much, if any, of a discount you obtain depends on competition and trade practices in your area, and on the dealer's standard practices. It's always worth trying to negotiate on price in a businesslike way. As a rule, you should expect to receive a discount in inverse proportion to service and other side benefits. Some big-city high-volume retailers customarily discount 40 percent, as do many mail-order houses. Street prices on *your* street, though, might be 20 percent off at best, and, in places where there's little competition among dealers, you might be lucky to get much of a discount at all.

Remember that if you're buying a case, strings, and any accessories, these are also subject to price negotiation. Look at the total price when you're all done. There's no point haggling for a discount on the guitar and losing it all back on the accessories.

Mail-order Brides

I can't imagine myself ordering an instrument sight unseen. Then again, I've always lived in or near a population center with an ample selection of competitively priced instruments to choose from. If you're out in the sticks, you're facing a much more limited set of choices. You're better off if you can sample an instrument before you buy it, but if your neighborhood offers a meaninglessly small range of instruments to sample from, then maybe you're as well off taking your chances with a mail-order bride (or groom). A few mail-order dealers are listed in the *Resources* section at the end of this book, and you'll find advertisements for more in the guitar magazines.

Almost every mail-order dealer offers approval terms by which you may return the instrument within a few days if you don't like it for any reason. Usually you eat the freight and insurance fees, a fair enough bite to swallow.

If you order by mail, you should have complete and unconditional approval privileges (except if you mar or damage the instrument) and it should be understood that the refund, minus freight and insurance, should go back to you at your discretion, not into credit from the retailer toward another purchase. Warranty and any other terms should be spelled out to your satisfaction. Using a credit card gives you some extra protection in case of dispute. To avoid misunderstanding, you should also clarify whether it's going to be your responsibility or the seller's to deal with the shipping agent in case of damage in transit.

Checking Out the Guitar

The problems described here are discussed in greater deal in other sections of this book. This is just a quick checklist of things to look for and ask about.

Structure

1. Are the woods laminate or solid? Ask! Industry standards in labelling and describing merchandise in catalogs and on the sales floor are in my opinion far too lax when it comes to woods.
2. Are there any cracks or other obvious faults?
3. As you sight down the neck from the fingerboard toward the bridge, does the neck seem to conform to the standards discussed in the earlier sections of this book on neck angle and fingerboard relief? It takes an expert to tell if it's perfect or not, but you should be able to see at least whether something appears to be grossly wrong.
4. Do the tuners work smoothly and sensitively?
5. Is anything obviously loose? Does it rattle when you shake it? (Be gentle!)

Playing Qualities

Is it comfortable to play? Pay attention to how it feels under both the fretting and picking hands. Analyze your feelings in terms of the following:

1. How far and how hard it is to depress the strings.
2. Distance between strings.
3. Contour of the neck.
4. Do the strings seem too light or too heavy? You will have to learn from experience to judge the feel of a guitar itself independent of the string gauge. Ask the dealer what the string gauge is.

Does it sound clean?

1. Are there mechanical buzzes and rattles that might come from something loose?
2. Do the strings buzz against the frets when you play only fairly loud? (You can expect a certain amount of buzz if you really wham the guitar.)

Does it sound *good*? The way you are going to learn to make the following distinctions is by comparing different guitars. Trying to learn what these words mean by playing only one guitar will get you nowhere.

1. Is it loud enough? Don't expect an inexpensive guitar to produce the volume of a better guitar. Just ask whether it seems loud enough to satisfy you. It probably does.
2. Is it soft enough? This is a hard test. A fine guitar gives a sense of fullness and presence even at low volume. Expect an inexpensive

guitar not to be as satisfying when you play it softly. But if it sounds too weak to give you pleasure, then reject it.

3. Is the tone balanced? Try to detect whether loudness of the low notes comes at the expense of the highs. This is a lot to ask of you, because it implies that you have a cultivated ear and enough playing technique to produce emphasis on either the high or low strings at will. Do the best you can. Try to hear whether the high strings have the same fullness that the low strings have. Play some chords and see whether the note on the second string can be heard as clearly as the others, or whether it gets lost. (On a nylon-string guitar, by the way, a weak third rather than second string is a more accurate giveaway of poor balance.)

4. Is the tone pure? Listen for rawness or abrasiveness, particularly on the high strings. Comparison will teach you to hear the difference between a ringing sound and an abrasive one.

5. Does the guitar sustain? Listen for how long its sounds linger in the air, and in your ear, after you've strummed or plucked it. Try playing one high note, say the first string tenth fret, and listen to how long it lasts. (However, if you're a beginner with weak fingers, you may not yet have enough strength to hold down the strings long enough for the notes to die naturally. Do the best you can.)

6. Does the guitar sing? Sustain is the most important component of the singing quality, but (once you've made sure the guitar is accurately in tune) also listen for the total sense of fullness and strength in individual notes, and for how well the different notes within a chord seem to fit together. Listen also for a clean, ringing quality that hangs in your ear like a pleasant aftertaste. The guitar's voice should have a sense of presence; it should sound as if it's right next to you, not as if heard through a closed door.

7. Is the guitar clear? Try strumming just the three bass strings with different chords. Do you hear three clean notes, or a muddy glob of sound?

What If You Can't Play Yet?

No two ways about it, you've got a problem. I'd certainly recommend that you try to learn to play at least a little on a rented or borrowed guitar before you go out to buy one. Try to enlist the help of an experienced friend. If you're planning to take lessons, ask your prospective teacher for help. (It would be unprofessional, though, to ask your teacher to put more than a nominal amount of time and energy into looking and checking. Offer to pay the teacher's usual hourly rate for this service. It'll probably be well worth it.)

If none of these options are available, then you are simply going to have to depend entirely on your dealer. If you find a good dealer, you'll do just fine.

12

Taking Care of
Your Guitar

Around the House

I don't think you'll ever meet a repairperson who won't urge you to keep your guitar in its case whenever you're not playing it. To hear them talk you'd think that it shouldn't be taken out of its case ever. But these are the people who see busted-up, shattered, bent, stepped-on, dropped, and spilled-on guitars day after day, and they have a pretty good idea of how many of those accidents occur to instruments that have been left in a corner or in an armchair or against a bookcase instead of being put back in their case.

You are, however, entitled to temper their advice with your own judgment. Just because so many home accidents happen on the stairs doesn't mean you should quit using the stairs. If you take out your guitar once a day for a one-hour playing session, it makes sense to put it back in its case when you're done. But if your habit is to grab the guitar for a few minutes every now and then in the course of the day, then you'll want it accessible. It might be unreasonable to trade off risk for convenience, just as long as you know what you're doing. Sometimes when you have five or ten minutes to kill, the handiness of your guitar determines whether you'll play it or grab some junk food out of the fridge instead. You tell me: which of these choices makes you a better person?

Bearing in mind that your guitar is more vulnerable when you leave it lying around, here are some tips for minimizing the dangers.

1. A favorite place for musicians to keep their guitar cases is horizontal across the arms of an armchair. It's a convenient height, and the guitar is protected. Tabletops are good for this too, but it's much more likely you'll have a free armchair than a free tabletop. Taking up an armchair with your guitar is easier to get away with if you're single.

2. If you keep your case on that armchair, you'll find it easier to get the guitar in and out impulsively if you keep only one latch locked. (To get away with this, though, you've got to train yourself to latch up the case completely whenever it comes off the armchair.) Don't ever leave a guitar in a case with the top down and all the latches undone. You're too likely to pick up the case and have the top fly open and the guitar fall out. Does this sound like a paranoid warning? Ask a repairperson how often it happens!

3. If you want to leave your guitar leaning up against a wall or bookcase, then at least find the safest spot for it. A corner is good, a corner behind an armchair is better. Make sure there's no radiator or other heat source (including even a lamp) too close, and clear the area of moveable objects that might fall.

4. Think about investing in a store-bought guitar stand. Spend a few extra bucks to get one that's got soft coated surfaces at all contact points, and that has enough weight, coupled with a low enough center of gravity, to keep stable. Lightweight cheapies don't do the job as well.

5. Some people like to hang their guitar on the wall—though it's definitely better to do this with a second knock-around guitar than with your primary instrument. Find an out-of-the-way spot away from heat sources, humidity, direct sunlight, and any other possible dangers. Mount something soft, like a foot-square piece of bulletin-board cork, on the wall where the guitar's back will touch it. Make sure it won't harm the guitar's finish, as many synthetics might. Hang the guitar from a secure hook by a secure material (say, strong leather thong, venetian blind cord, or coated 18-gauge grounding wire) tied securely around the third and fourth string tuning pegs. Check to see that everything is secure every so often, and when you put the guitar back on the wall, make sure that it's hanging securely before you let go of it. Even so, there are risks. Nothing is secure. I like to keep a couple of guitars on the wall, and so far, I've been lucky.

If you have cats, dogs, ferrets, kids, airhead friends and relatives, or other strange creatures wandering around your home, rethink the above suggestions accordingly.

Temperature and Humidity

Climate Changes

Changes in humidity are the greatest danger to your guitar. High humidity, especially when combined with heat, can loosen glue joints. Sometimes humidity can even cause wood to swell and distort. Low humidity is also bad for guitars, since the resulting shrinkage causes cracking and seam separation. The greatest danger, though, is an abrupt and extreme change in humidity—especially from damp to dry.

Heat causes wood to expand and cold to contract, so avoid abrupt temperature changes as well. In addition to cracking, temperature change can cause a condition called crazing or temperature checking, in which the finish develops tiny cracks similar to the texture of the cracked lacquer finishes of old paintings. It happens because the wood and finish expand and contract at different rates. The effect is only skin-deep, but it doesn't look good. When you bring a chilled guitar in from the cold, try to leave it in its case for a while so it can warm up gradually.

Cracking isn't the only problem caused by climate. Different woods (for example, a spruce top and ebony fingerboard) expand and contract at different rates and are likely to pull apart as well as to impart cracking stress on each other. And since wood expands and contracts along its grain pattern, abutting sections of wood with unmatched grain patterns, like back and sides, will expand and contract in different directions with similar results. (Please review chapter 4 for more on wood behavior.)

January Is the Cruelest Month

An arid climate, especially the arid microclimate of a heated home in wintertime, is another of the guitar's greatest enemies. There are various humidifiers on the market, all of which are basically neater and more elegant variations on the idea of a wet sponge. (Damp-It™ is probably the best-known brand, though there are others.) The problem with all of them is that if you forget, or are unable, to keep the device consistently moist, you may be in worse trouble that you'd have been without it. Home humidifiers have similar pros and cons. Bear in mind that home humidifiers, whether of the steam or ultrasonic variety, don't have much effect outside the room they're in.

Many repairpeople strongly recommend humidifiers. Somehow I've gotten through 30 years of owning guitars without a humidifier with only minor cracking problems—and few at that—that might have happened anyway.

Plywood won't crack from dryness, at least not all the way through. However, there are those who feel that the sound of plywood guitars deteriorates when they get excessively dry, and that humidification improves them.

It goes without saying that you should keep your guitar away from radiators, hot-air ducts (and the walls around them), freezing drafts, attics or garages with no climate control, and so on.

No Cure for the Summertime Blues

I once had a knock-around guitar made by one of the cheap American manufacturers of the sixties. It survived the first couple of decades of its life in the arid Southwest, but during its first summer in the steampits of northeastern Pennsylvania the back absorbed so much moisture that it swelled up into ripples like the sands of the Sahara. Then when it dried out in winter forced-air heat, the back straightened out a bit, developed lots of cracks, and shrank away from the sides. The top and neck also moved around some. After one more summer-winter cycle, it became unplayable and not worth fixing. My third-rate classical guitar, made with low-grade mahogany back and sides in Albuquerque during the sixties, also went through a similar set of changes, though not so badly that it turned unusable, as did a low-grade flattop guitar made during the thirties.

Also part of the southwest-to-northeast move were three fine 60-year-old flattops and a fine archtop, age about 30. They stayed perfectly stable after the move and for 10 years after, except for inconsequential action changes with the seasons. The flattops are back in the southwest, and doing fine. I hope I play as well when I'm their age.

The other great summer guitar-killer is the superheated car interior. Guitar glues are not permanent. They are deliberately intended to be soluble under conditions of heat and humidity so that instruments can be disassembled and repairs made. The way a repairperson gets a neck loose, for example, is to pry it off with a spatula dipped in boiling water, with additional injections of hot water from a syringe, under infrared heat lamps. The effect when you leave your guitar inside your car in the hot sun is very similar. So is leaving you guitar, in its case, outdoors on a lawn or patio in the sun. Don't do it.

Good Guitars Finish Last

The best way to deal with climate change is to buy a well-made guitar in the first place. Aged, properly finished air-dried quartersawn wood has the greatest stability. In less-expensive instruments, a decent grade of laminate (plywood) stays more stable than a bad piece of solid wood. Cheap plywood with a junk core is probably worst of all.

Instruments built under conditions of factory-controlled humidity tend to stay more stable than those built under high-humidity conditions. (Around 40 percent relative humidity is the textbook figure.) As a rule, American and Japanese guitars are built in factories with sufficient humidity control, as are the better Korean and Taiwanese instruments. Not so the cheap Korean and Taiwanese junkers.

Taking care helps the guitar, but a healthy mental attitude helps you. Take reasonable precautions, but avoid paranoia. Remember that the guitar is there for you to use, and that things that get used, no matter how precious, are subject to peril. Wood cracks. Cracks can be fixed.

Routine Cleaning and Maintenance

Spit 'n' Polish

Well, save the spit for your parade-dress shoes, but polish is a good thing to apply to your guitar now and then. Nothing personal, but I've never understood people who let their guitars get grungy. I don't much care how they look, really, but they're less pleasant to play when they're covered with dust, dried sweat, dead skin tissue, banana oil, chip dip, and other souvenirs. And even if you don't care about how grunge feels or looks, you'll find that your wood vibrates more freely, your fingerboard plays more smoothly, and that you're more attractive to (most) members of the opposite sex if you keep your guitar clean.

Go over your guitar with a little oil polish a couple of times a year. (I use "lemon oil," but I'm told it can darken some finishes, though I've never had that experience. A proprietary guitar polish from a music store should be safer.) I once heard of a viola player who uses olive oil, but I've never tried it. Waxes are no good—they coat the guitar—nor are heavy-duty treatments like tung oil that are more properly associated with finishing than with maintaining cleanliness.

Usually just a little polish on a clean cotton rag will do the job of keeping your guitar looking and feeling clean. Wipe it on, then wipe it off with a clean dry rag. You can keep your frets and fingerboard feeling neat and smooth by rubbing them down with a polish-moistened wad of 0000-grade (extra-fine) steel wool. Don't let it scratch any of the finished parts of your guitar and don't wipe it down with the same rag you use for polishing the finish, because the rag will pick up steel particles. Polish the bridge too. Keeping the fingerboard and bridge regularly oiled may also help get them through a period of dry climate without cracking.

When a guitar gets really dirty, you might need more than elbow grease. Many music stores carry one brand or another of heavy-duty guitar/violin polish containing a little grit to get the real grunge off. This stuff creates the same tradeoff problems for your guitar that rubbing compound does for your car: it invariably removes a bit of the finish along with the grunge, even though it's not supposed to. So use it only when absolutely necessary. (I used to know a repairperson whose favorite grunge remover was Pepsodent™. I mention this as an anecdote, not as a suggestion.)

It's also good to blow or vacuum the dust out of the inside of your guitar whenever there's an accumulation, which might mean every couple of weeks or years depending on your environment. There's more to this than just being compulsive. Dust globs may accumulate potentially harmful moisture.

You'll also find that you wind up with a friendlier-feeling guitar, and longer-lasting strings as well, if you make sure your hands are clean before you take out your guitar, and keep away from finger foods during a playing session.

Tuning Machine Maintenance

Your tuners have gears—probably of the usual metal screw-and-worm variety, though some of the lightweight enclosed gears are nylon. Gears wear out over the years, and they'll wear out faster if they're made nylon or cheap metal, or are poorly machined. Unless you have enclosed self-lubricating geartrains, you can help them feel smoother and live longer if you wipe off the grit once or twice a year and relubricate them. White grease (such as Lubri-Plate™) is better than machine oil, because it doesn't run. Just before a string change, spread a small dab over the gear worm using the end of a toothpick. As you wind and unwind the gear during the string change, the worm and screw will become coated with grease. Wipe off the excess when you're done.

Many tuners have a friction-adjusting screw in the peg shaft. It should be tight enough to put a comfortable amount of friction into the peg, not tightened down all the way. Adjust all six of them to your satisfaction once or twice a year. Of course, each tuner considered individually should feel smooth (but not loose enough to have any play). But you'll also find that you can tune more quickly and easily if all your tuners feel about the same. If your guitar has a slotted headstock then it probably has classical-style tuners. The danger with these is that the adjusting screw can get loose and rattle, or even fall out. Get into the habit of making sure it's properly adjusted whenever you change strings, if not more often.

Most tuners are held in place by small mounting screws on the back of the headstock (or on the side for classical-style machines), and perhaps by a hex-nut collar on the front of the headstock as well. Check them every so often (with a string change, for example) to make sure they haven't worked loose.

Cases

If you own an instrument of even medium value, you should have a hard case for it—what the music trade calls a "hard shell" case, abbreviated HSC in dealers' catalogs. The old-fashioned wooden ones work about as well as the new molded synthetic ones that some manufacturers (like Martin) offer, and both wood and synthetics come at different levels of quality. Synthetic cases are more waterproof, but can warp if left in the sun. (You should never leave a guitar in its case out in the sun anyway, but remember to never overheat an empty case either—no matter what it's made of.)

At the low end are inexpensive cardboard cases that don't really offer much puncture or extreme trauma protection. Soft shell cases, abbreviated SSC, are available. I wouldn't use one for a fine guitar, but lots of people store ordinary guitars in them for years. They'll do for around-the-house storage and an occasional car trip.

Strength is only one issue in a hard case. There also has to be a sufficiently thick layer of soft, resilient material between the outer shell and the guitar in order to provide a cushioning effect. The role of the cushioning material is extremely important; a mere shell, no matter how strong, will not sufficiently protect the instrument unless a resilient intermediate layer is also present.

The quality of latch hardware, hinges, and other fittings also contributes to the effectiveness and longevity of the case. Latches with a hinged catch, like the ones on steamer trunks, are preferable because they're a little harder to dislodge by accident.

Expect to pay upwards of $100 for a new hard case. Used ones are hard to find, but try looking anyway. It doesn't matter if a case looks a little beat up as long as it's sound.

At the high end are the specialized travel cases for professional use. The best-known are the fiberglass cases made by Mark Leaf, and the trunk-like Anvil cases. Leaf cases are good (and expensive), but overkill unless you're on the road a lot. Anvil cases are for guitarists who have roadies to carry their equipment, and tractor-trailers to move the show from town to town. Otherwise, forget them unless you've been pumping iron lately.

Some Specialized Case Manufacturers

Mark Leaf, 322 N. Ash, McPherson, KS 67460 makes extremely sturdy, triangular fiberglass cases with pressure/humidity seals.

Calton Cases, 4215 Brandon St. SE, Bay 3, Calgary, Alberta, Canada T2G 4A7 is the Canadian division of a respected English case maker. Calton fiberglass cases are guitar-shaped and not quite as robust as Leaf cases (which has the advantage of making them more manageable), while still being stronger than ordinary hard-shell cases.

Contour Products, 39 John St., Thornhill, Ontario, Canada L3T 1Y1 makes a padded overcase for hard-shell cases.

Another kind of case to consider is the padded soft carrying bag known among professionals as a gig bag. Gig bags are light, convenient, and dangerous, a broken neck or headstock being the main peril. Convenience outweighs peril for knock-around instruments, and aren't as risky to the bodies of solidbody electric guitars as to others, but the neck, if you'll permit me to run a metaphor through the Cuisinart, is their Achilles heel. Many musicians find the convenience worth trading off against the risk, and have gone a lifetime without damaging an instrument; others haven't.

Just as important as the case's material is the way it holds the guitar. Often damage comes from a guitar being knocked around within the case. A case should fit fairly snugly, like a shoe, and there should be some resilient, trauma-absorbing material between the shell and the instrument. If you acquire a mismatched case that's a little too loose, experiment with towels, closed-cell foam, or some other suitable padding until you fix it so the guitar doesn't move around. (Don't use vinyl or other such material that could harm your guitar's finish.) It's especially important that the neck shouldn't move around—be sure to check it for up and down as well as sideways movement, and if necessary add a little padding to the top over the place where the neck rests to hold it in place.

Also be careful of what you put into your case. Loose pens, capos, strap buckles, and tape cassettes can do lots of cosmetic damage and may even cause some real trauma. Don't carry liquids in your case. Vinyl articles and straps, as well as some other plastics, chemically interact with the finish and may cause blemishes if left in contact with the instrument. Buckle-less leather or cloth straps are safest. Finally, remember to loosen the strings whenever you ship your guitar or place it in foreseeable danger—in an airplane cargo hold, for example. If the guitar does suffer trauma, whatever happens will only be made worse by the tension of the strings.

Cracks and Breaks

Many of the things that can go wrong with your guitar are discussed in the pertinent sections of chapters 5 and 6. Accept the fact that with time and use (or abuse) things will go wrong, just as they do with your car, your body, and your elected public officials.

A guitar with almost any crack or break, no matter how bad, can be repaired or restored, even if it means replacing an entire neck or top. The question is whether it's worth the repairperson's time, skills, and material——which translates into your money——to do the job. You also have to find a person suited to the job. Most repairpeople know how to deal well enough with the equivalents of cuts, bruises, and the common cold, but extensive restoration work calls for luthiery skills that only select members of the profession possess.

Routine Crack Repair

Get it into your head that, in spite of all precautions, guitars sometimes crack. It's not necessarily the wood's fault nor the maker's. It's nature. It's wood's thing to crack. A crack may diminish your guitar's resale value somewhat. But, if properly repaired, it won't diminish the instrument's acoustic or structural integrity.

It's a good idea to have cracks and separations taken care of as soon as you notice them. Serious cracks need professional attention—especially long cracks, cracks where the wood has separated, and cracks where the wood is not on the same level on both sides of the split. They need to be clamped after gluing, and perhaps reinforced by tiny wooden studs (also called cleats) glued into the inside of the crack through the soundhole. The worst cracks, where the wood has separated and left a gap, need to be repaired by inserting wood splints into the gap. These repairs involve special tools and complicated techniques. Leave them to a pro.

But you may be able to deal with baby cracks on your own. Most cracks begin as tiny hairline splits. If you're handy, self-confident, and promise not to get mad at me when your finish shows some glue marks when you're done, you can fix it yourself. If you follow these steps you may be able to stop the crack from growing larger, or at least slow it down. Just try rubbing in a thin bead of white polyvinyl resin glue (like Elmer's™), and then quickly wipe off the excess with a moist rag. (White glue is better for tiny cracks than aliphatic resin glue, like Titebond™, because it's less viscous and so penetrates tiny cracks better. But for most other repairs, the pros prefer aliphatic resin glue.)

Bridge and Fingerboard Cracks

You may be able to slow down a bridge crack with the above method for a while, but the bridge crack always wins in the end, so you're probably better off having it repaired or replaced promptly. Sometimes a repairperson can save a cracked bridge by gluing, clamping, and running thin dowelling through it to reinforce the joint. It depends on the bridge shape and where the crack is. But usually cracked bridges need to be replaced. It's a routine procedure. Replacement bridges in common shapes and sizes are easily available from trade suppliers, but replacements for exotic bridges may have to be carved from scratch, requiring expert skills.

Ebony wears and feels better than rosewood, but it's more prone to shrinkage, so ebony fingerboards commonly develop hairline cracks over the years. People usually just leave them until they become unsightly, at which point a repairperson can easily fill them with a mixture of epoxy and ebony dust, making them invisible until they appear again five or ten years later. It's a situation you can live with.

The Trauma Unit

It may be wood's thing to crack, but it's definitely not wood's thing to have the pointy end of a guitar case latch shoved through its face, to fall four feet to a concrete floor, or to be swung at the speed of an Apollo liftoff into a mike stand. Let any of these things happen and you'll break your heart as well as your guitar. Somehow, I've gotten this far through life without these experiences. (Knock on wood. Or, come to think of it, maybe that's not such a good idea.) But my friends who have had them all speak of a sinking feeling in the pit of the stomach, a slowing down of reality, an adrenal rush, and a rising feeling of mingled anger and despair. In the end, they all got their guitars back in perfect playing condition, and with few or no scars to show for it.

This isn't a repair book, so I'm not going to go into repair techniques in detail. But it's important for you to know that just about anything in the way of repair is possible. Whether it's cost-effective or not is another story. And, of course, a job as serious as replacing an entire top is roughly the equivalent of a brain transplant. For better or worse, your guitar won't be the same guitar any more.

Trauma is one area where laminate guitars can be a problem. Plywood resists cracking and is probably also a bit stronger than solid wood when it comes to trauma, but once you do manage to punch your way through it, it doesn't just break: it shatters. Remember that in plywood, the plies are glued with their grain structure perpendicular to each other for maximum strength, similar to the plies in corrugated cardboard. Each ply fractures separately along its grain pattern, so instead of getting the comparatively neat, easy-to-patch gap as you would in solid wood, you wind up with a messy, jagged-edged hole that looks like a cartoonist's representation of an explosion. The only solution is to neatly cut out and replace an entire section. Twenty years ago, only student guitars were laminate, and repairpeople usually advised you to replace the instrument or settle for a quick-and-dirty repair solution. Now that laminates are also used for pricey, good-sounding instruments that are worth repairing, most repairpeople have had to learn to accept plywood repair and do their best.

PART II

Market Survey

How to Use This Section

This part of the book lists guitar models currently available, along with manufacturers' addresses and a brief history and description of each company and its products. Many of these companies also make other instruments, but, because this is a guitar book, you won't find out much about them here.

Most manufacturers will be happy to send you catalogs that have genuinely useful information in addition to hype and flashy pictures. Because you're an intelligent and sophisticated person, you know that you should take sales literature with a grain of salt.

HOW TO READ GUITAR SALES LITERATURE
A selection of hype from the catalogs of manufacturers who will remain nameless.

What they say:	What they mean:
"Reality will slowly disappear when the player touches the strings."	Reality quickly disappeared when the copywriter touched the typewriter. *or* Touch strings only at your own risk!
"... puts out a really big, robust sound at the same time delicate and expressive."	We can't make up our minds what kind of guitar this is, so maybe it's for you if you can't decide what kind of guitar you want.
"We've searched the world over to supply our luthiers with the finest available materials."	Traditional guitarmaking woods and sources are too expensive for us.
"The legend continues."	We're coasting on our reputation.
"Classic designs with modern technologies."	We switched from solid woods to laminates.
"Our instruments combine the skills of both craftspeople and engineers."	Our instruments combine the skills of craftspeople, engineers, and accountants.
"This guitar will make you a star."	Everyone will be famous for fifteen minutes, anyway.
"... finely aged woods."	We discovered a pile of old lumber at the back of our warehouse.
"An instrument that brings out all your native talent."	Six years of lessons didn't help, so what makes you think spending 900 bucks on a new guitar will?
(No words. Just a picture of a good-lookin' young guy with a guitar and a good-lookin' young woman staring adoringly at the good-lookin' guy.)	Sex sells. Good luck, dude.

If you take manufacturers' hype with a grain of salt, you should take this book with an equal dose as well. Not all my opinions are shared by everyone. There's also the (unfortunately) realistic possibility that somewhere in the writing or publishing process some of the factual data—especially in this half of the book, which is filled with numbers and specifications—has gotten botched. So please double-check before you buy.

I've divided the manufacturers up into domestic (U.S. and Canadian) and imported (mostly Asian) categories. To some extent this division reflects product similarities, but mostly it's just an arbitrary choice intended to make the book a little less unwieldy by breaking things up into smaller sections. There's also an extra section on private luthiers, which is a small sampling intended simply to give you some idea of what's out there.

In order to make the best use of this section, it's a good idea to make yourself familiar with the information in the first part of this book. For example, learning that an instrument has "scalloped bracing" isn't much good if you don't know what scalloped bracing is, and how meaningful the term (or buzzword) actually may be in the case of your particular instrument. This is the sort of stuff you find out in Part I.

Information Categories

In a few cases in this section, I've converted manufacturer's metric specifications to the nearest fraction of an inch, so there may be some minor discrepancies due to rounding-off.

Model

Under this heading you'll find the manufacturer's designation (name, alphanumeric code, etc.) for the guitar model being discussed. Sometimes I save space by grouping several similar models together.

Manufacturers respond to market forces by discontinuing some models and adding others with different feature sets over the years. This is especially true of the Asian importers, but is also true of companies like Martin that from time to time offer limited-production runs of unique or historical models.

Size/Shape

This heading gives the general size and shape of each instrument. Also look here to see whether the instrument is 12-string (assume 6-string unless stated) and what electronics, if any, are included as standard features. (Many makers also offer factory-installed electronics as an extra-price option.) You should also assume that, unless otherwise stated, all instruments have the now-standard 14 frets clear of the body (not counting a cutaway, if any).

The standard names used to describe guitar sizes and shapes derive, like so many other standards in the guitar world, from the practices of the Martin Guitar Company. In this section I use these standards *only* *approximately* so you can get a quick general idea of the size and shape of the instrument. (This is especially true when it comes to instruments described as "jumbo" and "grand auditorium".) You need to know some important basics: Whether the instrument is larger or smaller, whether it has a dreadnought or standard shape, and whether it has a cutaway, are all primary considerations. For more subtle distinctions, check the manufacturer's catalog or make it your business to examine the instruments in person.

You'll also find the term "shallow bodied" used in this section. It generally refers to electro-acoustic models around 3 inches deep. These guitars are designed with shallow bodies (approximating those of electric guitars) in order to make electric guitarists feel at home with them. They have the tone properties of acoustic guitars but (because of their shallowness) very weak volume, and are intended to be used electrified.

APPROXIMATE STANDARD GUITAR SIZES
Body length is for 14-fret models (except classical); 12-fret guitars usually have slightly longer bodies. Dimensions are in inches.

Name	Body length	Upper bout width	Lower bout width	Maximum depth
Concert	18⅜	10	13½	4¼
Grand Concert	18⅞	10⅞	14⁵⁄₁₆	4⅛
Classical	19⅛	11	14½	4⅛+
Auditorium	19⅜	11¼	15	4⅛
Grand Auditorium	20⅛	11¹¹⁄₁₆	16	4⅛
Jumbo	20⅛+	11¹¹⁄₁₆+	16+	4⅞
Dreadnought	20	11½	15⅝	4⅞

Scale

Scale, the length of the vibrating portion of the string, is given in inches. You can mostly divide the guitar world into short-scale (24.9 inches) and long-scale (25.4 inches) instruments. Long-scale is pretty much the standard these days (except that classical guitars are a tad longer). I've mostly quoted the figures from the manufacturer's spec sheets, though I suspect that the specs that say "25½" may be rounded-off fractions from 25.4.

Nut Width

This is the width of the nut at the fingerboard. It's conventional to give this measurement as a basic indication of fingerboard width.

A nut width of 1¹¹⁄₁₆ inches is pretty standard, and is a safe all-purpose width for most individuals and styles of playing. Many fingerpickers prefer a slightly wider fingerboard. Most fingerboards also widen out a bit as they go up the neck, and the degree to which they do so varies from model to model or maker to maker. A width of 2⅛ inches at the twelfth fret is pretty typical when the nut width is 1¹¹⁄₁₆ inches.

Sometimes I save space by grouping several similar models together in one entry. In cases where one of these models is a 12-string, you should figure on the 12-string nut width being greater by ⅛ to ¼ inch than the nut width given for the corresponding 6-string model.

Top, Back and Sides, Neck

These sections tell you the kind and species of wood used. My information depends on manufacturer's spec sheets, which are notoriously sloppy about stating whether wood is solid or laminate. Be sure to read the general description of the manufacturer's products that appears above the individual model listings. Unless the general description line indicates that solid woods are used, it would be wise to assume that any wood is laminate. Check the actual instrument with your dealer to be sure. Remember that laminated body woods are inferior to solid woods, but laminated necks are okay.

Fingerboard and Bridge

Generally these are made of the same wood. Where they differ, or when the manufacturer supplies specs for only one, this is made explicit.

Ornamentation

Only the basic, most salient features of ornamentation are given. I've adopted this space-saving tactic because it's hard for me to imagine anyone making a purchasing decision based on the very small differences in trim that distinguish most guitars. Generally speaking, the manufacturers are quite scrupulous about using more extensive trim as prices go up. For the same reason, I've also generally omitted details about nut and saddle material and tuning hardware. You may expect both the cosmetic and functional quality of the hardware to get better as prices increase, but I'd suggest you make your purchasing decision based on the sound and playability of the guitar, without worrying too much about the quality of the tuners or of the nut and saddle material. It's easy enough to replace them.

Bracing

Most instruments use bracing similar to the standard Martin X-brace pattern. Assume this is the case except when other information is stated. When words such as "scalloped" or "voiced" are used, you should assume that these refer to X-bracing, unless otherwise indicated.

Nonstandard bracing patterns are indicated, generally following the manufacturers' own descriptions and terminology.

Remarks

Important points and features (if any) not covered under any of the other headings are listed here.

Price

Manufacturer's list prices furnished to us at the time of writing are given here. Although they'll change over time (and you know in which direction), they should remain useful as a comparative index of the prices of different brands and models.

Depending on the degree of retailer competition in your area, you can expect to find prices discounted to a certain degree, and perhaps even negotiable beyond the stated discount price. Sometimes prestigious brands and models are less likely to be discounted. Don't expect private luthiers to discount instruments, because their price structure is not based on retail markup.

13

North American Manufacturers

Martin Guitar Company

Nazareth, PA 18064
See also Sigma and Goya (chapter 14)

The history of the Martin company is to a large extent the history of the American guitar. Martin more than any other manufacturer has defined the flattop guitar as we know it today. I'd guess that something like 98 percent of the steel-string guitars sold today are influenced by (or are outright copies of) Martin's looks, proportions, and bracing patterns. For that reason I've put Martin first in this section, even though everyone else is in alphabetical order.

Martin's headstock decals still read: "C. F. Martin & Co." But Martin's stationery these days says "Martin Guitar Company," and that's what I use in this book.

Because of continuous family management and the stability of Martin's work site, the history of the Martin business and its product designs are documented to a much greater degree than this short sketch suggests. Martin product lore takes up a book of its own, so for deeper reading, consult Mike Longworth's *Martin Guitars: A History*. Once you've memorized that, you'll need an apprenticeship of several years of hands-on experience to really become a Martin expert—especially if you want to know enough of Martin's product history to swim safely in the shark-ridden seas of the vintage Martin guitar market. This chapter includes most major points, but there are many more details to learn, including past models no longer in production.

C. F. Martin and the Martin Bracing System

Many Europeans came to young America because of religious strife, but it was a craft guild jurisdictional dispute that led Christian Frederick

Christian Frederick Martin (1796-1873). *Photo courtesy Martin Guitar Co.*

Martin (1796–1873) to emigrate from Saxony to New York City in 1833. Like his father before him, he was a guitar maker and a member of the Cabinet Makers Guild in Mark Neukirchen, a town of small woodworking industries. The Violin Makers Guild wanted the guitar business all for itself, and Martin decided it was better to run than fight. He was right.

Martin got off to a good enough start running a general-service music store and guitar workshop in New York but didn't much care to live there, even then. In 1839 he moved his workshop to the rolling hills of Nazareth, a congenial Moravian German community in Pennsylvania's Lehigh Valley. There the Martin company has remained to the present day. (Incidentally, Martin kept stamping its instruments "C. F. Martin & Co., New York" until 1898, because its instruments were distributed by a separate New York City company until then.)

C. F. Martin brought with him to New York a guitar shape and a simple diagonal bracing system which he had learned from his own master, the Viennese luthier Johann Stauffer. But by the time he moved to Nazareth his instruments no longer looked like Stauffer's on the outside, and he was experimenting on the inside as well. By the end of the 1850s, what we now know as the characteristic Martin X-bracing pattern had taken shape. It was used more and more over the years, and by the end of the century it became a standard feature of all Martin guitars.

Remember that early Martin guitars were originally made to be gut-strung. The X-brace was not originally conceived for steel strings. In that sense, it was an accident waiting to happen, and when it did happen, it was a fortunate accident indeed. Many early Martins can tolerate being strung with low-tension steel strings (like compound bronze or silk-and-steel sets). They function effectively, sometimes magnificently, this way, but usually with a voice and tonal balance not particularly suited to today's fashions in either sound or playing touch. Guitars were also generally built smaller in those days, too.

Martins tended to become somewhat stronger and heavier during the years after 1900, as the public's taste turned more and more toward steel strings. But they weren't officially and consistently beefed up until the late twenties, when Martin formally accommodated its product line to steel strings by embedding an ebony reinforcing strip in the neck. (The reinforcement became a metal T-bar in 1934, a square channel bar in 1967, and finally an adjustable tension rod inside a channel bar in 1985.)

Martin tops of this time tended to "belly"—to bulge a little below the bridge under the pressure of the medium-to-heavy gauge steel strings fashionable at that time. (Most guitars belly a bit, and should.) It wasn't really bad for the guitars, but the public found it disconcerting. In 1939, Martin accommodated by moving the crossing point of the two main braces that make up the X about an inch further away from the soundhole. This created space for a larger bridge plate and also made smaller the amount of bridge area between the braces. (The original configuration is known as the *high X-brace* position.)

Lightness of the bracing also contributed to the tendency to belly. Part of the standard Martin bracing design involved scooping out crescents of wood from the tops of the bracing struts, giving the strut an overall parabolic shape like that of a suspension bridge. This is known as *scalloping* the bracing. In 1944, Martin stopped scalloping the braces and increased their thickness from 1/4 inch to 5/16 inch in order to keep the tops from bellying as much.

Many feel that, as a result of these two bracing changes, the tops lost some punch and volume, and high notes became less transparent and less well-balanced. (Some also feel that this was abetted by a changeover to Sitka from Adirondack spruce tops at about this time, though the effects of this changeover, or even whether there really was one, are questionable.)

Since the mid-seventies, Martin has again offered scalloped bracing on selected models. Some models even recreate the pre-1939 bracing position. Many other manufacturers now offer scalloped bracing as well.

It's good to remember than guitar sound is the result of the interaction of many complex variables. Scalloped bracing is only one of them. It may produce a meaningful tonal difference or it may be merely a buzzword, depending on the manufacturer and on the individual instrument. And even though the scalloped bracing does make an audible difference on Martins and other fine instruments, whether you prefer the sound or not is still a matter of taste. There are a number of excellent, good-sounding players out there who could and would have a scalloped instrument if they wanted to, but don't. When you're listening to guitars, don't listen for whether the bracing seems to be scalloped. Listen for whether you like the sound of the instrument.

The Martin Mystique: Prewar Martins

The prewar Martins set the standard by which all other flattop guitars are judged. It runs against every spiritual presupposition of luthiery that the greatest instruments of their type ever made should have come out of a factory rather than from the single-minded, single-handed shop of a private luthier, but somehow that's what happened.

The Martin factory is an assembly line in the sense that no one person is responsible for a given guitar. Martin line employees are not luthiers, but skilled craftspeople who have been trained in a particular operation. Each operation, neck shaping, top gluing, inlaying, and so on, is done by a different person. But there the resemblance to an assembly line ends, because it moves more slowly than, say, Henry Ford's line. Instruments are typically on the Martin line for four months, because they're set aside to stabilize in between major operations.

The more handwork and personal concern there is in a manufacturing process, the more variation there is in the character and even the quality of the individual products. This give us the fascinating differences that exist among individual fine guitars, even of the same model. It also means that some Martins sound better than others, and this, in turn, means that some Martins sound worse than others. To debate just what "better" or "worse" means in terms of taste is irrelevant. The point is that, because differences do exist, you'd better learn to hear them and to be able to decide what you like and what you don't.

Most players feel that there's a definite sound characteristic of "prewar" Martins. But there are also a lot of great-sounding Martins that were made after that time, and some sound better and more "prewar" than some of the prewar ones do. You can also find unexceptional instruments and some real dogs among prewar Martins. Because the market for them is a collectors' market based in part on cosmetic condition, production statistics, and other nonmusical considerations, you can expect to see some of these dogs offered at top dollar, too.

Is it possible to get a new Martin that's as good a guitar as a vintage Martin? Yes and no. No, because age does certain things to a guitar that only age can do, so no new guitar can ever be like an old one. Yes, because some individual modern Martins, among those where quarter-sawn body woods are still used, are better than some individual old ones. (It's also important to remember that, although the Martin legend comes from the days when it was the best game in town, nowadays other fine American manufacturers and luthiers make instruments of comparable quality.) But there's a certain unique character to the older instruments that cannot, I think, be recaptured.

Martin's traditional cosmetic features of herringbone-pattern marquetry and inlay of abalone and mother-of-pearl have also achieved a mystical status (even though they are not causally related to sound quality), and are widely copied throughout the guitar industry. For more details, see the discussion of inlay and ornamentation in chapter 7.

The Martin Dreadnought Guitar

As American music moved into the early decades of the 20th century, public taste demanded larger and larger guitars. The age of young ladies entertaining guests in the front parlor with light classical pieces was over. The age of country and western singers was about to begin.

The new generation of solo singers wanted a booming, powerful bass to fill in under their voice. Mountain stringband guitarists wanted the same sound to help them fill the space of a nonexistent bass player, and they also needed lots of power to be heard. The names Martin gave to its guitars over the past several decades tell the story. For a long time, Martin's largest size was the *concert* guitar. By today's standards, it's so small a guitar that it's only available on special order. Then came the *grand concert* size, and finally the *auditorium* size. (I guess they didn't have stadium rock concerts back then.) But people hungered for an even bigger sound.

The progression of Martin guitar sizes, in a variety of styles and vintages. Left to right: Model 0-21 (c. 1920); 00-42 (early 1930s); 000-18 (late 1930s); D-28 (mid-1950s); and D-45S (special custom model with 12-fret neck and solid headstock, 1937). *Photo by George Gruhn, courtesy Gruhn Guitars, Inc.*

MARTIN'S LARGEST-SIZED GUITARS SINCE 1854

Concert (0)	introduced 1854
Grand Concert (00)	introduced 1877
Auditorium (000)	introduced 1902
Largest size custom Ditson	1916–30
Dreadnought (D)	introduced 1931
Grand Auditorium (M)	introduced 1977
Jumbo (J)	introduced 1980

Flashback to 1916. In that year, Martin began to custom build a small number of oddly-shaped guitars for the Ditson company, a music retailer. These instruments had a very wide waist (similar to some early 19th-century French guitars), and were made in small, medium, and large sizes. They bore the Ditson name and were not at first even stamped with Martin-series serial numbers. Conflicting testimony survives about whether the design was the brainchild of Ditson guitar department manager Harry Hunt or Martin foreman John Deichman, but one or the other of these gentlemen, it seems, deserves a prominent place in guitar history. The shape ranks second only to Christian Martin's X-brace as the most influential design innovation in the history of the flattop guitar.

Flashback to 1931. The country was caught up in the Depression. Ditson was no longer ordering guitars, and not too many other people were either. Martin factory shifts were cut down to part-time and a desperate management had gone so far as to develop a prototype line of rosewood trinkets (they were never actually marketed) in order to try to boost total revenues. Stimulated by the perception that the world wanted larger guitars and by the desire to try anything new that might increase sales, Martin introduced its own version of the largest-size Ditson model. They named it after HMS Dreadnought, then the largest battleship afloat. (According to factory legend, the name had to begin with D because the custom Ditson models were already referred to inhouse as the D-series.)

The pace began to pick up through the early thirties as the public began to get used to the mahogany-bodied model D-1 and the rosewood-bodied D-2. At that time the dreadnoughts, like many of Martin's other instruments were still being made with 12-fret necks. But these were the waning years of 12-fret guitars, and by 1934 most models, including the dreadnoughts, were fitted with 14-fret necks and their concomitantly smaller upper bout size (to make room to expose the two extra frets). In that year Martin changed the mahogany dreadnought designation to D-18 and the rosewood to D-28. That was when sales really began to take off. These two instruments have remained as the Martin's best-known workhorse guitars to the present day.

The dreadnought shape has now become the usual shape people think of when they think of steel-string guitars. Many other makers have copied it, though in the case of cheap imitations it's merely the shape, and not the sound, that's being copied. It's so often thought of as *the* most desirable guitar shape, but in fact there are many advantages to other shapes as well, whether the equally large jumbo guitar, or other smaller sizes. The dreadnought style is almost every bluegrass guitarist's first choice, but other styles may make much greater sense for other styles, or as all-purpose guitars.

Martin Since 1950

Martin moved into the fifties with a line of guitars ranging from the small concert size to the massive dreadnoughts. Sales were about 6000 instruments a year during that period, thanks to the musical tastes of the times, but they began to pick up when the sixties generation came along. They picked up so well, in fact, that, by the middle of the decade, there was a three years' back-order for new guitars, and a new factory was built in Nazareth to accommodate the demand.

Martin also, about this time, introduced the D-35 model, essentially a D-28 with a three-piece (rather than the traditional two-piece) back. Brazilian rosewood was beginning to get scarce and it was hard to find sections large enough to make the backs of an instrument as large as a dreadnought. Three-piece backs are attractive, the wood grains, when properly selected, make a pleasing contrast, and the extra seam means an extra strip of ornamental marquetry at the joint. In a clever bit of marketing, Martin added a few more cosmetic features (like fingerboard binding) and charged *more* for an instrument whose origins were in a desire to economize on rosewood. (In the end, the difference between the D-28 and D-35 is generally one of looks more than of sound or sturdiness, so you should simply get whichever pleases you if these are the guitars you're looking at. Martin sales literature claims a consistently more bass-heavy sound for the D-35s, but I can't say I've noticed this.)

The late sixties were a time of change. Martin had always used Brazilian rosewood for it's top models, but export restrictions made it impossible to obtain on as large a scale as Martin required, and the company began to use somewhat lighter-colored, more highly textured Indian rosewood instead. Most players and luthiers believe that there is no perceptible sound difference between Brazilian and Indian rosewood, and both woods seem equally durable. Nonetheless, Brazilian Martins immediately began to acquire a mystique and a collector's value apart from any real value as a playing instrument.

Aside from looks, the only validity for preferring Brazilian rosewood is that along about the same time as the change to Indian, Martin was in its peak production years (over 22,000 instruments in the record year 1970, as opposed to around 6500 per year during the fifties, and 7500 in the late eighties.) Many feel that during these high-production years from the late sixties into the mid-seventies, a higher-than-usual percentage of mediocre-sounding Martins came out of the factory. However, there were also many excellent instruments produced during those years. Anyone who has been around the music retail business has shared my own experience of seeing customers reject reasonably-priced, fine-sounding Indian guitars in favor of more expensive Brazilian models that sounded no better, or even worse.

During the 1970s public taste began to shift definitively away from smaller guitars and Martin began to produce fewer and fewer of them, to the point where they are now offered only as special-order or limited-edition instruments. For decades, Martin relied on the dreadnought to serve the large-guitar market, and its next-largest guitar was the auditorium size, which by today's standards is a small instrument. It was probably a point of pride that Martin was reluctant to develop jumbo-size instruments, leaving them to Gibson and Guild. The problem was that Gibson and Guild, and now the Japanese as well, were offering both dreadnoughts and jumbos. It made little sense, especially in the shrinking market of the seventies, to leave the entire market share of jumbo guitars to the competition.

In 1977, Martin introduced its "grand auditorium" M-series guitars, with large jumbo-size bodies comparable in breadth to the Gibson J-200 jumbo prototype and its Guild and Japanese derivatives, but more shallow in depth. Martin already had the molds and templates for such a body size. They had been used for a long-defunct series of archtop guitars that Martin had offered, with limited success, in the thirties and forties. The idea came in part from Berkeley craftsmen John Lundberg and Marc Silber, who had been putting flat tops onto archtop Martins and similarly-sized archtop Prairie State guitars. Their conversions demonstrated that this body size could produce a large sound with most of the dreadnought's bite and volume, but with fewer of the dreadnought's problems toward bass-heaviness. But for those who want a bassier instrument closer to the dreadnought's sound, Martin waited only three years after it introduced the M series before launching the J ("Jumbo M") series, having the same breadth as the M but every bit as deep as a dreadnought.

Martin's aggressive marketing of the M and J series is only part of a new set of marketing strategies the company had to come up with during the eighties. Competition has been fierce. The Japanese have completely dominated the low-end plywood market (in which Martin's imported Sigma line has only a small share). In the midrange, the all-solid-wood guitar is a creature of the past, and Martin had to counter Guild and the better Japanese models by introducing its Shenandoah line of guitars with solid-tops and plywood-bodies. At the high end, Martin has to compete against an army of private luthiers and limited-production makers who did not exist in earlier generations, as well as against the excellent products of the Santa Cruz and Taylor companies.

Once upon a time the competition was Martin versus Gibson, with Guild running a derivative third place. Each company had its own sound and its own style, and customers chose on the basis of differentiated taste. Now the competition is essentially over parity products—dreadnoughts and jumbos—differentiated by small feature differences rather that major differences in shape and sound. Santa Cruz and Taylor each produce a few styles that are unique, but when it comes down to the reality of market share, the big battle is over the dreadnought and jumbo guitars. In this arena, what Santa Cruz and Taylor (and, for that matter, a good many of the private luthiers as well) offer are Martin-style guitars with slightly different structural and cosmetic features. They're all Martin's children, and now they're competing with their parent.

Martin also has to compete with its own past. Martin fanatics will

Martin acknowledged contemporary taste by introducing new models like this MC, beginning in the late seventies. *Photo courtesy Martin Guitar Co.*

only be happy with a true "vintage" model, but ordinary players looking for a good used instrument can with a little patience usually find a more recent Martin at a far lower price than comparable new instruments.

Martin's response to the conditions of the eighties and nineties has been to position itself solidly as a "conservatively innovative" high-end company, and it's done a good job of keeping its balance on the high-wire rope of this apparent self-contradiction.

The past several years have seen an increasing number of revivals of structural designs and cosmetic features from the prewar period. Abalone and pearl inlay, discontinued in the early forties, were reintroduced on a limited scale as early as the mid-sixties, and are now used on a good many standard models. Scalloped bracing, herringbone inlay, pre-1939 bracing, bridge-plate modifications, and other features are also available as standard features on several models, and as options on others.

Martin has capitalized on the collectibility of its older instruments by offering a bewildering array of special-issue and limited-edition models in recent years. (They're not included in the listings below, which only include the standard catalog models.) The entire special-issue program is highly promotional and somewhat gimmicky in nature (though the instruments that come out of it are fine). Included are instruments with special structural or cosmetic features, labels and interiors with signatures of Martin staff, recreations of older instruments, instruments made of unique or unusual materials, and so on. In addition to Martin's own programs, every so often one of the major acoustic guitar dealers will order a special custom run of some model with special features, for sale by that dealer only.

The special-issue instruments are usually touted as collectors' items of the future. Whether this will be the case, and to what degree their value will increase compared to the value of other guitars, will depend on factors that are unrelated to the qualities of the instruments themselves. I recommend that you buy an instrument because you like it, not primarily as an investment. However, it's easy to imagine you might find an instrument you like among these special-issue Martins. Some of the special-issue models have seemed to me a bit pricey for what you're getting (given that dealers don't usually discount them), while others have seemed to me to be reasonable deals.

Martin has also kept up with changing tastes. The shallow-contoured "low-profile" neck was introduced in 1985, to accommodate the tastes of a generation of guitarists used to the light strings and fast necks of electric guitars. (Santa Cruz and especially Taylor ship guitars with fast necks as a rule; Taylor in particular positions itself as an "easy-to-play" guitar.) Martin just can't allow market share to slip over this issue without putting up a fight.

But because many guitarists prefer the feel of the standard neck and the tonal advantages of stiffer action, Martin did not give it up completely. While most models now have the low-profile neck, the standard neck is available as a special order item or, on some models, as a standard feature. And because Martin necks have too much handwork to be absolutely uniform anyway, enough variation exists that sooner or later you'll find a neck exactly suited to your taste.

Another feature that appeals to people who customarily play electric guitar are the cutaways now available on a few models in the M and J series. Martin has yet to make a cutaway dreadnought. They probably reason, quite sensibly, that the styles of music the dreadnought is best for are the styles least likely to ever call for a cutaway. But because it's not necessarily the nature of the guitar-buying public to be sensible, I expect that the pressures of competition will someday lead Martin to make a cutaway dreadnought as well. It's another question of market share.

Also in 1985, Martin finally adopted the adjustable truss rod. Even though the Gibson patent on the adjustable truss rod expired decades ago, Martin steadfastly refused to adopt it, asserting that a properly made, properly aged guitar would not need one. In Martin's own case, at least, the assertion was mostly correct. Traditionally, Martins have been extremely stable. Nonetheless, seasonal changes do occur with all wooden instruments, and neck adjustments are also routine when changing string gauge. And the new thin necks, with less wood mass to help them stabilize themselves, would be intrinsically less stable than the old-style, thicker necks. This is probably why the adjustable rod and new neck style were introduced at the same time.

Finally, Martin has also revived koa wood on a number of models (some standard, some special-issue), and has issued an entirely new series of maple-bodied guitars in many of its most popular sizes and shapes. The traditional Martin sounds are the brilliant sound of rosewood and the sweet, full sound of mahogany—if you wanted the bright, brittle sound of maple you used to have to go to Guild, Gibson, or the Japanese. No longer. It's a matter of market share again. In the guitar market of the nineties, no one can afford to send any business to the competition.

Other Martin Products

Over the years Martin made or distributed lines other than guitars, and still does. (In the 19th century, there was even a flirtation with zithers!) Mandolins (of various sizes and styles) were a big item for a while, particularly in the early years of this century, and flat back mandolins are still included as special-order items in the Martin catalog. In fact, in 1898 Martin split with the company that had distributed its instruments since the earliest days over the issue of mandolins; Martin wanted to start making them for the new wave of Italian immigrants, and the distributor was reluctant to handle them. To the taste of many, Gibson outclassed Martin by a long way as a mandolin maker, and bluegrassers in particular favor the gruff Gibson sound. However, there are some (especially classical and European-style mandolinists) who prefer the sweeter Martin sound.

Martin also did well with ukuleles, taro-patches, and tiples (in various sizes and styles) during the Hawaiian music craze of the twenties, having jumped on the bandwagon in 1916 just as the fad was beginning. The ukulele was so popular that a Martin uke was part of the baggage in Admiral Byrd's flight over the North Pole in 1926. (Ukulele production figures aren't well documented, but recollections suggest that perhaps twice as many ukes as guitars came out of the Martin factory during the twenties!) Martin ukuleles are still available today on special order, and are highly regarded.

The Hawaiian craze was also responsible for the H-series guitars Martin produced during the twenties and thirties in Hawaiian style (high nuts, vestigial ornamental frets, and uncompensated bridge saddle placement). Most of the surviving H-series instruments have by now been converted to standard configuration by their owners.

There were also several adventures over the years with archtop and electric guitars, none of which really went anywhere. They were never even competitive. Martin's heart just wasn't in these kinds of instruments, but Gibson gave them their all. However, Martin's sideline of tenor guitars are probably the best ever made, and possibly the only ones made by a first-rate manufacturer.

Martin made several styles of nylon-string guitars over the years, but in sound and feel they were well removed from the mainstream tastes of classical guitarists. They gave pleasure to many individual players, but never achieved acceptance or recognition in the classical guitar world. A few models are still available on special order.

Martin has also recently introduced a line of 4-string acoustic bass guitars.

Several other lines of musical instruments and products have been distributed by Martin over the years. In the seventies there were Fibes Drums and Vega Banjos, both of which were spun off at the end of the decade. Today Martin imports its acoustic Sigma and electric Stinger guitar lines from Asia, and also distributes the less expensive Goya line. Parts for the laminate-bodied Shenandoah line are imported, then assembled in Nazareth. Martin also operates several distinct divisions related to guitar crafts and supplies. Darco Strings, once an independent company, has been part of Martin since 1970. Martin's wood products division supplies standard and exotic guitar woods and guitar kits, and offers custom milling services. The 1833 shop offers a mail-order service for guitar accessories, doodads, gift items, and books relating to instrument-making and guitar lore. Martin also markets several transducers and transducer interfaces under its own name.

Name that Number:
Martin's Size and Style Designations

Since the days of C. F. Martin himself, the Martin company has used a system consisting of an alphabetic prefix and number suffix (for example, D-28) to designate its models. Guitarists bandy these letters and numbers about the way cyclists talk about gear ratios, computer nuts about processor speed, and fitness freaks about aerobic threshold. If you don't know how the Martin numbering system works, you're just not cool, so pay close attention to this section.

The alphabetic prefix refers to the instrument's size and shape, which Martin calls "size." The numeric suffix refers to the wood, ornamentation, and other details of material, which Martin calls "style." For example, in "000-28" (pronounced triple-oh twenty-eight), the "000" tells you that the guitar is auditorium size and the "28" tells you that the guitar has rosewood back and sides, ebony bridge and fingerboard, and certain other details of ornamentation.

Martin Size Prefixes

The following table lists all Martin guitar sizes from the beginning of the company. (Because small guitars are now sadly out of fashion, though, only the D, M, J, and, just barely, 000 sizes are currently in standard production. A few models in size 0 and 00 are available as special-order items, as is one model in the tiny size 5, which may serve as a child-size guitar.)

Because Martin guitars are made with much handwork, and because many custom-modified instruments have been produced over the years, and because some changes occur during experimental and transitional periods, the specs in the prefix table are subject to minor change—especially as applied to early instruments.

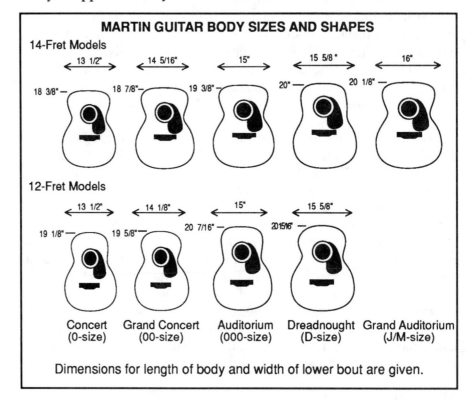

MARTIN GUITAR BODY SIZES AND SHAPES

14-Fret Models

| | Concert (0-size) | Grand Concert (00-size) | Auditorium (000-size) | Dreadnought (D-size) | Grand Auditorium (J/M-size) |

12-Fret Models

Concert (0-size) Grand Concert (00-size) Auditorium (000-size) Dreadnought (D-size) Grand Auditorium (J/M-size)

Dimensions for length of body and width of lower bout are given.

MARTIN GUITAR SIZE PREFIXES

(certain unusual and limited-production sizes are omitted)

Martin number	Appellation	Frets clear of body	Scale length (in.)	Body length (in.)	Upper bout width (in.)	Lower bout width (in.)	Max. depth(in.)
5	*(smallest)*	12	21.4	16	8 1/4	11 1/4	3 7/8
4		12	22	16	8 5/16	11 1/2	3 3/4
3		12	23.9	17 3/8	8 1/8	11 1/4	3 13/16
2 1/2		12	24.5	17 7/8	8 1/4	11 5/8	3 7/8
2		12	24.5	18 1/4	8 1/2	12	4
1		12	24.9	18 7/8	9 1/4	12 3/4	4 3/16
O	Concert	12[a] 14	24.9 24.9	19 1/8 18 3/8	9 1/2 10	13 1/2 13 1/2	4 3/16 4 1/4
OO	Grand Concert	12[a] 14	24.9 24.9	19 5/8 18 7/8	9 3/4 10 7/8	14 1/8 14 5/16	4 1/16 4 1/8
OOO	Auditorium	12[a] 14	24.9 24.9	20 7/16 19 3/8	10 3/4 11 1/4	15 15	4 1/16 4 1/8
OM[b]	Orchestra Model	14	25.4	19 3/8	11 1/4	15	4 1/8
M	Grand Auditorium	14	25.4	20 1/8	11 11/16	16	4 1/8
J[c]	Jumbo M	14	25.4	20 1/8	11 11/16	16	4 7/8
D	Dreadnought	12[a] 14	25.4 25.4	20 15/16 20	11 1/2 11 1/2	15 5/8 15 5/8	4 3/4 4 7/8

[a]Early models and some later recreations were 12-fret. 14 is now standard. Some late 12-fret OOO models had a 25.4-inch scale. [b]OM was used to indicate what were essentially the first 14-fret OOO models (there were other minor design distinctions as well). Eventually all OOOs went to 14 frets. [c]The J model is like the M, but with the greater depth of a dreadnought.

Martin also uses the following characters as part of the size prefix, when applicable.

H–	Herringbone purfling (usually scalloped bracing also)
–C	Cutaway
–12	12-string model

Martin also uses the following prefixes to describe several of its guitar models that are not pertinent to this book:

C, F	1930s–1940s carved-tops and archtops
E	Early 1980s solidbody electric guitar series
F, GT	1960s solidbody electric guitar series
N	Nylon-strung classical guitar
R	1930s carved-tops and archtops

Martin Style Suffixes

The following list includes all Martin styles in production as of the date of writing of this book, as well as several discontinued styles produced in large enough numbers that you're likely to encounter them on the used guitar market. Various antique and short-run styles are not included. Only the largest features (type of wood, major inlay work, etc.) are cited here, though styles are also distinguished by more subtle features of ornamentation, hardware, and other details. Certain variations in the specifications below occur at different periods and in occasional individual instruments. "Body" refers to back and sides. All tops are spruce unless otherwise specified. With a few exceptions (mostly among earlier instruments), bridges and fingerboards are rosewood in styles 15 through 21, and ebony in styles 28 through 45. Generally Martin reserves its best woods for the higher-numbered styles.

MARTIN GUITAR STYLE SUFFIXES

Style suffix	Basic features
15	Mahogany top and body, no binding
16	Mahogany body, very simple detailing
17	Mahogany top and body
18	Mahogany body
21	Rosewood body (rosewood neck/fingerboard)
28	Rosewood body (ebony neck/fingerboard)
35	Like -28 but 3-piece back and bound fingerboard
40, 41, 42	Increasing degrees of pearl/abalone inlay and top purfling
45	More extensive pearl/abalone inlays and purfling round most top and body joints; top of the line
60-series	Maple body

The following characters sometimes appear directly after the style suffix on special models. (Martin creates additional character suffixes for limited-production styles as the occasion warrants.)

A	Ash body
B	Special edition with Brazilian rather than Indian rosewood
C	Cutaway
C, G	Nylon-strung classical guitar
Deluxe	Uses extra-high quality materials and/or extra ornamentation
E	1960s guitars with magnetic pickups installed
H	Hawaiian (lap-style) setup
K	Koa body
LE	Limited edition including special features
M	Jumbo M model
NY	Design based on pre-1898 model from period when Martin label still read "New York" rather than "Nazareth"
P	(For "Profile") Low-profile neck; used on early models before low-profile was made standard
S	(For "Standard") Used on 12-fret versions of normally 14-fret guitars
SE	(For "Signature Edition") Special collector's edition with underside of top signed by Martin officers and staff
T	Tenor (4-string) guitar
V or Vintage	Recreation of vintage model

Martin Statistics

When Martin started putting serial numbers on its guitars in 1898 it began with number 8000, having estimated its 1833–1898 production totals at about 8000 instruments. Here are some Martin guitar production totals over the years. They reflect not only the growth of the company but also the history of musical taste and, in the case of the year 1939, of the American economy as well. By the end of the 1980s, a total approaching a half million Martin guitars had been built. The following chart of Martin serial numbers is useful for dating used Martins.

ANNUAL MARTIN PRODUCTION FIGURES FOR SELECTED YEARS

Year	Guitars made
1833 to 1897	est. total 8000
1898	348
1899	568
1919	1,062
1929	3,275
1939	2,195
1949	4,692
1959	5,471
1969	15,630
1971 (peak)	22,627
1979	12,100
1987	8,041

MARTIN SERIAL NUMBERS

Year ending	Last number	Year ending	Last number	Year ending	Last number	Year ending	Last number
1898	8348	1921	16758	1944	90149	1967	230095
1899	8716	1922	17839	1945	93623	1968	241925
1900	9128	1923	19891	1946	98158	1969	256003
1901	9310	1924	22008	1947	103468	1970	271633
1902	9528	1925	24116	1948	108269	1971	294270
1903	9810	1926	28689	1949	112961	1972	313302
1904	9988	1927	34435	1950	117961	1973	333873
1905	10120	1928	37568	1951	122799	1974	353387
1906	10329	1929	40843	1952	128436	1975	371828
1907	10727	1930	45317	1953	134501	1976	388800
1908	10883	1931	49589	1954	141345	1977	399625
1909	11018	1932	52590	1955	147328	1978	407800
1910	11203	1933	55084	1956	152775	1979	419900
1911	11413	1934	58679	1957	159061	1980	430300
1912	11565	1935	61947	1958	165576	1981	436474
1913	11821	1936	65176	1959	171047	1982	439627
1914	12047	1937	68865	1960	175689	1983	446101
1915	12209	1938	71866	1961	181297	1984	453300
1916	12390	1939	74061	1962	187384	1985	460575
1917	12988	1940	76734	1963	193327	1986	468175
1918	13450	1941	80013	1964	199626	1987	476216
1919	14512	1942	83107	1965	207030		
1920	15848	1943	86724	1966	217215		

Models

Martin

The following Martin models are all made entirely of solid wood (except the Shenandoah series). Tops of all models are quartersawn, but the Martin catalog at the time of this writing specs only the sides and backs of dreadnought-series guitars as quartersawn (I do not recommend nonquartersawn woods in guitars in this price range.) Standard X-bracing is used unless otherwise indicated. Most models are now being made with Martin's thinly contoured "low-profile" neck, but old-style necks are occasionally produced, and are available as a special option. Adjustable truss rods are standard, except on certain special-order instruments and limited-issue recreations of older models. Indian rosewood is standard, though Brazilian is sometimes available on special-order and limited-edition instruments. 14-fret necks are standard. A strong synthetic hard shell case is included in the price.

The listings below are the standard-order and special-order items listed in Martin's most recent catalog as this book goes to press. Short-run, limited-edition, and discontinued models—recent as well as vintage—are not included. Thus, for example, such instruments as the S (for "Special") series of 12-fret dreadnoughts, which petered in in the late sixties and petered out in the late eighties, are not mentioned here.

With Martins, as with instruments from most other manufacturers, you may expect the ornateness of bindings, position markers, tuning hardware, and other details to increase toward the top of the product line.

Model/ Size	Scale/ Nut width	Top	Back/ Sides	Neck	Fingerboard/ Bridge	Ornamentation/ Bracing	Price
5-18 12-fret	¾-size (kid-size)	spruce	mahogany	mahogany	mahogany		special order
0-16NY 12-fret concert	24.9 1⅞	spruce	mahogany	mahogany	rosewood		special order
00-21 12-fret grand concert	24.9 1⅞	spruce	rosewood	mahogany	rosewood		special order
00-45 12-fret grand concert	25.4 1⅞	spruce	rosewood	mahogany	ebony	extensive abalone and pearl purfling and inlay	special order
000-16M auditorium		spruce	mahogany	mahogany	new model just announced	scalloped bracing	$1325
000-18 auditorium	25.4 1¹¹⁄₁₆	spruce	mahogany	mahogany	rosewood		special order
000-28 auditorium	25.4 1¹¹⁄₁₆	spruce	rosewood	mahogany	ebony		special order
D-18 dreadnought	25.4 1¹¹⁄₁₆	spruce	mahogany	mahogany	ebony		$1560
D-28 dreadnought	25.4 1¹¹⁄₁₆	spruce	rosewood	mahogany	ebony		$1790
D-35 dreadnought	25.4 1¹¹⁄₁₆	spruce	rosewood; 3-piece back	mahogany	ebony	thin X-braces to balance response of 3-piece back	$1880

Martin models, cont.

Model/ Size	Scale/ Nut width	Top	Back/ Sides	Neck	Fingerboard/ Bridge	Ornamentation/ Bracing	Price
D-41 dreadnought	25.4 1¹¹⁄₁₆	select spruce	rosewood	mahogany	ebony	abalone top purfling, rosette, and position markers; bound fingerboard and headstock; scalloped bracing	$2820
D-45 dreadnought	25.4 1¹¹⁄₁₆	spruce	rosewood	mahogany	ebony	abalone top, sides, and fingerboard purfling, rosette, and position markers; bound fingerboard and headstock; scalloped bracing	$5330
D-62 dreadnought	25.4 1¹¹⁄₁₆	spruce	maple	mahogany	ebony	scalloped bracing; pre-1939 position	$1980
D12-28 12-string dreadnought	24.9 1⁷⁄₈	spruce	rosewood	mahogany	ebony	lightweight modified X-bracing	$1880
HD-28 dreadnought	25.4 1¹¹⁄₁₆	spruce	rosewood	mahogany	ebony	herringbone purfling; scalloped bracing	$2140
HD-35 dreadnought	25.4 1¹¹⁄₁₆	spruce	rosewood; 3-piece back	mahogany	ebony	herringbone purfling; thin X-braces to balance response of 3-piece back; scalloped bracing	$2430
J-18M jumbo		spruce	mahogany	mahogany	rosewood	scalloped bracing	$1710
J-21M jumbo		spruce	rosewood	mahogany			$1900
J-40M jumbo[a]	25.4 1¹¹⁄₁₆	spruce	rosewood	mahogany	ebony	abalone position markers; scalloped bracing	$2120
J-65M jumbo	25.4 1¹¹⁄₁₆	spruce	maple	mahogany	ebony	scalloped bracing	$2060
J12-40M 12-string jumbo	25.4 1¹³⁄₁₆	spruce	rosewood	mahogany	ebony	abalone position markers; modified bracing	$2190
J12-65M 12-string jumbo	25.4 1¹³⁄₁₆	spruce	maple	mahogany	ebony		$2140
M-64 shallow jumbo (grand auditorium)	25.4 1¹¹⁄₁₆	spruce	maple	mahogany	ebony	scalloped bracing	$1990
M-36 shallow jumbo (grand auditorium)	25.4 1¹¹⁄₁₆	spruce	rosewood; 3-piece back	mahogany	ebony fingerboard; rosewood bridge for tonal balance	scalloped bracing	$1890

[a]J-40 also available at extra cost as model J-40MC with cutaway and oval soundhole, or model J-40MBK with black finish.

Model/ Size	Scale/ Nut width	Top	Back/ Sides	Neck	Fingerboard/ Bridge	Ornamentation/ Bracing	Price
M-38 shallow jumbo (grand auditorium)	25.4 1¹¹⁄₁₆	spruce	rosewood; 3- piece back	mahogany	ebony finger- board; rosewood bridge for tonal balance	abalone rosette; bound finger- board and headstock;scal- loped bracing	$2350; add'l specs n/a
MC-28 cutaway shallow jumbo (grand auditorium)	25.4 1¹¹⁄₁₆	spruce	rosewood	mahogany	ebony	scalloped bracing; modified with oval soundhole	$2170
MC-68 cutaway shallow jumbo (grand auditorium)	25.4 1¹¹⁄₁₆	spruce	maple	mahogany	ebony	abalone lettered headstock inlay; bound finger- board and headstock;scal- loped bracing	$2400

Shenandoah

The lower-priced Shenandoah line, begun in 1983, was Martin's response to the marketing challenge from Guild, Alvarez-Yairi, and the other makers of high-quality, good-sounding guitars with laminate bodies and solid spruce tops. Martin imports neck and body components from Japan, and assembles them in its Pennsylvania factory. Shenandoah instruments preserve to a satisfying degree many characteristics of the traditional Martin sound—and, of course, appearance. Models are styled after traditional Martin designs and come with solid tops, laminate bodies, low-profile nato necks, ebonized rosewood fingerboard and bridge, built-in pickups, a wooden hard shell case, and a limited lifetime warranty (one year warranty on electronics).

Model/ Size	Scale/ Nut width	Top	Back/ Sides	Neck	Fingerboard/ Bridge	Ornamentation/ Bracing	Price
000-2832 auditorium with built-in pickup	24.9 1¹¹⁄₁₆	spruce	rosewood laminate	nato	ebonized rosewood	mother-of-pearl headstock inlay; scalloped bracing	$1150
D-1832 dreadnought with built-in pickup	25.4 1¹¹⁄₁₆	spruce	mahogany laminate	nato	ebonized rosewood		$1020
D-2832 dreadnought with built-in pickup	25.4 1¹¹⁄₁₆	spruce	rosewood laminate	nato	ebonized rosewood		$1070
D-3532 dreadnought with built-in pickup	25.4 1¹¹⁄₁₆	spruce	rosewood laminate; 3-piece back	nato	ebonized rosewood		$1110
D-4132 dreadnought with built-in pickup	25.4 1¹¹⁄₁₆	spruce	rosewood laminate	nato	ebonized rosewood	extra pearl inlay; scalloped bracing	$1670
D-6032 dreadnought with built-in pickup	25.4 1¹¹⁄₁₆	spruce	bird's-eye maple laminate; 3-piece back	nato	ebonized rosewood	scalloped bracing	$1250

Model/Size	Scale/ Nut width	Top	Back/ Sides	Neck	Fingerboard/ Bridge	Ornamentation/ Bracing	Price
D-6732 dreadnought with built-in pickup	25.4 1¹¹⁄₁₆	spruce	quilted (highly figured) ash laminate	nato	ebonized rosewood	scalloped bracing	$1430
D12-1932 12-string dread-nought with built-in pickup		spruce	mahogany laminate	(new model announced as this book goes to press)			$1270
D12-2832 12-string dread-nought with built-in pickup	25.4 1¹¹⁄₁₆	spruce	rosewood laminate	nato	ebonized rosewood		$1130
HD-2832 dreadnought with built-in pickup	25.4 1¹¹⁄₁₆	spruce	rosewood laminate	nato	ebonized rosewood	herringbone purfling; scalloped bracing	$1150
SE-2832 cutaway shal-low jumbo with built-in pickups and tone/vol-ume controls	25.4 1¹¹⁄₁₆	spruce	rosewood laminate	nato	ebonized rosewood		$1400
SE-6032 cutaway shal-low jumbo with built-in pickups and tone/vol-ume controls	25.4 1¹¹⁄₁₆	spruce	bird's-eye maple laminate	nato	ebonized rosewood		$1460

J. W. Gallagher and Son Guitars

Wartrace, TN 37183

Background

John W. Gallagher, a cabinetmaker since 1939, turned to guitars in the mid-sixties and soon developed a reputation as a maker of distinguished high-quality instruments. The small Gallagher shop, now run by J. W.'s son Donald, turns out only about 75 guitars a year. Gallaghers are used by many folk and country performers and recording artists, including Don Potter (the studio guitarist who has done such exquisite recording work with The Judds) and Doc Watson. Enough musicians to be worth mentioning tell me that they prefer older Gallaghers to more recent models; I haven't played enough Gallaghers of different vintages to have formed an opinion of my own.

Gallagher offers bodies of both rosewood and mahogany, but understands and respects mahogany better than most makers. (The distinctive qualities of Gallagher instruments are a rather heavy sweetness, medium separation, and balance across all the strings—the very things mahogany is best at—as well as a thick, dark bottom to the sound that you might say is more like molasses than like Martin's maple syrup.)

A photo of a Gallagher dreadnought appears on the cover of this book.

Doc Watson performs with his Gallagher guitar. *Photo by Larry Sandberg.*

Models

Gallaghers have adjustable tension rods and (at this writing) ivory nuts and saddles. Woods are solid and air-dried for at least three years. Cutaway body and slotted headstock options are available on all models at extra cost. Note the 12-string and 12-fret options on the G-70 and G-45.

Model/Size	Scale/ Nut width	Top	Back/ Sides	Neck	Fingerboard/ Bridge	Ornamentation/ Bracing	Price
72 Special, 71 Special dreadnought	25¼ 1¹¹/₁₆	spruce (select tight-grained on 72)	rosewood	mahogany	ebony	abalone purfling (72), herring-bone purfling (71), other inlay; voiced top and back bracing	$1985, $1640
A-70 auditorium	25¼ 1¹¹/₁₆	spruce	rosewood	mahogany	ebony	herringbone pur-fling; voiced bracing	$1490
DW (Doc Watson Model) dreadnought[a]	25¼ 1¹¹/₁₆	spruce	mahogany	mahogany	ebony	herringbone purfling; voiced bracing	$1290
G-45, G-45M, G-45-12 dreadnought[b]	25¼ 1¹¹/₁₆	spruce	mahogany	mahogany	rosewood		$1070, $1015, $1165
G-50 dreadnought[c]	25¼ 1¹¹/₁₆	spruce	mahogany	mahogany	rosewood		$1100
G-65 dreadnought	25¼ 1¹¹/₁₆	spruce	rosewood	mahogany	ebony		$1260
G-70, G-70M, G-70-12 dreadnought[d]	25¼ 1¹¹/₁₆	spruce	rosewood	mahogany	ebony	herringbone purfling	$1510, $1540, $1600
GC-7012-fret grand concert	25¼ 1¹¹/₁₆	spruce	rosewood	mahogany	ebony	herringbone purfling; voiced bracing	$1490
Ragtime Special auditorium[e]	25¼ 1¾	spruce	mahogany	mahogany	ebony	herringbone purfling, other inlay; voiced bracing	$1290

[a]Based on Doc Watson's custom specifications. [b]M model is 12-fret; 12 model is 12-string; both have 1⅞-inch nuts. [c]The original 1965 J. W. Gallagher model. [d]M model is 12-fret; 12 model is 12-string; both have 1⅞-inch nuts. [e]Designed for fingerpicking.

Gibson Guitar Corp.

641 Massman Dr., Nashville, TN 37210
See also Epiphone

Background

Orville Gibson (1856–1918) was a Michigan guitarist, woodworker, and luthier of whose early life we know little. He possessed enough acumen, though, to persuade a group of businessmen to found The Gibson

Mandolin-Guitar Manufacturing Company in Kalamazoo, Michigan, in 1902. (By the twenties, the company was also a major banjo maker as well.) Orville Gibson was never actually a principal in the firm. Instead he drew fees and royalties as a design consultant, and made most of his contributions within the first two years of the company's existence. His design principles, which chiefly involved the careful shaping of arched tops and backs, seem for the most part to have been worked out in his private shop by the 1880s.

Orville Gibson's work with both guitars and mandolins was influenced by the arched-top and -back design of violins. The first Gibson guitars were archtop models with round soundholes. These instruments represent an evolutionary step that never went anywhere, like the platypus. They largely disappeared from fashion by the twenties. Dark-sounding and slow to speak, they were unable to provide the crispness and rhythmic pliability American music demanded of the guitar as it moved into the thirties.

By the twenties, the legendary acoustical engineer Lloyd Loar had guided the Gibson company to preeminence as a manufacturer of banjos and archtop guitars and mandolins. (The now-classic designs of the Mastertone banjo, the L-5 f-hole guitar, and the F-5 mandolin date from this period.) Gibson was also turning out a number of interesting round-hole guitars at this time. Gibson was also the pioneer of the adjustable tension rod, on which it held the exclusive patent until the late fifties.

For the most part Gibson's better flattops were overshadowed in the marketplace by Martin (as they have been throughout Gibson's history). Gibson's low end, however, was lower than Martin's (and even still lower if you take into account the cheapie Kalamazoo line that Gibson started during the Depression). Gibsons became the Model T of American guitars during this period.

The best Gibson banjos, mandolins, electric guitars, and f-hole acoustic guitars are outstanding instruments, ranking among the greatest of their kind ever produced. Gibson has also made some excellent flattops. The Nick Lucas models (1928–38) and the J-200 (originating in the 1938 model then called the Super Jumbo, and still made today) are among the all-time classics. Of earlier (pre-World War II) Gibsons, even the low-end models are instruments of character.

Historically, Gibsons have had a characteristic sound quite definably distinct from Martins. What most people now think of as the Gibson sound is typified by the guitars designated as the "Jumbo" model. The Jumbos are plump, large-bodied guitars, like dreadnoughts with more rounded shoulders, pigeons rather than robins, but Gibson's smaller guitars have the same sound quality, too. Compared to Martins (Martins being the usual standard of comparison), Gibsons have traditionally been darker sounding and with less separation, sweeter and not as loud. Woods have something to do with this also. Martin's sound has always been rosewood-oriented. Gibson's past adventures with rosewood (like the Advanced Jumbo and rosewood J-200) were brilliant departures from habit. Historically, Gibson has designed its guitars around the sounds of mahogany or maple.

Gibson's corporate history has been as varied as its catalog. By the late forties, control of the company passed from the original consortium to a company called CMI (Chicago Musical Instruments), which installed an innovative president named Ted McCarty in 1958. During McCarty's sixteen-year tenure, Gibson's sales increased well over a thousand percent, in good part because of McCarty's vision in adopting the Les Paul solidbody guitar and developing a range of other electrics as well. It's arguable that Gibson's emphasis on electric guitars was accompanied during this period by a decline in the quality of its acoustic guitars.

Gibson also acquired the Epiphone company in the late fifties. To avoid franchise conflicts, Gibson manufactured Epiphones as an independent line until 1967.

In the late sixties, CMI was sold to the Norlin conglomerate, which dismantled Epiphone as an entity and used the name for a line of inexpensive oriental imports based on Gibson models. Gibson quality became extremely inconsistent during this period, as so often happens when an independent product-oriented company becomes part of a bottom-line-oriented conglomerate.

In 1986, CMI was purchased and moved to Nashville by a new consortium of music-oriented businessmen, with the intention of restoring the company's lost quality and reputation. The first Nashville Gibsons did not, in my opinion, accomplish this. More recently, Gibson purchased Flatiron Mandolins (a high-quality company), and began making acoustic guitars at Flatiron's Bozeman, Montana shop.

I was able to play a number of the new Montana Gibsons before this book went to press. The Montana Division seems to have set out to capture the feel and sound qualities of the 1940s Gibsons, and for the most part has done so admirably. There were a few minor and cosmetic problems and the finish seemed rather thick, even by today's heavy-handed standards. Though most instruments gave me pleasure, I found considerable inconsistencies in sound from instrument to instrument even within the same model line. These differences seemed to me to be on the level of taste rather than absolute quality, so be sure to try out lots of different instruments and base your decision on the individual guitar in hand. I played a number of first-rate Advanced (rosewood) Jumbos and some that were not so good, but one of the liveliest tops I found was on a considerably less expensive J-45. Of all the models, only the J-200s were consistently disappointing, offering a thin cutting sound appropriate to their maple bodies, but without the punch and bottom that Gibson was able to build into the J-200s of earlier times. Perhaps you'll find better ones than I did. They'd be worth looking for, and the other models are certainly worth looking at.

The Montana Division has demonstrated that it can make good guitars and that it can get the sound the makers want. It's a good alternative to the Martin, Taylor, Santa Cruz, and Guild sounds, which, while different from each other, are all much closer to each other on the spectrum than the classic Gibson sound is to any of them. It will be interesting to see now if the Montana people care to develop their sound in new directions; I, for one, would look forward to this.

It will be interesting, as well, to see if the Montana Division can free itself from classic Gibson tradition in other ways, too. Some people like

National fingerpicking champion Rollie Brown playing a Gibson J-200. *Photo by Larry Sandberg.*

the clubby feel of the classic Gibson neck, for example, but the popular taste these days is for faster necks, and I'm not at all sure that Gibson will be able to compete successfully without some accommodation. And it would be wonderful if Gibson at least looked into the marketing feasibility of recreating a grand concert-sized guitar—their small instruments of the thirties are cult items especially suitable for country blues, and treasured by those own them.

Old Gibsons for Gibson Lovers

Many older Gibsons have become collector's items: harp guitars, archtop roundholes, and certain ornamental models because they're old and odd, f-hole models with Lloyd Loar's signature on the label because they're rare and cultish and for the most part superb, J-185s and rosewood models because they're good and only a few were made, and so on.

But older Gibsons are also good player's guitars. There are people playing every kind of music—even in bluegrass where the Martin dreadnought reigns supreme—who just plain prefer the sound of their Gibson. There are traditional country blues stylists who find that the Gibson balance, thumpy bass strings, and thick, sweet sound of the high strings are much more suitable to their style than anything they can get out of other guitars. There are rhythm guitarists who find that the compressed, fisty chord sounds of their J-200 or Everly Brothers model punch their way into places in the ensemble that the Martin sound will never reach. And there are lots of player/collectors who own three, five, a dozen Martins, and also one or two Gibsons from the thirties, forties, or early fifties that they use for a knock-around guitar or for a change of pace.

Some older Gibsons, particularly smaller and less glamorous models, were once good bargains, but unfortunately (for you and me, at least) the entire Gibson collectible market has taken an upswing in recent years. It's still sometimes possible to get a reasonable deal. For some reason, fewer Gibson flattops than Martins seem to have held up over the years. I've heard it suggested that they just weren't as well made to begin with, but I'm not at all sure that that's the case. I suspect that Gibsons have simply tended to suffer more hard use, abuse, neglect, and disrespect from their owners over the years.

Models

The models listed below all have adjustable tension rods. They are available in a variety of finishes and (at additional cost) with a factory-installed saddle-mounted pickup. I regret that Gibson has not cared to answer our request for more detailed specifications about their woods. Check with your dealer. I suspect (or at any rate, hope) that they're using more solid woods than their somewhat erratically written sales literature lets on.

There is also a less expensive five-model line (in the $900 range) called the Blueridge Acoustic Collection, for which Gibson did not furnish us specs or other information. I'd expect body woods in this price range to be laminates.

Model/ Size	Scale	Top	Back/ Sides	Neck	Fingerboard/ Bridge	Ornamentation	Price
Dove dreadnought	25½	solid spruce	maple	maple	rosewood	ornate bridge and pickguard	$1815
Humming-bird dreadnought	24½	spruce	mahogany		rosewood	ornate pickguard	$1685
J-100 jumbo	25½	spruce	maple		rosewood	differs from J-200 only in trim	$1435
J-180 jumbo	24¾	spruce	maple		rosewood	based on the old Everly Brothers model: star position markers, over-size pickguard, black finish	$1535
J-200 jumbo	25½	spruce	maple			ornate bridge and pickguard	$1775
J-30 dreadnought	24¾	spruce	mahogany		rosewood		$1125
J-45 rounded dreadnought	24¾	spruce	solid mahogany		rosewood		$1319

Gretsch

Fred Gretsch Enterprises, Box 1175, Savannah, GA 31402

Background

Gretsch began in Brooklyn in 1883 as the banjo, tambourine, and drum workshop of German emigrant Friedrich Gretsch. After Friedrich's death in 1895, his son, Fred, Sr., added mandolins to the line and gradually built the company to international proportions. By the thirties Gretsch had acquired distribution rights for the highly regarded K. Zildjian cymbal company and added a line of guitars. Gretsch guitars of the period were f-hole archtops, befitting the big-band era. Most Gretsch facilities had by then moved to Chicago, which at the time was the center of the American musical instrument industry. However, the guitar line remained based in New York City.

In the post-World War II period, the guitar line expanded under the presidency of Fred Gretsch, Jr. Gretsch f-hole models were never competitive with Gibson and Epiphone, but in the fifties Gretsch introduced a series of electric guitars designed in consultation with Chet Atkins. They had a character all their own, and a sound very similar to that of a lap steel guitar (which Gretsch also then made). They became popular in the south among country-and-western musicians, and helped define the sound of that style, time, and place. The Baldwin Piano and Organ Company acquired Gretsch in 1967, and proceeded to decimate the guitar and banjo lines as the sixties acoustic music boom began to fade. In 1985, Fred Gretsch (great-grandson of the founder) satisfied a long-standing personal ambition by repurchasing the company. Current models are based on original Gretsch designs of the forties and fifties.

Models

At several points in its history, Gretsch marketed flattop guitars aimed at country players (after all, Gretsch had the distribution), but these were not traditionally the company's strongest suit or major interest. The current catalog lists several interesting flattops that promise to offer a playing feel similar to that of the well-known f-hole guitars. These electro-acoustic models, on which Gretsch's reputation as a guitar manufacturer is based, are quintessential rockabilly, cowboy jazz, and fifties-sound guitars. If you want that sound and feel, there's nothing else like them.

Unfortunately I haven't been able to find any recent Gretsch instruments to submit to a hands-on examination for you. New and newly-managed American companies like Gretsch, Gibson, and Heritage are going to have a tough time getting their products back into stores dominated by less expensive Asian imports and by higher-end instruments from makers like Guild and Martin that didn't forsake their markets or their standards when the bottom dropped out of acoustic music in the seventies.

The new Gretsch management strongly asserts its devotion to reestablishing traditional model lines with contemporary refinements. Its well-done catalogs succeed in making the following instruments appear to be substantial and well worth considering. All are made with distinctive round-cornered triangular soundholes.

Gretsch sales information current at this writing is at times unclear as to whether solid, laminate, or quartersawn woods are used. Such specifications as were made available to us are given in this section.

Model	Size	Top	Back/Sides	Neck	Fingerboard/Bridge	Ornamentation	Price
Crimson Flyer	cutaway dreadnought with pickup	spruce	chestnut	2-piece mahogany	ebony-stained rosewood	ornate rosette, inlaid bridge, shaded finish	$1350
Night Bird	cutaway jumbo with pickup	spruce	maple	2-piece mahogany	ebony-stained rosewood fingerboard	ornate rosette, inlaid bridge, black finish, elbow rest on top of upper bout	$1200
Rancher	jumbo	spruce	maple	multipiece rock maple	rosewood fingerboard	headstock inlay, other appointments	$1050
Sun Valley	dreadnought	spruce	rosewood	mahogany	ebony-stained rosewood	ornate rosette, headstock and bridge inlays	$1250

Django Reinhardt playing a Gretsch acoustic guitar. *Photo courtesy of Fred Gretsch Enterprises.*

Guild

Sales: 2885 S. James Dr., New Berlin, WI 53151
Factory: 60 Industrial Dr., Westerly, RI 02891

Background

The Guild company was formed by guitarist and music-store owner Al Dronge in 1952, after the demise of the original Epiphone company. Dronge was able to hire many of Epiphone's craftsmen and, according to rumor, to acquire some of Epiphone's molds, templates, and fixtures as well. Guild got off to a good start on the strength of its archtop models, and was compelled by increased production demands to move from New York City to larger quarters in Hoboken, New Jersey, in 1956.

Once in larger quarters, the company turned to classical and flattop guitars as well. Guild's top-of-the-line flattop, from the beginning, was the jumbo-sized model. Smaller guitars were also available, but Guild didn't add a dreadnought to the line until the mid-sixties.

Guild was purchased by the Avnet conglomerate in 1967, at which time it moved to its present Rhode Island facility. In 1986 it was purchased by a small guitar-oriented consortium, but passed through some hard times. Recently Guild was purchased by U. S. Music Corporation (formerly the Faas Corporation), which also owns Randall, the noted amplifier company. Guild's standards have remained high over the years, and it appears that the new owner aims to preserve them.

Old Guilds never really became collector's items, and recent Guilds may never become collectible, since they're being made with laminate sides and backs. (Some top-of-the line models were being made with solid back and sides, and this may still be the case under the new management, though the specs they supplied us don't make this clear. Guild would serve itself, its customers, and its dealers better if its sales literature were more accurate about the nature of its woods.) A new Guild may be harder to resell than a new Martin, and probably would command a smaller percentage of its original cost, but if you stick with it you'll get a well-made, excellent-sounding instrument that provides good value for your money. Because they have never acquired the mystique of collectibility, and are underrated in general, used Guilds can usually be had at lower prices than other instruments that deliver no better sound or durability. I especially recommend that you look at Guilds if you're looking for a 12-string.

The best-sounding individual Guilds have their own sound, powerful, balanced, clean, without the separation and bark that distinguishes Martins and makes them so desirable for those who must have that sound. Guilds can sound terrific in their own way. They typically come out of the factory very well set up, with a neck shape and setup more reminiscent of a smooth-feeling f-hole jazz guitar than of the stiffer bluegrass feel characteristic of Martins. I suspect that a certain number of finicky Martin owners keep their repairpeople busy trying to customize a Guild feel onto a Martin neck, and it can't really be done. If you want a guitar that feels like a Guild, get a Guild.

Guitarists as diverse as Eric Clapton, Holly Dunn, Randy Travis, John

Denver, Richie Havens, Bonnie Raitt, and John Renbourn have used Guild flattops.

Guild also markets the Madeira line of less expensive imports.

Models

If memory serves me right, Guild was the first prestigious manufacturer to go from solid to plywood back and sides, beginning in the mid-seventies. They did a good job of it, coming up with some slightly arched pressed plywood back designs that projected a strong, clear sound.

Until a few years ago, Guild models were designated by an annoyingly inconsistent alphanumeric system—you couldn't tell from the model prefix whether you were getting a dreadnought, a jumbo, or what. In 1986, Guild rationalized its acoustic guitar model designations into the Dreadnought Series D-models, the Jumbo Series JF-models, and the Traditional Series GF-models of auditorium-size guitars. All have a 25⅝-inch scale, adjustable tension rod, and 1¹¹⁄₁₆-inch nut (add ⅛ inch for 12-strings). Most are available with a choice of natural or sunburst finish and (with a surcharge) in left-handed configuration. An electro-acoustic model, the Songbird, is also available.

The specs for Guild body woods in this chapter reflect the poor quality of information in the Guild catalog available at the time this manuscript was prepared. Guild assures me that by the time you read this, dealers should have a better catalog accurately reflecting the use of solid verses laminate body woods. Basically, the picture is this: All current models designated archback (you can tell by looking for the arch and for the absence of interior back bracing) have laminate bodies. All current flatback models (distinguished by the presence of interior back-bracing as well as by the flatness of the back) have solid quartersawn wood bodies. All rosewood guitars are flatbacks. As for the tops, they're all solid quartersawn wood.

Given my usual reservations about laminates, it's interesting to note that, in most of the new Guilds I've played, I prefer the tone and response of the laminate instruments—and so do many other players, as well as the Guild tech rep with whom I spoke.

Model	Size	Top	Back/sides	Neck	Fingerboard/bridge	Ornamentation/bracing	Price
D-15	dreadnought	mahogany	mahogany	mahogany	rosewood		$795
D-25, D-25-12	dreadnought (12 model is 12-string)	spruce	mahogany	mahogany	rosewood		$945, $1045
D-30, D-40, D-40C	dreadnought (C model is cutaway)	spruce	(30) maple, (40) mahogany	(30) maple, (40) mahogany	rosewood	scalloped bracing	$1095, $1145, $1295
D-50	dreadnought	spruce	rosewood	maple	ebony	scalloped bracing	$1395
D-100[a]	dreadnought	select hand-crafted solid spruce	rosewood	mahogany	ebony	abalone top and neck inlay; scalloped bracing	$2895
GF-25[b], GF-30	auditorium	spruce	(25) mahogany, (30) maple	(25) mahogany, (30) maple	rosewood	natural finish; 30 has scalloped bracing	$945, $1095
GF-55	auditorium	spruce	rosewood	mahogany	ebony	mother-of-pearl and abalone inlays; scalloped bracing	$1595
JF-30, JF-30-12	jumbo (12 model is 12-string)	spruce	maple	maple	rosewood	scalloped bracing	$1195, $1295
JF-55, JF-65-12	jumbo (65-12 model is 12-string)	spruce	available with rosewood or maple	available with rosewood or maple	ebony	mother-of-pearl and abalone inlay; hand shaved bracing	$1695 (both)
Songbird	cutaway auditorium with pickup and preamp	spruce	mahogany	mahogany	rosewood	available in natural, black, and white finish	$1195

[a]Model D-100C is available with additional features including hand-carved neck heel. [b]Model GF-25 is available at a slightly lower price in sunburst.

Heritage

225 Parsons St., Kalamazoo, MI 49007

Background

When Gibson moved to Nashville a few years ago, some ex-Gibson employees who had stayed behind in Kalamazoo found the backing to form Heritage Guitars, Inc. (Perhaps it's not such a good name, because they also make other fretted instruments.) Heritage is seriously trying to become a major manufacturer. I regret that I haven't seen any Heritage flattops yet. I did get to play a couple of archtop electrics and thought they were comparable to the products the same workers were turning out when they worked for Gibson—which is just what you'd expect.

The Heritage instrument line includes these three flattop guitars with adjustable tension rods and either natural or sunburst tops.

Heritage acoustic guitars have solid quartersawn spruce tops. Information available at this writing does not specify the nature of body wood in detail.

Model	Size	Scale	Top	Back/ Sides	Neck	Fingerboard/ bridge	Price
H-445	dreadnought	25½	solid spruce	mahogany	maple	rosewood	$850
H-450	dreadnought	25½	solid spruce	solid mahogany	mahogany	rosewood	$1015
H-480	cutaway carved-back dreadnought; small oval soundhole	25½	solid spruce	solid mahogany	mahogany	rosewood	$1115

La-Si-Do (Minstrel, Seagull, Simon & Patrick)

42 Principal Sud, La Patrie, Québec, Canada J0B 1Y0

Background

You've probably never heard of La-Si-Do, but they're one of North America's largest manufacturers. (I guess they must sell their guitars to all those people in the Yukon and Northwest Territories.)

La-Si-Do has sent us a minimal response to our survey of manufacturers, so instead of listing their specs, I'll have to just give you a quick summary of their model lines based on what I've seen in the stores. These guitars seem to be finding increased distribution in the United States. If you can't find a local dealer, one reputable mail-order source for them is Elderly Instruments, Box 14210, Lansing, MI 48901.

The characteristic sound of the La-Si-Do instruments I've played is dry and clean, with surprisingly good sustain for the money in each price bracket. They're not particularly loud. As a rule, beginners don't appreciate that this is a much better sound than boomy apparent loudness. But it's precisely this kind of balanced sound, hard to come by in a beginner's guitar, that will let you develop the best playing touch you can. The instrument's playing feel is also important for your growth as a guitarist. While not thoroughly consistent (no manufacturer is), the La-Si-Dos I saw were as a rule more nicely set up than other instruments in their price ranges.

Models

La-Si-Do guitars are available in sizes from grand concert (or so) to dreadnought, and as 12-string or left-handed models as well—even both at once! (I think the Seagull lefty 12-string must be the only such instrument in anywhere near its price-class, and one of the few at any price.) At the lower end of the line, La-Si-Do products are definitely built to play, not to look at. Your money's worth goes to your ear and fingers, not your eye.

I haven't seen La-Si-Do's recommended retail price list, so the prices below are *roughly* street prices for 6-string models at the time of this writing. The following models are also available with factory-installed L.R. Baggs pickups at extra cost. There is also a Godin Guitars series of electro-acoustic guitars that I haven't seen.

Minstrel Series ($200+ range). In the Minstrel series, you get good sound and feel for the price.

Body and top are made of a brownish-dyed wild cherry laminate, and the overall look is, well, not really crude, but certainly not slick. If you think people will snicker at you for having a guitar that doesn't look real neat and shiny, you'd better keep away from the Minstrels. On the other hand, every Minstrel series guitar I picked up was one I would have been content to see in the hands of a beginning student, in terms of both playability and sound. In fact, I enjoyed playing them, and much more than many Asian imports at twice the price.

Seagull Series ($275+ range). The ones I've seen actually have solid cedar tops on their wild cherry laminate bodies, and are a bit better appointed and more polished looking than the Minstrels. They're equally good deals.

Simon and Patrick Series ($550-$650) These are nicely made, nicely appointed, and nice-looking solid-topped laminate guitars that are also good deals for the money. But in this price range, some instruments from other manufacturers are also competitive, so do your comparison shopping.

Larrivée

Factory: 267 E. First St., N. Vancouver, BC, Canada V7L 1B4
Larrivée USA: 716 1/2 W. Lincoln, DeKalb, IL 60115

Background

Larrivée Guitars was founded in 1968 by classically trained luthier Jean Larrivée. The small Vancouver factory makes a number of standard models, each of which is available in several grades distinguished by increasing complexity of ornamentation. I haven't had the chance to play more than four or five Larrivées over the years. They were finely, often ornately, made, with a sweet sound, very dark, not highly separated, and so thick that it was heavy. I've only played showroom Larriveés; never one that's been in use. Tops were slow to speak and the voices somewhat suppressed, but it was my sense that the tops would open up considerably once the instruments were played in a little more, so take this into account when you sample Larrivées.

Models

Larrivée guitars have solid quartersawn tops and bodies. They are made with adjustable tension rods, Sitka spruce tops, Honduras mahogany necks, Indian rosewood or maple back and sides (except as indicated), and ebony fingerboards and bridges. Woods are aged at least five years at the factory before use.

Natural finish is standard but sunbursts are also available. Factory-installed Fishman pickups with preamps and controls and custom finish and inlay work are available at extra cost. All guitars carry a limited lifetime warranty.

In addition to the 6-string models offered below, Larrivée also offers

12-string "Larrivée body" and dreadnought models at approximately $150 over the cost of the 6-string models.

The following chart shows the price of each of the standard body sizes at each of the four progressively ornate inlay levels. (Chez Larrivée, inlay is a *specialité de la maison*.) The "Larrivée body" is about auditorium size, with the silhouette of a classical guitar—likely a reflection of Jean Larrivée's training as a classical luthier. The inlay levels are:

- **Standard:** fairly straightforward.
- **Special:** mother-of-pearl and abalone fingerboard inlays, mother-of-pearl eagle headstock inlay.
- **DeLuxe:** engraved mother-of-pearl and abalone fingerboard inlays, silver-bordered headstock with mother-of-pearl and abalone gryphon inlay, and abalone top purfling.
- **Presentation:** abalone and mother-of-pearl position markers, silver-bordered headstock with mother-of-pearl and abalone unicorn inlay, and abalone body purfling on all bound joints.

Inlay level	Dreadnought & Larrivée bodies	Larrivée cutaway body	Jumbo body
Standard grade, mahogany body	$964	(n/a)	$1064
Standard grade	1240	1480	1340
Special grade	1470	1710	1570
Deluxe grade	1700	1940	1800
Presentation grade	3600	4000	3700

Norman Guitars

U.S. distributor: MMS, Inc., Box 1071, Neptune, NJ 07754

Norman did not respond to our questionnaire directed to their Québec Province office. However, just before going to press we were able to obtain the address of Norman's new U. S. distributor, which is given above.

Ovation, Adamas, Applause (Kaman)

Background

The fortunes of Kaman Corporation's founder Charles H. Kaman were based on a new design for a helicopter rotor blade, but he was an avid guitarist who had turned down a chance at a professional career to go to college. When Kaman Corporation's board decided, in the late sixties, that diversification into consumer products would help balance the ups and downs of aerospace contracting, it was natural that Charles Kaman's background would lead the company toward guitars.

In the spirit of its aerospace heritage, Ovation is a pioneer in the use of factory automation and of synthetics for guitar construction. The standard Ovation models have spruce tops, graded in quality to match the price category of each model. A variety of new bracing patterns were developed through acoustical research. The radical Ovation bodies are made of a single bowl-shaped moulding of the synthetic fiberglass material that Kaman uses for covering its rotor blades. This highly sound-reflective material was shaped, after much design testing by engineers, to focus the sound waves out through the sound hole. Letting the sound "out" is not necessarily the most important function of a soundhole (it's there to form what acousticians call a reflex chamber), but in any case the guitar works well. Ovation called it the "Lyrachord" body. Some purists hate the very idea of Ovation guitars, but I've always liked them for what they are. I find the Ovation body shape a bit tricky to hold in the lap, though, but it may not bother you as much as it does me, and it probably won't bother you at all if you use a strap.

Ovation was also a pioneer in the use of built-in pickups, having developed the technique, now in common use by other manufacturers as well, of seating in the bridge an individual piezo-electric pickup for each string. Ovations are good guitars to look at especially if you're in the market for an instrument which you'll primarily be playing amplified. Kaman continues to be a leader in the development of built-in amplification and connectivity.

In 1975, Ovation introduced its Adamas model, a revolutionary (and pricey) design with a top of synthetic graphic-fiber laminates sandwiching a birch veneer inner core, and an unusual array of small soundholes in the upper bouts. They call it the "Fibronic" soundboard. Purists hate the Adamas even more than they hated the original Ovation. I can't say I care much for its looks, but I enjoy its sound: crisp, clear, extremely well-balanced, and with effective built-in pickups. But's it's not a sound with a soul of its own. It's a sound that follows orders, and the people giving the orders are engineers. The keyword is efficiency over character.

The better Ovations have achieved wide acceptance as trustworthy, roadworthy journeyman-quality professional instruments—especially by guitarists who use Ovation's built-in pickups and preamps. (Some of the less expensive models offer simpler electronics.)

Graphite fiber

Graphite fiber is a modern synthetic perhaps best known for its use in fishing rods and tennis rackets—in other words, as a wood substitute in precisely those applications which, like a guitar, require a combination of strength and elasticity. The material is created by high-temperature treatment of polyacrylonitrate fiber, which results in graphite fibers about $\frac{1}{10}$ the thickness of a human hair. These fibers are then embedded in epoxy resin.

Graphite resins have been used by several makers for guitar necks (mostly on electric guitars), in addition to Ovation's use of it on Adamas tops.

Models

The following list summarizes the Ovation and Adamas lines and refers to the other variations that are available at prices appropriately adjusted from that of the cited model: cutaway, shallow body, 12-string, electronics, and so on. In addition, a variety of color and finish options are available on most models.

All Ovation guitars are approximately auditorium-size and have the molded synthetic body described above. Adamas bodies are slightly deeper. Scale length is 25¼ inches and nut width is 1¹¹⁄₁₆ inches throughout the line, except for 1⅞-inches on 12-strings. A wide-neck Adamas 6-string is also available.

The quality of Ovation tops increases with the price range of each model line, and sound quality tends to increase very consistently along with them. All Ovations are built with an adjustable tension rod set inside a sturdy oversize channel bar. The shallow-bodied model variations (that are designed primarily to make players of thin bodied electric guitars feel at home with the body shape) come with wide frets to make the players feel at home on the fingerboard as well. Ovation also markets the Applause line of Korean-made, less expensive, lower-quality guitars based on the standard Ovation model. They are not listed here, since Kaman declined to send us spec sheets for them.

Ovation's sythetic bodies have solid quartersawn tops, except in the Adamas line, which uses a high-quality laminate of carbon graphite with a birch veneer core.

Model	Top	Neck	Fingerboard/ Bridge	Ornamentation/ Bracing	Price	Remarks
1117 Legend	Sitka spruce	mahogany/ maple laminate	ebony finger-board; walnut bridge	proprietary A-shaped bracing pattern	$1099	other Legend series guitars are available in shallow-bowl cutaway and 12-string configurations and with built-in electronics
1312 Ultra	Sitka spruce laminate	mahogany/ maple laminate	rosewood fingerboard; walnut bridge	proprietary bracing design	$449	other Ultra series guitars are available in shallow-bowl, cutaway, and 12-string configurations with and without built-in electronics
1712 Custom Balladeer	Sitka spruce	mahogany/ maple laminate	ebony fingerboard; walnut bridge	proprietary bracing design	$949	has built-in pickups and preamp. other Custom Balladeers guitars available as shallow-bowl, cutaway, and 12-string
1718 Elite	Sitka spruce; birch veneer reinforcement	mahogany/ maple laminate	rosewood fingerboard; walnut bridge	Adamas-style soundholes with leaf-pattern marquetry; proprietary fan bracing pattern	$1199	has built-in pickups and preamp, other Elites include shallow-bowl, cutaway, and 12-string
1719 Custom Legend	Sitka spruce	mahogany/ maple laminate	ebony finger-board; walnut bridge	abalone purfling and inlay; proprietary A-pattern bracing	$1429	has built-in pickups and preamp, other Custom Legends include shallow-bowl, cutaway, and 12-string
1990-7 Collector's Series	bird's eye maple laminate	mahogany/ maple laminate	ebony finger-board; walnut bridge	proprietary fan bracing pattern	$1599	has cutaway, built-in pickups and equalizer, shallow-body model 199S-7 is also available.
Adamas 1187	carbon graphite with birch veneer	walnut	walnut	leaf-pattern soundhole marquetry; proprietary fan bracing pattern	$2299	wide-neck, cutaway, and 12-string, models and simpler Adamas II series available
Ovation CC11 Celebrity Acoustic	Sitka spruce laminate	mahogany/ maple laminate	rosewood fingerboard; walnut bridge	proprietary design	$349	Other Celebrity guitars include shallow-bowl, cutaway, and 12-string configurations, optional electronics

Santa Cruz Guitar Company

328 Ingalls Ave., Santa Cruz, CA 95060

Background

Luthier Richard Hoover and repairpeople William Davis and Bruce Ross started the Santa Cruz Guitar Company in 1976. (Davis left the company in 1978 and Ross in 1989.) The company's philosophy remains based on its original principle of turning out fine work by luthier-level craftspeople in a limited-production setting. Current production is around 250 instruments a year, a small figure that helps keep quality control high. Santa Cruz instruments are among the finest new factory guitars you're going to find, in a class with Martins, Schoenbergs, and very few others.

Much of the company's success is based on its association with Tony Rice, the leading guitar exponent of new acoustic music on the guitar, who endorses the model named after him. This very lightly-built dreadnought is designed in collaboration with Rice and modelled after his legendary Martin, an eccentrically modified instrument once owned by the legendary Clarence White. But I'd advise prospective buyers to consider other Santa Cruz models as well.

Santa Cruz Model OM. *Photo courtesy Santa Cruz Guitar Co.*

Whether you prefer the Santa Cruz sound to Martin's is your own decision. It's a good sound, and an authentic one, and the guitar's voice sounds like it's all there even on brand-new instruments. The dozen or so Santa Cruz instruments I've played were consistently well-made. They tended to be more balanced and more luscious in tone than many contemporary Martins, but less punchy, lacking Martin's characteristic bark and bite. If you're looking for a smaller-size guitar, Martin has nothing (except on special order or limited edition) to compare to the Santa Cruz Model H, a model based on the superb, unusual, sweet-sounding but long-forgotten Nick Lucas model Gibson of the twenties.

Models

The prices given below are base prices for each given model. Actual prices are determined by the various mix-and-match options that Santa Cruz offers, including additional choices of wood, ornamentation, neck configuration, and so on. Cutaway, left-handed, and 12-string designs are available as options for each model. The company also accepts custom orders.

Adjustable tension rods and a limited lifetime warranty are standard on all Santa Cruz guitars. Price includes a hard shell case. Santa Cruz guitars have solid quartersawn tops and bodies.

Model/ Size	Scale/ Nut width	Top	Back/ Sides	Neck	Fingerboard/ Bridge	Ornamentation/ Bracing	Price
Model D dreadnought	25.4 $1^{13}/_{16}$	quartersawn Sitka or German spruce	rosewood or koa	mahogany	ebony	tapered bracing	$1850
Tony Rice Model D dreadnought; oversize soundhole[a]	25.4 $1^{11}/_{16}$	quartersawn Sitka or German spruce	rosewood	mahogany	ebony	scalloped bracing	$2350
Model D, 12-fret rounded dreadnought	25.4 $1^3/_4$	quartersawn Sitka or German spruce	rosewood or koa	mahogany	ebony	tapered or scalloped bracing	$2450
Model F jumbo[b]	$24^3/_4$ $1^{13}/_{16}$	quartersawn Sitka or German spruce	koa, maple, or rosewood	multipiece mahogany and maple	ebony	tapered	$2050
Model FS jumbo with cutaway	$24^3/_4$ $1^{13}/_{16}$	quartersawn cedar	rosewood	mahogany	ebony	bindings and purfling of various ornamental woods; tapered bracing	$3200
Model H extra deep grand concert[c]	25.4 $1^{13}/_{16}$	quartersawn Sitka or German spruce or koa	koa, maple, or rosewood	mahogany	ebony	tapered X-braces and scalloped tone bars	$1900
Model OM auditorium	25.4 $1^{13}/_{16}$	quartersawn Sitka or German spruce	rosewood or koa	thin profile V-shaped mahogany	ebony	herringbone rosette; scalloped bracing	$2250

[a]Designed in collaboration with Tony Rice. [b]Model F has arched back designed for acoustic jazz sound. [c]Model H is a 14-fret guitar based on the 1920s Nick Lucas model.

Schoenberg Guitars

38 Shore Drive, Concord, MA 01742
Available from the manufacturer or selected dealers

Background

Schoenberg Guitars began in 1986 as a collaboration between collector/dealer/fingerpicking virtuoso Eric Schoenberg, luthier Dana Bourgeois, and the Martin Guitar Company. In 1990, Bourgeois was replaced by T. J. Thompson. The Schoenberg company produces about thirty instruments each year.

The guitars are made to Schoenberg's specifications at the Martin factory, with attention, handwork, and decision-making by Thompson at critical production stages. Quartersawn solid woods are selected at the Schoenberg workshop, then sent to Martin for assembly. At the Martin shop, Thompson hand shapes the bracing, voices both the bracing and the tops themselves, and acoustically matches all top and body components. After assembly, the guitars go back to the Schoenberg workshop for final adjustments and setup.

The instruments themselves say "Schoenberg" on the headstock but carry Martin serial numbers. You can think of them as Martins that have been given more-than-standard handwork and quality control, to a degree otherwise received only by guitars from private luthiers and limited-production shops.

I regret that I've never had a chance to play a Schoenberg guitar. People who have, and who know a fine guitar when they play one, enthusiastically describe them as superb instruments on a par with the great original Martins after which they are modelled—which would put them in the absolute top rank. Past acquaintance with Eric Schoenberg gives me every reason to believe these reports.

Models

The prototype for the Schoenberg guitar is the Martin OM. (OM, short for Orchestra Model, was the designation Martin used around 1930 for its first 14-fret auditorium-size guitars.) Schoenberg guitars are set up and acoustically optimized for fingerpicking. (That is to say, with fast, relatively low action and a sound that in response to a light touch is clear, well-balanced, and well-separated.) Necks are relatively slim, with the slight V-contour found on some early Martins. As it happens, such an instrument may also suit some flatpickers as well—especially soloists and lead players.

Schoenberg guitars have solid quartersawn tops and bodies. Price includes a hard case and humidifying gadget. Instruments carry Schoenberg's limited lifetime warranty, which is also honored by select Martin authorized warranty centers. Many custom options, including other grades and types of wood, inlay work, neck widths, installed pickup, etc., are available at extra cost.

In addition to the models listed below, Schoenberg has from time to time produced limited-edition reissues of other classic Martin models.

Model/ Size	Scale/ Nut width	Top	Back/ Sides	Neck	Fingerboard/ Bridge	Ornamentation/ Bracing	Price
12-Fret Soloist 12-fret auditorium (noncutaway)	1⅞	Engelmann spruce	rosewood	mahogany	ebony	pyramid bridge, slotted head-stock; no pick-guard; scalloped bracing, hand-voiced	$3015
Soloist cutaway auditorium (optional non-cutaway)	25.4 1¾	Sitka spruce	rosewood	mahogany	ebony	pyramid bridge, fine bindings and position markers;scalloped bracing, hand-voiced	$2765
Standard cutaway auditorium (optional non-cutaway)	25.4 1¾	Sitka spruce	rosewood	mahogany	ebony	pyramid bridge; scalloped brac-ing, hand-voiced	$1860

Soloist cutaway guitar by Schoenberg. *Photo courtesy of Schoenberg Guitars.*

Taylor Guitars

9353 Abraham Way, Santee, CA 92071

Background

Taylor was founded in the mid-seventies. Their well-made, good-sounding instruments are first rate and are generally priced somewhat below Martin and Santa Cruz. Subjectively, I've enjoyed the sound of Martin and Santa Cruz instruments a bit more, but you might disagree, and I'd hardly think you foolish if you did. Plenty of people do, evidently, because new Taylors sell well (the company turns out over 2000 instruments a year), and used ones are hard to find.

Taylors sound good and are made of good woods, but they owe most of their success, I think, to the fast necks and congenial action which they have made a strong sales point. Taylor seems deliberately to have sought out a niche at the upper price and quality level based on these characteristics, and they've done a good job of it. If you are looking at Martin and Santa Cruz instruments, you are doing yourself a disservice if you don't also look at Taylors.

Models

Taylors are equipped with an adjustable tension rod. All tops, necks, and bodies are of solid quartersawn wood. Scale length is 25½ inches. X-braces are scalloped (except on 12-strings and on the Dan Crary model, as noted) and nut width is 1¹¹⁄₁₆ inches (except 1⅞ inches on 12-strings and 1¾ on auditorium-sized models). All instruments have (at least) pearl position markers and Schaller tuners (gold-plated on higher models); as is the case with most makers; ornamentation increases as prices go up.

National fingerpicking champion Chris Proctor and his Taylor guitar. *Photo courtesy Flying Fish records.*

Model	Size	Top	Back/Sides	Neck	Fingerboard/Bridge	Ornamentation	Price
555	12-string jumbo	Sitka spruce	mahogany	mahogany	Indian ebony		$1328
610	dreadnought	Sitka spruce	German maple	mahogany	Indian ebony		$1148
615	jumbo	Sitka spruce	German maple	mahogany	Indian ebony		$1264
1452	12-string jumbo	Sitka spruce	German maple	mahogany	Indian ebony		$1452
710	dreadnought	Sitka spruce	Indian rosewood	mahogany	Indian ebony		$1226
712	auditorium	Sitka spruce	Indian rosewood	mahogany	Indian ebony		$1288
750	12-string dreadnought	Sitka spruce	Indian rosewood	mahogany	Indian ebony		$1410
810	dreadnought	Sitka spruce	Indian rosewood	mahogany	Indian ebony	abalone rosette	$1480
812	auditorium	Sitka spruce	Indian rosewood	mahogany	Indian ebony	abalone rosette	$1554
815	jumbo	Sitka spruce	Indian rosewood	mahogany	Indian ebony	abalone rosette, other inlay	$1628
855	12-string jumbo	Sitka spruce	Indian rosewood	mahogany	Indian ebony	abalone rosette, other inlay	$1872
910	dreadnought	Sitka spruce	Indian rosewood	mahogany	Indian ebony	abalone rosette, other inlay	$2116
912	auditorium	Sitka spruce	Indian rosewood	mahogany	Indian ebony	abalone rosette, other inlay	$2222
915	jumbo	Sitka spruce	Indian rosewood	mahogany	Indian ebony	abalone rosette, other inlay	$2328
955	12-string jumbo	Sitka spruce	Indian rosewood	mahogany	Indian ebony	abalone rosette, other inlay	$2678
DCSM [a]	cutaway dreadnought	Sitka spruce	Indian rosewood	mahogany	Indian ebony	unscalloped X-brace	$1750
K-20	dreadnought	koa	koa	mahogany	Indian ebony		$1688
K-22	auditorium	Sitka spruce	koa	mahogany	Indian ebony		$1756

[a]Dan Crary Signature Model.

Other North American Manufacturers

Favilla
(defunct)

Favilla Guitars was established in Manhattan in 1890. I'm not familiar with their early work but have seen many good, creditable, sweet-sounding guitars from the fifties and early sixties. However, they seem not to have held up over the years; you hardly see them around these days.

Favilla wound up being hurt more than helped by the 60s folk boom, it seems. They built a large factory and increased production in 1965, and brought in a Japanese import line in 1970. (The Japanese instruments were also called Favillas, but with a script headstock logo rather than the coat-of-arms used on domestic instruments.) Apparently they overextended themselves, for they ceased operation in 1973.

Fender
1130 Columbia Avenue, Brea, CA 92621

Leo Fender ranks with Les Paul as one of the great pioneers of the electric solidbody guitar, and was the first to successfully mass-produce and market it. While the company that has borne his name since the 1940s (he is no longer associated with it) has made its greatest contributions with its solidbody Telecasters and Stratocasters, it has from time to time marketed acoustic guitars as well.

In my street research, I found a few current Fender acoustic guitars of varying quality, and apparently of Korean origin, on sale at prices from $100 to $300. Several dreadnoughts at a street price of around $200 played well and sounded quite good for the price. However, Fender did not reply to our manufacturer's questionnaire, so no specific model information is given here.

Gurian
(defunct)

Beginning in 1971, the Gurian company produced attractive, well-made, good-sounding steel-string guitars of distinctive design (that is to say, not Martin clones) which represented good value, though their sound and the feel of their necks was not to everyone's taste. Unfortunately, the company was not able to recover from a major fire, and went out of business in 1981.

Used Gurians these days still represent good value as long as they are priced as used instruments; unfortunately some sellers price them as collectibles at too high a figure.

La Jolla Luthiers (Bi-Level Guitars)
Box 23366, San Diego, CA 92123
Available through dealers

This small shop run by luthier Wayne Harris produces about a hundred instruments a year, including both steel-string and classical models. They are based on an unusual design developed by Roger Pytlewski, in which the top is bent into two levels connected by a 10-degree ramp precisely at the latitude where the bridge is placed. The purpose, and advertised result, of this design is to increase the instrument's high overtones and overall perceived brilliancy and volume.

The steel-string model is the Collector's Series Bilevel, a dreadnought-sized instrument with Sitka top, Brazilian rosewood body, and mahogany neck (all quartersawn) and fan bracing, with a list price of $2167. The instrument is built with an adjustable truss rod and carries a 5-year limited warranty.

Lo Prinzi and Augustino

(defunct)

These companies, created by Thomas LoPrinzi and his brother Augustino, each produced several thousand good-quality instruments during the seventies. A used one can provide satisfaction and value if not priced as a collectible.

Mossman

2914 National Ct., Garland, TX 75041

After several years as a private luthier, Stuart Mossman founded the S. L. Mossman Company in Winfield, Kansas, in 1969. The company rebuilt from a severe 1975 fire only to close in 1977 after a dispute with distributors. Eventually the company was taken over by luthier Scott Baxendale, an original Mossman employee, and production was resumed in the mid-eighties.

The original Mossmans were guitars influenced by the classic Martin dreadnought design, and built specifically for bluegrass. I haven't sampled, or heard any second-hand reports, of the instruments made in Mossman's current incarnation, and the company has not participated in our survey of manufacturers.

Stelling

Stelling Banjo Works, Ltd., Rt. 2, Box 302, Afton, VA 22920

Just as this manuscript is being prepared for press, Stelling has introduced their first guitar: a bluegrass dreadnought with Sitka spruce top and quartersawn cherry (!) body, priced at $2100. Stelling is well known as a manufacturer of excellent bluegrass banjos. If their guitar is of the same quality, it's certainly worth looking for.

Imported Models

The following sections list the major imported brands. With the exception of Lowden, these are instruments made in Asia (mostly Japan or Korea). Some are imported by the Japanese or Korean companies themselves; others are made abroad to the specifications of the American companies that import them. Approximately 90 percent of the guitars sold each year in the U.S. are now imports.

The extreme low end of the guitar market is for the large part filled by Asian-made instruments not listed here (their importers did not respond to our survey of manufacturers). You'll find them in music stores with names like Bentley, Carlos, Kingston, Franciscan, Kay, Hohner, Schmidt, Harmony, Almirez, and others. For the most part they're somewhat less expensive than the instruments of the major importers and of proportionally poorer quality. I have not seen any that I would particularly recommend, except for the small nylon-string children's-size models. These do their job adequately.

Alvarez and Alvarez-Yairi

Dist. by St. Louis Music, 1400 Ferguson Ave., St. Louis, MO 63133

Background

You'll find that the Alvarez and Alvarez-Yairi lines of laminate-bodied Asian imports are well worth looking at. They offer good sound and appearance for the money. The top-of-the-line instruments are nicely appointed, and setup seems somewhat consistently better than with many competing brands.

Alvarez, which began in 1965, was a pioneer among Asian companies in offering laminate-body guitars with solid tops, fancy inlays and appointments, and other amenities in its top-of-the-line models, many of which may be found in professional use. This is especially true of the Alvarez-Yairi line, a series of instruments manufactured under the supervision of luthier/designer Kazuo Yairi. (However, you'll find that prices at the top of the line are in a league with Guild's, and worth comparing with other domestic products as well.)

The following selections will give you a representative idea of the Alvarez and Alvarez-Yairi lines. I've left out several in-between model variations, and also a few models for which product specifications were not provided by the distributor. All instruments are available with factory-installed pickups at additional cost.

Alvarez Models

All Alvarez guitars are fitted with an adjustable tension rod mounted in a U-shaped channel bar, and carry a five-year limited warranty. Alvarez guitars have laminate tops and bodies in the lower price ranges and solid quartersawn tops in the higher ranges. Again, always ask to be sure.

Model	Size/ Shape	Top	Back/ Sides	Neck	Fingerboard/ Bridge	Ornamentation/ Remarks	Price
5212 Regent Special, 5214 Regent Deluxe, 5214-12 Regent, 5220C Regent	similar to dreadnought (5214-12 is 12-string; 5220C is cutaway)	spruce	mahogany	nato	rosewood	5212 has adjustable bridge	$199, $249, $340, $299
5224 Mahogany Solid Top	dreadnought	solid spruce	mahogany	nato	rosewood		$369
5227 Rosewood Special, 5225 Rosewood Solid Top	dreadnought	spruce (solid on 5225)	rosewood	nato	rosewood		$349, $459
5022 Glenbrook Solid Top	dreadnought	solid spruce	rosewood	nato	rosewood	herringbone purfling	$525
5021 Foxmore Mahogany	12-string dreadnought	spruce	mahogany	nato	rosewood		$425
5054 Golden Chorus	12-string dreadnought	solid spruce	rosewood	nato	rosewood		$599
5086 Wildwood Bi-Phonic	cutaway shallow-bodied rounded dreadnought with pickup and equalizer	cedar	ovangkol	nato	rosewood	thin profile neck; pickups have separate controls for bass and treble strings	$750
5041 Fusion Electric, 5088 Fusion EQ Special	dreadnought with pickup (and equalizer in 5088)		mahogany	5041 nato; 5088 mahogany	rosewood		$515, $565
5080-Series Fusion Cutaways	shallowbodied cutaway dread-nought with pickup	curly maple	curly maple	nato	rosewood	available in various colored finishes; serial numbers differ with finish	$649
5063 Wildwood Special	rounded dread-nought	spruce (cedar on 12-string)	ovangkol	nato	rosewood		$430, $599
510	dreadnought		mahogany				$1050
512	auditorium		mahogany				$1104

Alvarez-Yairi Models

The inconsistencies and seemingly important omissions (like some top woods!) in some of these listings are a reflection of the spec sheets provided to us by the distributor. These are good-sounding instruments worth checking out. As models move toward the high end, a lot of attention goes into cosmetic details as well. Yairi-series guitars have laminate tops and bodies in the lower price ranges and solid quarter-sawn tops in the higher. Some special Yairi series instruments (none of which are current at this writing) may have solid bodies as well.

Model	Size/Shape	Top	Back/Sides	Fingerboard/Bridge	Ornamentation/Bracing/Price
GY-1 Virtuoso Tradition	cutaway dreadnought with pickup and equalizer	solid spruce		ebony	shell inlay on fingerboard and headstock; $1199
WY-1 Virtuoso Folk	cutaway auditorium with pickup and equalizer	solid cedar	rosewood	2-piece bridge	herringbone top edge purfling; shell soundhole purfling; $1199
DY-50 Wind River Deluxe	dreadnought	cedar	jacaranda		shell soundhole purfling, ornamental bridge shape; $899
DY-52, DY-80 Canyon Creek	dreadnought (80 is 12-string)		coral rosewood	2-piece bridge	ivory and shell soundhole inlay; parabolic bracing; $699, $825
DY-53 Canyon Creek Jumbo	small jumbo		pecan		parabolic bracing; $725
DY-54, DY-55 Wind River	dreadnought		54 is rosewood; 55 is black jacaranda		abalone soundhole purfling; $725, $799
DY-74, DY-74C, and DY-76 Wellington	dreadnought (74C is cutaway; 76 is 12-string)	solid Canadian spruce	rosewood	ebony	shell inlay on fingerboard and headstock; parabolic bracing; $875, $899, $925
DY-75DCB Lexington	dreadnought		rosewood	ebony fingerboard; 2-piece bridge	marquetry purfling and other trim; $950
DY-87 Express	thin-bodied cutaway auditorium with pickup and equalizer	curly maple	curly maple		transparent blue, black, or red finish; $899

Aria

Dist. by Matao Corp., Box 583, Bellevue, WA 98009

Background

Aria seems to be best represented in retail stores by their inexpensive nylon-string guitars. In my part of the world, at least, there are hardly any steel-string models on display and I've seen few over the years, so I can't report any definite impressions of the product line. The few steel-string guitars I've seen have struck me, like the nylon-string ones, as adequate, reasonably priced instruments that compare to competitive models from other makers.

Models

Aria's somewhat ambiguous sales information implies laminate tops and bodies on less expensive models and solid quartersawn tops on better models, presumably with laminate bodies, but you must check for yourself.

Model	Size/ Shape	Top	Back/ Sides	Neck	Fingerboard/ Bridge	Ornamentation/ Remarks	Price
AW-100	dreadnought	spruce	mahogany	mahogany	rosewood fingerboard		$209
AW-200, AW-220E, AW-200T	dreadnought (E model has pick-up, T model is 12-string)	spruce	mahogany	mahogany	rosewood		$259, $439, $319
AW-200F	grand concert	spruce	mahogany	mahogany	rosewood		$259
FET Elecord Series	cutaway shallow-bodied auditor-ium with built-in pickup (preamp and equalizer on more expensive models)	arched laminates: spruce, spruce/ chestnut, maple, or sycamore	chestnut, rosewood, maple, sycamore, or mahogany; arched back	mahogany	ebony or rosewood fingerboard; rosewood bridge	electronics im-prove in each price bracket	$619 to $1775
LW-12, LW-12BC, LW-12HBT	dreadnought (BC has cut-away; HBT is 12-string)	cedar	mahogany	mahogany	rosewood fingerboard; ebonized maple bridge	herringbone purfling	$469, $609, $499
SW-8; SW-8T	dreadnought (T is 12-string)	solid cedar	mahogany	mahogany	rosewood fingerboard; ebonized maple bridge		$669, $729

Aspen

International Music Company, Box 2344, Fort Worth, TX 76113

Background

Aspen is a U.S.-based company that has successfully combined the economics of exchange rates and the Asian labor market with intelligent design using laminated wood bodies and (on many models) solid wood tops.

I've only sampled instruments at the low end of the Aspen line. I found them okay for the money, but couldn't get enthusiastic. I haven't come across any of the high-end Aspen Luthier (AL-series) instruments, but people I'm inclined to trust tell me they offer good sound and high manufacturing quality, comparable to, say, the similarly priced instruments of the more widely distributed Alvarez-Yairi line. Aspen shares a niche with Alvarez-Yairi in combining cost-saving laminated bodies not only with solid tops, but with many cosmetic amenities. (You'll find when you compare fittings that the two companies' feature sets are slightly different.)

Models

Aspen warranties run from two years at the low end to limited lifetime at the top of the line. Aspen uses laminate tops on its less expensive models and quartersawn solid tops with laminate bodies on its mid-range standard and Luthier models. The top-of-the-line Luthier Studio series models have quartersawn tops and bodies.

Model	Size/Shape	Top	Back/Sides	Neck	Bracing	Price
A-118S	dreadnought; nut width 1¾	spruce	mahogany		scalloped	$359
A-124, A-124E	dreadnought	mahogany	mahogany	mahogany		$189, $269
A-125SEC	cutaway dreadnought with built-in pickup; nut width 1¾	cedar	Indian rosewood		scalloped	$499
A-128S, A-128SE	dreadnought; nut width 1¾	spruce	Indian rosewood		scalloped	$459, $549
A-135SF	jumbo; nut width 1⅝	Sitka spruce	maple		scalloped	$549
A-18, A-18EC	dreadnought	spruce	mahogany		voiced	$229, $379
A-28	dreadnought	spruce	rosewood		voiced	$299
AL-18, AL-18E	dreadnought	solid German spruce	mahogany	5-piece mahogany laminate	scalloped	$789, $1029
AL-28, AL-28E	dreadnought	solid German spruce	rosewood	5-piece mahogany laminate	scalloped	$879, $1129
AL-35	dreadnought	solid German spruce	solid rosewood, 3-piece back		shaved	$1249, $1489
AL-F	jumbo	solid German spruce	solid maple	5-piece mahogany laminate	scalloped	$1269

Note: "E" designates built-in pickup; "C" designates cutaway.

Epiphone

Gibson Guitar Corp., 641 Massman Dr., Nashville, TN 37210

Background

Epiphone is now nothing more than a name used by Gibson for its line of Asian imports, but it was once a proud and important domestic manufacturer.

The Epiphone Company began as the stringed-instrument workshop of Anastasios Stathopoulo in New York City in 1873. In 1928, it changed its name to Epiphone after the name of the new boss, Anastasios's son Epi (short for Epaminondas).

With changing times and tastes, the company specialized more and more in guitars. During the thirties, Epiphone developed a wide range of f-hole guitars, the best of which were highly coveted by big-band rhythm guitarists. Epiphone and Gibson were the major f-hole guitar factories, and each had its partisans. Epiphones were characteristically cruder-sounding, harsher, and louder, with a punch that could slice right through the middle of the horns. Epiphone electrified many of their models in the thirties and forties and won some fans, but never really succeeded in matching Gibson's quality or marketing success. Epiphone also included at least one flattop guitar, the mid-priced Navarre, in their catalog, but their heart wasn't really in it.

Family problems, union disputes, and an inability to regain competitive footing with Gibson after the war-production years led to a move from New York to Philadelphia in the early fifties, but the company was already moribund. Many of the fine Epiphone craftsmen elected not to follow the plant from New York to Philadelphia, and some eventually went to work for the newly-formed Guild company. Philadelphia production never really got off the ground, and in 1957 the company was sold to Gibson. As a way of avoiding franchise territory conflicts, Gibson manufactured Epiphones as an independent line until 1967, when the named shifted over to use for imports.

Models

The current Epiphone import line consists of inexpensive laminate 25½-inch-scale models with adjustable tension rods. Instruments are monitored for quality by Gibson and carry a three-year limited warranty.

I've sampled a fair number of imported Epiphones. They represent a fair value for their price, and they've neither excited nor dismayed me. Setup struck me as more inconsistent than with other brands.

Epiphone uses laminate tops and bodies, except, as indicated in the specs, for the top of the line models.

Model	Size/ Shape	Top	Back / Sides	Neck	Fingerboard/ Bridge	Ornamentation	Price
PR-350, PR-350S, PR-350-12	dreadnought (350-12 is 12-string)	spruce (solid on 350S)	mahogany		rosewood fingerboard	extra-price options: saddle-mounted pickup; black finish (350); left-handed config-uration (350S).	$244, $339, $359
PR-715	dreadnought	spruce	rosewood	mahogany	rosewood fingerboard	herringbone purfling	$399
SQ-180	jumbo	spruce	mahogany		rosewood fingerboard	based on Gibson Everly Brothers model: star position markers, over-size pickguard, black finish	$389

Goya

Martin Guitar Company, Nazareth, PA 18064

Background

Goya and Sigma are the two laminate-body import lines handled by Martin, Goya being the cheaper. Martin acquired rights to Goya in 1976.

I've played only a few Goyas, and enthusiastically thought them good deals for what they are. They were decently set up, with a clean well-balanced sound rather than the boomy false loudness which beginners often fall for, to their later regret. I'd be pleased if all my beginning students had guitars as good.

The Goya name is also remembered from the fifties and early sixties as a line of Swedish-made instruments with small, sweet voices, and necks that were none too stable.

Models

Selected models are available (at extra cost) in left-handed configuration and with factory-installed pickups. They are designed by the Martin company and warranted by Martin for one year.

Goyas have laminate tops and bodies, except as indicated in the specs, for the top of the line models.

Model	Size/Shape	Top	Back/Sides	Fingerboard/Bridge	Ornamentation/Bracing/Price
G-215	grand concert	spruce	mahogany	rosewood	scalloped bracing; $299
G-235	grand auditorium	solid spruce	rosewood	rosewood	scalloped bracing; $458
G-300, G-312, G-318C, G-415	dreadnought (C model has cutaway; 415 is 12-string)	spruce	mahogany		$222, $274, $320, $323
G-316H	dreadnought	spruce	rosewood	rosewood	herringbone purfling; scalloped bracing; $393
G-335S Deluxe Dreadnought	dreadnought	solid spruce	rosewood	rosewood	herringbone purfling, inlaid headstock and other appointments; scalloped bracing; $520
G-518	grand auditorium	spruce	rosewood	ebonized hardwood	inlaid headstock and other appointments; $434
G-610 Mini-Dreadnought[a]	¾-size (kid-size); approx. dreadnought shape	spruce	mahogany	rosewood	scalloped bracing; $224

[a] G-610 weight is imbalanced toward headstock; make sure your kid is comfortable with it first.

Ibanez

Chesbro Music Co., distributor (western states)
Box 2009, Idaho Falls, ID 83403

Hoshino USA, distributor (eastern states and California)
1726 Windham Rd., Bensalem, PA 19020

Background

To judge from their presence in American music stores, Ibanez must sell a lot of instruments. Ibanez seems very concerned with looks and features, but in general I haven't liked the sound and feel of Ibanez instruments as much as others. You may disagree, however, especially when you compare this seemingly ubiquitous brand to whatever else may be available in your market area.

Models

The following list gives a representative selection of Ibanez instruments. I've left out a few in-between models. Ibanez uses laminate tops and bodies except as indicated in the specs for the top-of-the-line models.

Model/ Size	Scale/ Nut width	Top	Back/ Sides	Neck	Fingerboard/ Bridge	Ornamen- tation/bracing	Price
AE300 cutaway dreadnought[a]	25.4 1¹¹⁄₁₆	spruce	mahogany	nato	rosewood		$549
AE400 cutaway jumbo[b]	25.4 1¹¹⁄₁₆	spruce	mahogany	nato	rosewood		$599
AE500 cutaway shallowbody auditorium[b]	25.4 1¹¹⁄₁₆	spruce	rosewood	nato	rosewood		$629
AW18, AW18-12 dreadnought[c]	25.2 1¹¹⁄₁₆	solid spruce	mahogany	nato	rosewood	rosewood; scalloped bracing	$599, $699
Model: AW28 dreadnought	25.2 1¹¹⁄₁₆	solid spruce	rosewood	nato	rosewood	scalloped bracing	$699
PF10, PF10-12 dreadnought[d]	25.4 1¹¹⁄₁₆	spruce	mahogany	nato	rosewood		$259, $289
PF15-S dreadnought	25.4 1¹¹⁄₁₆	solid spruce	mahogany	mahogany	rosewood		$449
PF40; PF40-12 dreadnought	25.4 1¹¹⁄₁₆	spruce	maple	nato	rosewood		$349, $399
PF45S dreadnought	25.4 1¹¹⁄₁₆	solid spruce	maple	mahogany	rosewood		$549
V300L left-handed dreadnought	25.2 1¹¹⁄₁₆	spruce	mahogany	nato	rosewood		$439

[a]Built-in pickup . [b]Built-in pickup and equalizer. [c]18-12 is 12-string. [d]10-12 is 12-string.

Lowden

U.S. sales address: Box 245, Lake Luzerne, NY 12846

George Lowden is a northern Irish builder of high-quality instruments characterized by a sweet tone and good separation, sustain, clarity, balance, and tonal equivalence from string to string. These are qualities particularly well suited to contemporary Celtic and "new age" styles. They encourage thoughtful playing and sound full and strong when played with a soft or moderate touch, but as you play them with a harder touch, volume no longer increases in proportion to the energy of your stroke. These are instruments for weaving textures, not for spraying out bullets of sound.

The Lowdens I've played have been approximately auditorium-size guitars, but very deep. Instruments that had been played in had full voices, but the voices of fresh showroom instruments were somewhat contained, implying that Lowdens need to be played in more than guitars of other makers do. Your best bet is to find a dealer that will let you play the instrument for several hours over several days.

The availability of Lowden guitars in the United States has been inconsistent over the years. At one time a line of Lowden-designed Asian-made guitars came and just as quickly went. Lowden instruments can again be found at selected dealers, but because Lowden's U.S. distributor has not responded to our request for information, no further information is given here.

Eileen Niehouse of the band Myles na Gopaleen and her Lowden guitar. *Photo by Larry Sandberg.*

Madeira

Guild Guitars, 2550 S. 170th., New Berlin, WI 53151

Background

Madeira is the name Guild uses for its small line of import models. Although they're not as easy to find in stores as Guilds themselves, they're competitive within their price brackets. The A-5 is one of the few grand concert size guitars you'll find in this price range.

Models

Madeira's sales information does not make specifications available. I would assume laminate throughout.

Model	Size/Shape	Top	Back/ Sides	Price
A-10, A-10/12, A-30R, A35CE	dreadnought (model /12 is 12-string; CE has cutaway and pickup)	spruce	mahogany (A-30R is rosewood)	$229, $269, $299, $379
A-5	grand concert	spruce	mahogany	$219

Saga Musical Instruments

Box 2841, 429 Littlefield, South San Francisco, CA 94080

Background

Saga started off as an instrument parts supplier (it still is), and made a good reputation for itself in the seventies with a neat little do-it-yourself banjo kit. It now imports and distributes its own line of folk instruments made in Japan, including the guitars listed below. (In addition, a very low-priced Korean-made student model dreadnought, the BR-05S, is in the planning stages as we go to press.) Saga has also revived the old "Regal" mark for its line of imported resophonic guitars.

I haven't seen these instruments, but on the basis of past experience with Saga I'd expect them to be forthright, decently-made products that offer value commensurate with their prices. Try to sample them if you can.

Models

All dreadnoughts have a mahogany neck with 25½- inch scales and an adjustable tension rod. Saga's low range begins with an all-laminate student model, progressing through a midrange with solid quartersawn tops and laminate bodies, to all solid-wood models at the top of the line.

Model	Size/Shape	Top	Back/Sides	Fingerboard/Bridge	Ornamentation/Bracing	Price
BR-35; BR-3512 Blueridge	dreadnought; 3512 is 12-string	solid spruce	mahogany	rosewood	scalloped bracing	$549/$625
BR-65, BR-6512 Blueridge	dreadnought; 6512 is 12-string	solid spruce	rosewood	rosewood	scalloped bracing	$575/$650
BR-75, BR-85	dreadnought	solid spruce	solid mahogany; BR-85 is solid rosewood	rosewood	herringbone purfling, abalone rosette; scalloped bracing	$625/$875
DG-series "Django" Guitar[a]	26.25 scale (this is quite a long scale!); 1 7/8 nut width		zero fret, archtop-style tailpiece and moveable bridge			$595 to $1150

[a]Based on the late-thirties Selmer Maccaferri model with small elliptical soundhole; five models available from the laminate mahogany DG-100 to solid rosewood DG-500; price depends on model.

The Saga BR-35 dreadnought. *Photo courtesy Saga Musical Instruments.*

Samick

Samick Music Corp., 8521 Railroad St., City of Industry, CA 91748

Background

A Korean company founded in 1958, Samick is one of the world's largest producers of pianos and fretted instruments. It has been doing business in the United States (mostly in pianos) since the 1970s, and over the years has conscientiously worked to improve the quality of its products, especially to make them durable in the U.S. climate. Its guitars run from relatively inexpensive to well into the middle price range. Samick is apparently seeking a niche by offering such features as solid wood tops and scalloped bracing in price brackets lower than those in which competing companies offer similar amenities. Unfortunately, I haven't had the chance to see or play any of them, so I can't evaluate how well these features work.

Models

All instruments are made with an adjustable tension rod, and all necks are one-piece solid wood. As usual, the side and back woods mentioned in this section are laminates unless labelled as solid. Most Samick guitars have laminate tops, with quartersawn solid wood appearing only at the top of the line.

I'd like to commend Samick USA for being the *only* Asian importer to supply me with explicit information for all models as to whether woods are laminate or solid (*every* company was asked to do so).

Model	Size/ Shape	Top	Back/ Sides	Neck	Fingerboard/ Bridge	Ornamentation/ Bracing	Price
EAG-88	shallow cutaway auditorium with built-in pickups; 25.6 scale	maple	maple	nato	rosewood	scalloped bracing; blue burst finish	$499
EAG-89	shallow cutaway auditorium with built-in pickups; 25.6 scale	solid spruce	rosewood	nato	rosewood	red burst finish	$599
S-7 Samick Yairi[a]	auditorium	solid cedar	rosewood	nato	ebony	multiple wood binding; scalloped bracing	$729
S-8	auditorium	solid spruce	jacaranda	nato	ebony	scalloped bracing	$899
SF-1241	dreadnought	mahogany	mahogany	mahogany	mahogany		$169
SF-1251[b]	dreadnought	spruce	nato	nato	nato		$199

[a]Also available: S-7EC with cutaway and built-in pickup. [b]Also available: SF-1251E with built-in pickup.

Model	Size/ Shape	Top	Back/ Sides	Neck	Fingerboard/ Bridge	Ornamen- tation/Bracing	Price
SF-1501	grand concert	spruce	mahogany	nato	rosewood	scalloped bracing	$219
SF-150SR	grand concert	spruce	rosewood	nato	rosewood	scalloped bracing	$219
SF-1812	12-string dreadnought	spruce	nato	nato	rosewood	scalloped bracing	$249
SF-18CE	cutaway dread- nought; built-in pickup	spruce	mahogany	nato	rosewood	scalloped bracing	$299
SF-2812	12-string dreadnought	spruce	rosewood	nato	rosewood	herringbone bind- ing; scalloped bracing	$399
SJ-215	jumbo	sycamore	nato	nato	rosewood	scalloped brac- ing; available in gray, white, or black burst	$299
SK-5 Samick Yairi	auditorium	solid spruce	ovangkol	mahogany	rosewood	scalloped brac- ing; bone nut and saddle	$399
SK-6 Samick Yairi	auditorium	solid cedar	sycamore	nato	rosewood	scalloped brac- ing; bone nut and saddle	$529
SK-7 Samick Yairi	auditorium	solid cedar	rosewood	nato	rosewood	scalloped bracing	$599
SW-218	dreadnought	spruce	mahogany	mahogany	rosewood	scalloped bracing	$229
SW-235HS	dreadnought	solid spruce	rosewood	nato	rosewood	tree-of-life finger- board inlay; scal- loped bracing	$349

Sigma

Martin Guitar Company, Nazareth, PA 18064

Sigma guitars are the better of the two laminate-body Asian import lines handled by Martin (the other is Goya). Martin has been selling them since 1970. They're made to Martin's specifications and are inspected and adjusted at the Martin factory before being shipped to retailers. Solid tops have been standard in recent years, but earlier models had laminate tops.

Sigmas are solidly made and are good for what they are. I've found in perusing display models that setup is not as consistent as I'd like or expect, but that's something the dealer should be able to fix easily before the guitar leaves the shop.

Note that the Sigma warranty varies according to model, and in some cases is more impressive than that of competitors.

Models

Because Martin did not make Sigma prices available to us, I've been able to give descriptions of the various series without having to break them down by model. You'll find that prices are competitive with those of similar products from other manufacturers.

Model/ Size	Scale/ Nut width	Top	Back/ Sides	Neck	Fingerboard/ Bridge	Ornamen- tation/Bracing	Remarks
1-Series D models dreadnought; 12-string available	25.4 1¹¹⁄₁₆	laminated spruce	mahogany	mahogany	ebonized hardwood	scalloped-style bracing	two-year limited warranty
2-Series D models dreadnought; 12-string available	25.4 1¹¹⁄₁₆	laminated spruce	mahogany or rosewood	mahogany	ebonized hardwood or rosewood	scalloped-style bracing	five-year limited warranty
GCS Series grand concert	24⁷⁄₈ 1¹¹⁄₁₆	laminated spruce	mahogany	mahogany	ebonized hardwood or rosewood		two to 10-year limited warranty
Marquis Series D models dreadnought; cutaway and 12-string available	25.4 1¹¹⁄₁₆	laminated spruce	mahogany, rosewood, ovangkol, or chestnut	mahogany	ebonized hardwood	herringbone purfling on some models; scalloped bracing	available in several finishes; 10-year limited warranty
SDM-18, SDR-28, SDR-28H, SDR-35, SDR- 41 dreadnought	25.4 1¹¹⁄₁₆	solid spruce	rosewood (18 is mahogany)	mahogany	ebonized hardwood	28H has her- ringbone pur- fling; 35 has 3- piece back; 41 has mother-of- pearl-style pur- fling and inlay; scalloped-style bracing	two-year limited warranty
SE 18, SE 40T shallowbodied cutaway dread- nought with pickup and equalizer	25.4 1¹¹⁄₁₆	laminated spruce or sycamore	mahogany	mahogany	rosewood	available in several finishes	limited lifetime warranty; one year on electronics

Takamine

C. Bruno & Son (division of Kaman Music Corp.), distributor
Box 525, Bloomfield, CT 06002

Background

By the early seventies, Takamine established an excellent reputation for sturdy, moderately priced Asian guitars of decent sound quality that a beginner could learn on without hinderance. Since then prices have risen and the line has become more hifalutin', but generally Takamines still provide good value.

Takamines are distributed in the United States by C. Bruno and Son, once a noteworthy 19th-century guitar firm, which now survives in name as the distributing arm of the Kaman Corporation. Unfortunately, neither Kaman nor Bruno could or would supply us with a price list.

You'll find that Takamine prices cover the midrange spectrum, and that they are competitive for the sound, sturdiness, and warranty you get.

Models

The following selection from the Takamine catalog omits Takamine's E-models. The E-models (prefixed with the letter E) are identical to the models listed below, except that they are equipped with good-quality pickups, preamps, and equalizers. Many Takamine models are also available in left-handed configuration. Takamines carry a limited lifetime warranty.

Takamine's somewhat ambiguous sales information implies laminate tops on the less expensive models and solid quartersawn tops on the better models, with laminate bodies throughout both ranges.

Model	Size/ Shape	Scale	Nut width	Top	Back/ Sides	Neck	Fingerboard/ Bridge
F-307	grand concert	24¹³⁄₁₆	1⅝	spruce	nato	nato	rosewood
F-340	dreadnought	25⅜	1⅝	spruce (F-341 with black finish)	nato	nato	rosewood
F-350M	dreadnought	25⅜	1⅝	spruce	maple	maple	rosewood
F-360S, F-360	dreadnought	25⅜	1⅝	solid spruce (F-360 is laminate)	rosewood	mahogany	rosewood
G-330, G335	dreadnought (G-335 is 12-string)	25⅜	1⅝	spruce	bubinga	nato	rosewood
N-10, N1012	auditorium (N-1012 is 12-string)	25⅜	1⅝	solid red cedar	mahogany	mahogany	rosewood
N-20	jumbo	25⅜	1⅝	solid red cedar	mahogany	nato	rosewood

Washburn

230 Lexington Dr., Buffalo Park, IL 60089

Background

The Washburn mark was used around the turn of the century for guitars made or distributed by the Chicago firm of Lyon and Healy, a giant of musical instrument manufacturing in that era. More recently the name has been picked up for use on a new line of instruments imported from the Orient. There is no historical continuity between the products of the two companies, in spite of loose suggestions to the contrary in the contemporary company's sales literature.

The current Washburn line includes thoughtfully designed instruments with prices from the low-to-high midrange. They're well made (as opposed to finely made) and offer good value for the money. The better Washburns are professional-quality instruments, and a good many working musicians use them—especially the electro-acoustic models—as journeyman instruments in addition to, or instead of, more expensive guitars.

During the eighties Washburn has been extremely aggressive in both promotion and marketing, so their instruments are available in many

Artie Traum playing a Washburn dreadnought. *Photo by Larry Sandberg.*

cities throughout the U.S. Unfortunately, they were unwilling or unable to get a copy of their price list to us by press time, so you'll have to check prices at your music store. Generally speaking, price and quality go up as the model number rises within each category. In the higher *list* price ranges, Washburns begin to compete with American-made guitars of better reputation and possibly better quality, so I'd suggest careful comparison shopping. Take a look at dealer discounts and also at what used instruments are available in that price range.

The people at Washburn also distribute Oscar Schmidt International. The Schmidt name was once associated solely with autoharps, but is now also used for school play and rhythm instruments and a small line of inexpensive, low-quality guitars.

Models

Note that the DC-series guitars have a special extended cutaway. In this design, which Washburn calls the "Stephen's Cutaway" after its inventor Stephen Davies, a deeply recessed heel block allows the cutaway to permit easier access to the very highest frets than standard cutaways do.

Most acoustic Washburns have solid quartersawn tops and laminate backs and sides. As noted, the more expensive models have solid tops; the tops on the lowest price instruments are presumably laminate.

Model	Size/Shape	Top	Back/Sides	Neck	Fingerboard/Bridge	Ornamentation/Bracing/Remarks
D12, D12CE	dreadnought	spruce	mahogany	mahogany	rosewood	CE version has cutaway and built-in pickup
D21, D21E	dreadnought	solid spruce	rosewood	mahogany	rosewood fingerboard	scalloped bracing; E version has built-in pickup
D25	dreadnought	solid spruce	ovangkol	five-piece mahogany and rosewood laminate	rosewood	scalloped bracing
D30	dreadnought	solid cedar	bird's-eye maple	mahogany	rosewood	walnut binding; shaved bracing
D61	dreadnought	solid Alaskan spruce	bookmatched solid rosewood	mahogany	rosewood	rosewood pickguard, maple binding; shaved bracing
D68 Harvest	dreadnought	solid Alaskan spruce	bookmatched solid Indian rosewood	five-piece mahogany and rosewood laminate	rosewood fingerboard; ebony bridge	rosewood pickguard, hand-rubbed finish; hand-shaved bracing
DC60, DC6012, DC60E Lexington	dreadnought with extended cutaway	solid spruce	ovangkol	mahogany	rosewood	D6012 has 12 strings, D60E has built-in pickup.
DC80 Charleston	dreadnought with extended cutaway	solid cedar	rosewood	mahagony	rosewood	
EA-series	grand concert cutaway with built-in pickup and equalizer	spruce				Available at several price levels with mahogany or maple bodies and different levels of finish and fittings.

Yamaha

Yamaha Corporation of America
6600 Orangethorpe Ave., Buena Park, CA 90620

Background

Yamaha is probably the largest of the Asian importers (its products don't necessarily all come from Japan). Countless students have learned to play on the cheaper models, while many working musicians have found the APX and solid-top FG models suitable for professional use. Yamahas are easy to find and mostly have a pleasing, somewhat throaty tone that is helped along by using phosphor bronze strings.

I'd recommend Yamahas without reservation as student guitars except that their fingerboards (except in the APX series) are a bit narrower than some people find comfortable. The problem is exacerbated because Yamaha likes to cut their nut grooves rather far in from the edges of the fingerboard. Many Yamaha owners find that their instruments become more comfortable after they have a repairperson cut a new nut—a cheap, easy job.

Models

Body woods are laminate unless otherwise specified. The shallow-bodied APX electro-acoustic models are available in a variety of colored finishes. Select models are available left-handed.

Yamaha calls its FG-series guitars "jumbos," but their broad-waisted shape makes them more like small dreadnoughts. The following representative selection omits a few in-between FG models that are distinguished by small differences in woods, fittings, and price.

Yamaha's ambiguous sales information implies laminate tops on the less expensive models and solid quartersawn tops on the better models, with laminate bodies throughout both ranges.

Model	Size/Shape	Top	Back/Sides	Neck	Fingerboard/Bridge	Ornamentation/Bracing	Price
APX 6 built-in pickup, preamp, equalizer	auditorium; scale 25.6, nut width 1.7	spruce	agathis	nato	rosewood		$669
APX 10 built-in stereo pickup, preamp, equalizer	auditorium; scale 25.6, nut width 1.7	spruce	sycamore	African mahogany	ebony	scalloped bracing	$1299
APX 20 built-in stereo pickup, preamp, equalizer	auditorium; scale 25.6, nut width 1.7	spruce	sycamore	African mahogany	ebony	abalone purfling, abalone and mother-of-pearl; scalloped bracing; bone nut and saddle	$1499
APX 9-12 built-in stereo pickup, preamp, equalizer	12-string auditorium; scale 25.1, nut width 1.8	spruce	agathis	African mahogany	rosewood		$1049
FG-450SA	dreadnought	solid spruce	ovangkol	nato	rosewood	scalloped bracing	$489
FG-400A	dreadnought	spruce	nato	nato	bubinga fingerboard		$259
FG-410A, FG-410-12A, FG-410-EA	dreadnought 12A is 12-string; EA has built-in pickup	spruce	nato	nato	bubinga fingerboard; nato bridge		$319, $349, $499
FG-420A, FG-420-12A	dreadnought 12A is 12-string	spruce	nato	nato	bubinga fingerboard; rosewood bridge		$359, $389
FG-460SA, FG-460S-12A	dreadnought 12A is 12-string	solid spruce	Indian rosewood	nato	rosewood	scalloped bracing	$539, $569
FG-470SA	dreadnought	select solid spruce	Indian rosewood	nato	rosewood	scalloped bracing	$619
FJ-645A	jumbo	spruce	nato	nato	Indian rosewood	reddish-brown sunburst top	$519
FS-310	grand concert	spruce	nato	nato	bubinga fingerboard; nato bridge		$309

A Luthiers' Gallery

Hardly anyone was building steel-string guitars by hand 25 years ago. Now there are dozens of luthiers who even manage to make a living at it. (Or almost a living—a good many also do an extensive business in repair as well as building.)

Some makers charge more and some less, but generally speaking you can expect to pay between two and four thousand dollars for a hand-made instrument. Why buy one? (You probably shouldn't if you have to ask!) But here are some reasons, for better or worse, that you might have:

- You're an experienced player and you've wished for years to have a certain neck shape or cutaway or cosmetic feature that's not available ready-made.
- You may think, and justly so, that your luthier's guitars are just plain better-sounding than factory guitars, or that they have exactly the sound you want.
- You're an amateur guitarist and guitar fan, you care about guitars, you play well enough to justify having a good instrument (or maybe not), you make good money, the kids are out of school, the car only has 10,000 miles on it, and this time you're going to damn well treat yourself for a change.
- You're convinced that the value of your luthier's instrument will increase over the years at a rate significantly exceeding the rate of inflation. (A lousy reason and probably a bad bet.)

The following sampling of luthiers is intended to give you an idea of what's out there. Please don't interpret anyone's presence (or absence) as a sign of approval or disapproval. (The only luthiers listed here whose current work I know and recommend firsthand are Harry Fleishman, Franklin Guitars, and D. W. Stevens; I know of everyone else's work only at second hand.) This chapter is necessarily limited only to those luthiers from whom I was able to obtain usuable information in time for my deadline, so a few well-reputed names do not appear here (for example, Danny Ferrington, Bozo Podunavac, and John Zeidler). Other respected luthiers are not listed here because at this writing they are not active in guitar making (for example, Max Krimmel, Mark Whitebook, David Russell Young), because they are primarily classical makers (for example, Gila Eban), or because of my own simple ignorance. In any case, the size of this section had to be kept manageable and we had to stop *somewhere*. Including both full-time makers and repairpersons who make an occasional instrument, there are several hundred luthiers now in business in North America.

Please also note that many of the luthiers listed here also make classical guitars or other instruments. Since those instruments are outside of the scope of this book, I haven't necessarily indicated their other activities or products.

Almost all luthiers are prepared to work with you in developing an instrument to suit your needs and style. You don't always have to know exactly what you want in the way of size, shape, and materials, since often a good luthier can make valuable suggestions based on an analysis of your playing style and musical taste. Sometimes you'll find a luthier who has a ready-made guitar for sale. If you're a bit leery about laying out a hefty down payment for an instrument that doesn't even exist yet, this is definitely the way to go. But at this point many luthiers are well-established in their own parts of the world. Through a track record that may include dozens or hundreds of instruments, they have earned the trust of local musicians who are eager to commission from them the guitar of their dreams.

Although many luthiers have supplied me with specs for their standard models, please note that these are only starting points. The whole point of going to a luthier is to have an instrument custom-made to your own tastes and specifications. You should be prepared to pay an additional fee for any custom features which require additional time, effort, or materials.

A few makers have achieved national reputations. But one of the things I like best about the current guitarmaking scene is that a good many luthiers seem able to get by simply by serving the musicians of their own community.

There are two national organizations for luthiers:

Association of String Instrument Artisans (ASIA)
    14 S. Broad St., Nazareth, PA 18064
Guild of American Luthiers (GAL)
    8222 S. Park Ave., Tacoma, WA 98408

Another source of information, though no longer up to date, is Susan C. Farrell's *Directory of Contemporary Instrument Makers*, University of Missouri Press, 1981. As we go to press, the following publication has been announced: *1991 Directory of North American Luthiers and Repair Shops*, A. B. Thel Publishing, 142-E2 Hilltop Drive, Sequim, WA 98382.

Andersen Stringed Instruments

503 N. 36th, Seattle, WA 98103

Steven Andersen builds a variety of instruments including about 10 acoustic guitars yearly. He has been in business since 1980. He builds custom instruments to suit client's needs. Also offered standard are dreadnought and auditorium-size models with 25^{11}/$_{32}$-inch scale, 1^{11}/$_{16}$-inch nut width, Engelmann spruce top, Brazilian rosewood back and sides, and scalloped bracing. Price is $2500.

Blue Lion (Robert and Janita Baker)

4665 Parkhill Rd., Santa Margarita, CA 93453

Blue Lion has mostly made dulcimers since 1975, but owners Robert and Janita Baker also produce six to eight acoustic guitars each year. Their model B1 Standard is a jumboish instrument of quartersawn woods with 25-inch scale and scalloped bracing. A variety of woods, inlays, and other custom features including pickup are available, and no two instruments are exactly alike. Prices begin at $1650 including case.

Cimarron Guitars (John Walsh)

566 Sherman, Box 254, Ridgway, CO 81432
Available from the maker and selected dealers

About 24 Cimarron Guitars are made each year by luthier John Walsh. Standard models are listed below; cutaways, electro-acoustics, and other custom configurations are also available. Cimarron guitars have scalloped or plain X-braces, adjustable tension rods, multipiece mahogany or maple necks, and are standard with ebony fingerboards and Sitka spruce tops. (Other woods are available on order, as are various ornamentation details.)

Prices for all models include hard case and are based on standard body woods: $1700 for Honduras mahogany, $1800 for American black walnut or northern hard maple, or $2000 for East Indian rosewood. The standard models are the jumbo New Tradition, dreadnought Silver Chord, and approximately-auditorium-sized Spanish Steel String.

Blue Lion's spruce-topped cutaway model. *Photo courtesy Blue Lion Instruments.*

Jeffrey R. Elliott

2812 SE 37th Ave., Portland, OR 97202

Elliott, established since 1966, makes six to eight classical and steel-string guitars a year, including 12-string, 7-string, harp guitars, and so on. His clients have included Leo Kottke, Ralph Towner, and Julian Bream.

Elliott's basic model is somewhat like a classical guitar in shape and feel, with a $25^{19}/_{32}$-inch scale and a nut width of $1\frac{7}{8}$ inch or less. Various quartersawn top and body woods are available, the Honduras mahogany neck has a nonadjustable aircraft aluminum reinforcing rod, and the bracing is a proprietary hybrid of fan- and X-patterns. Ornamentation and other features (cutaway, pickup, etc.) are customized. Prices begin at $4000, and instruments are warranted for the duration of the maker's career.

Evergreen Mountain Instruments (Jerry Nolte)

Rt. 1, Box 268-A, Cove, OR 97824

Luthier Jerry Nolte, in business since 1972, produces about a dozen Evergreen Mountain guitars each year. Among the standard features of his instruments are scalloped bracing, arched backs, cedar tops (spruce on request), 3-piece Honduras mahogany necks with adjustable truss rod, rosewood fingerboard and bridge, and hand-rubbed violin-varnish. Built-in pickup and other features of inlay, material, and design are available on special order. Nolte lists maple, koa, and cherry among body woods, but he favors American black walnut. All woods are quartersawn. He guarantees his instruments' materials and workmanship for the duration of his career. Price includes hard case.

Model	Size/Shape	Scale	Nut width	Price/remarks
New York	12-fret	24¼	1¹¹⁄₁₆	$700; based on early Washburn, smaller than concert size with total length of 35½ inches
Concert	12-fret auditorium-size (6- or 12-string)	25¼		$800
Auditorium	rounded dreadnought (6- or 12-string)	25¼	1¹¹⁄₁₆	$800
Studio	grand concert	25¼	1¹¹⁄₁₆	$700; tenor guitar model also available

Fleishman Instruments

c/o Starrett, 3500 Clay St., Denver, CO 80211

Harry Fleishman has been making guitars since 1975. Although his reputation is based most strongly on his electric guitars and basses, he also makes a small number of acoustic guitars yearly. Work is entirely custom, using quartersawn woods and an original variation of the X-bracing system. He works in a variety of woods, but especially likes mahogany bodies. Prices begin at $2500.

Franklin Guitar Co. (Nick Kukich)

604 Alaskan Way, Seattle, WA 98104

Luthier Nick Kukich has been in business as the Franklin Guitar Company since 1976. He builds about 36 instruments a year with the assistance of inlay cutter and finisher Jeanne Munro. Stefan Grossman, Larry Coryell, John Renbourn, and Chris Procter are among the guitarists who have performed or recorded with Franklin instruments. In addition to the models listed below, a copy of a thirties 12-string Stella (the instrument played by Leadbelly) is in the planning stage as we go to press.

Kukich uses Engelmann spruce tops from trees personally selected, milled, and aged. Top, body, and neck woods are quartersawn. Instruments are built with a modified X-brace, adjustable truss rod, and slightly arched fingerboard, and carry a limited lifetime warranty. Nut widths on all models are configured to customers' specifications. Cutaway, lefthanded, and custom features are available at extra cost.

Stephan Grossman performs with his Franklin OM model. *Photo by Larry Sandberg.*

Model	Size/Shape; Scale	Top	Back/ Sides	Neck	Fingerboard/ Bridge	Ornamentation	Price
OM 1, Jumbo 1	auditorium, jumbo; 25½	Engelmann spruce	koa	Honduras mahogany	ebony	herringbone purfling	$1450, $1500
OM 2, Jumbo 2	auditorium, jumbo; 25½	Engelmann spruce	East Indian rosewood	Honduras mahogany	ebony	herringbone purfling	$1600, $1650
OM 3, Jumbo 3, 3AA[a]	auditorium, jumbo; 25½	Engelmann spruce	Brazilian rosewood	Honduras mahogany	ebony	herringbone purfling	$2000, $2050
OM 5, Jumbo 5	auditorium, jumbo; 25½	Engelmann spruce	select Brazilian rosewood	Honduras mahogany	ebony	abalone binding, other inlay	$3000, $3050

[a] 3AA has bound, abalone-inlaid fingerboard and headstock and other ornamentation; add $500.

Klein Custom Guitars

2560 Knob Hill Rd., Sonoma, CA 95476
Available from the maker or selected dealers

Steve Klein builds about 10 acoustic instruments each year. He founded his company in 1972, four years after beginning as a luthier. Klein is highly regarded by his peers for his innovative designs, which include unusual body proportions, a slip-in bolted neck, Kasha-influenced bridges, and a proprietary bracing design consisting of a "flying" (elevated) main brace with radial ancillary struts. Much of his work is custom (he likes to call himself a "guitar tailor"), but his standard designs (using quartersawn woods) include Sitka tops, walnut or rosewood backs and sides, rosewood necks (with fingerboards in rosewood or ebony), adjustable graphite truss rod, and 25½-inch scale 14-fret fingerboards. Cutaways, 12-string, fancy ornamentation, and other custom features are available. Prices begin at $3750. Joni Mitchell, J. D. Souther, and Joe Walsh have recorded with Klein guitars.

Walter Lipton Guitars

Orford, NH 03777

Walter Lipton makes 10 or fewer instruments a year, including both classical and steel-string models, with prices starting at $2250. They are custom made to suit customer's needs, but one model is a fingerpicking guitar similar to the current Martin jumbo M style. Woods aged 10 to 20 years are used, and engraved pearl is a specialty. According to Lipton, his guitars "take up where Martin left off about 1935." Aged woods and engraved mother-of-pearl inlays are also a specialty.

Lipton also runs the Euphonon Co., a supply house which sells fretted instrument parts, strings, tools, and woods.

Lost Mountain Editions, Ltd. (Richard Schneider)

754 Lost Mountain Rd., Sequim, WA 98382

Richard Schneider has been a guitar maker since 1964, and has worked closely with acoustical theorist Michael Kasha since 1967. He is the leading exponent of Kasha-inspired soundboard design and an innovator in his own right (recent Schneider instruments have included such unusual features as backs made of spruce and braced similarly to top bracing). His instruments are reported to have an extrememely powerful, evenly balanced sound.

Schneider makes about four acoustic guitars each year. His steel-string models use quartersawn woods and a non-adjustable truss rod. Cutaway, built-in pickup, and 12-fret neck are available. Price includes Mark Leaf fiberglass case.

Model/Size/ Shape	Scale/ Nut width	Top	Back/ Sides	Neck	Fingerboard/ Bridge	Ornamentation/ Bracing	Price
Concert-SS Recording Guitar[a]	25.63 1.68	Sitka spruce	Sitka spruce back; Brazilian rosewood sides	Honduras mahogany	ebony fingerboard; maple, ebony, and fiber laminate bridge	dyed maple bindings and purfling; Kasha-principle top bracing; proprietary "Floating Double-X" back bracing	$7500 to $10,000

[a]This guitar is uniquely shaped, with angular shoulders, 40-inch length, and 14 13/16-inch lower bout. Also available as 12-fret model.

Manzer Guitars

Box 924, Station P, Toronto, Ontario, Canada M5S 2Z2

Linda Manzer has been an independent luthier since 1978, having apprenticed with Jean Larrivée and archtop guitar maker James D'Aquisto. She builds about 20 acoustic guitars a year, including archtop and classical instruments. Much of her time is spent on custom work including exotic, unique, and sculptural designs. Pat Metheny, Bruce Cockburn, Angél Parra, and Liona Boyd are among the players for whom she has executed commissions.

The standard models listed below use quartersawn woods, standard X-bracing, and nonadjustable reinforcing rods. Cutaway and 12-string configurations and built-in electronics are available at additional cost.

Model/ Size	Scale/ Nut width	Top	Back/ Sides	Neck	Fingerboard/ Bridge	Ornamentation	Price
Standard Steel-String auditorium	25½ 1¹¹⁄₁₆ or to spec	German spruce or cedar	Indian rosewood	South American mahogany	ebony	abalone rosette; other inlay	$2400
Cowpoke dreadnought size; classical shape	25½ 1¹¹⁄₁₆ or to spec	German spruce or cedar	Indian rosewood	South American mahogany	ebony	abalone rosette; other inlay	$2400
Midsize ("The Squirt") ⅔-size guitar	17 1¾ or to spec	cedar	Indian rosewood	South American mahogany	ebony	abalone rosette	$2000

MJH Guitars (Michael Jacobson-Hardy)

21 Garfield St., Florence, MA 01060

Michael Jacobson-Hardy, a luthier since 1976, makes about 10 acoustic guitars a year, including his standard jumbo rosewood cutaway model as well as custom instruments.

Monteleone Instruments

Box 52, Islip, NY 11751

John Monteleone has been making instruments professionally since 1973. He now makes about 20 acoustic guitars each year. His strong reputation is based primarily on his archtop carving (f-hole guitars and mandolin-family instruments), but he also offers the following flattop models.

All instruments include an adjustable tension rod, and custom inlay, cutaways, woods, and other features are available at additional cost.

Model/ Size	Scale/ Nut width	Top	Back/ Sides	Neck	Fingerboard/ Bridge	Ornamen- tation/Bracing	Price
Hot Club Model F[a]	25¼ 1¾	German or Alaskan spruce	Indian rosewood	mahogany	ebony	simply, classic- ally appointed with ivoroid binding and rosewood soundhole edging; asym- metric bracing with large ellipti- cal soundhole	$2900
Hot Club Model A[b]	25¼ 1¾	German or Alaskan spruce	curly maple	curly maple	ebony		$4900
Dreadnought	25¼ 1¾	German or Alaskan spruce	Indian rosewood	mahogany	ebony	asymmetrical X-brace	$2900
Hexaphone jumbo; ellipti- cal soundhole	25¼ 1¾	German or Alaskan spruce	Indian rosewood	mahogany	ebony		$3000

[a]Cutaway Maccaferri-style guitar, about auditorium size. [b]Cutaway archtop, f-hole adaptation of Maccaferri-style guitar, about auditorium size but only 3⅜ inches deep.

Instruments are warranteed for life to the original owner against defective materials and workmanship.

Petillo Masterpiece Guitars (Phillip Petillo)

1206 Herbert Ave., Ocean, NJ 07712.
Available from the maker or selected dealers

Phillip Petillo, a luthier since 1967, makes about a dozen acoustic guitars a year. Most of his work is customized to the customer's specs, and he works with both traditional and unconventional sizes and shapes, as well as individualized inlay designs, in a wide variety of quartersawn woods. Prices start at $1200.

Shanti Guitars (Michael Hornick)

Box 341, Avery, CA 95224
Available through select dealers or from the luthier

Luthier Michael Hornick has been established as Shanti Guitars since 1986, and makes 12 to 20 instruments a year. His standard models are listed below but custom features, including cutaways and elegant inlay work, are also available. Standard features include adjustable tension rod, a mother-of-pearl dove headstock inlay, snowflake inlay position markers, ivory or bone nut and saddle, and chrome Schaller tuners. Price includes hard-shell case. 12-string configuration, extra inlay, and some wood choices listed below are available as options above base price.

Shanti body shapes and sizes are slightly unusual, so the size/shape configurations below are approximate analogies only.

Model/ Size	Scale/ Nut width	Top	Back/ Sides	Neck	Fingerboard/ Bridge	Ornamentation/ Bracing	Price
D Shanti Dreadnought	25.4 1¹¹⁄₁₆ to 1¹³⁄₁₆	quartersawn Sitka, German, or Engelmann spruce	quartersawn Brazilian or Indian rosewood or koa	mahogany	ebony	choice of abalone or herringbone, etc., and other inlay; plain or scalloped bracing to spec	$1500
F Jazz Style jumbo	24¾ 1¹¹⁄₁₆ to 1¹³⁄₁₆	quartersawn Sitka or German spruce	quartersawn or slab-cut Indian or Brazilian rosewood or koa	quartersawn mahogany	ebony	inlay work	$1900
JS Jumbo	25.4 1¹¹⁄₁₆ to 1¾	quartersawn Sitka spruce	quartersawn or slab-cut Indian or Brazilian rosewood or koa	quartersawn mahogany	ebony	inlay work	$1825
SC Shanti Concert auditorium	24¾ 1¹¹⁄₁₆ to 1¾	quartersawn Sitka spruce	quartersawn or slab-cut Indian or Brazilian rosewood or koa	quartersawn mahogany	ebony	inlay workplain or scalloped bracing to spec	$1750
SL Shanti Lucas deep grand concert	25.4 1¹¹⁄₁₆ to 1¹³⁄₁₆	quartersawn Sitka spruce	quartersawn or slab-cut Indian or Brazilian rosewood or koa	quartersawn mahogany	ebony	body is based on 1920s Nick Lucas style	$1725
TD Telluride Dreadnought[a]	25.4 1¹¹⁄₁₆	quartersawn Sitka spruce	quartersawn Indian rosewood	quartersawn mahogany	ebony	herringbone purfling, other inlay; scalloped bracing	$1500

[a]Designed especially for bluegrass flatpicking.

Stefan Sobell Musical Instruments

The Old School, Whitley Chapel, Hexamshire, Northumberland, England NE47 0HB

U. S. distributor: Simpson Guitar Services, Box 4326, Ithaca, NY 14852. Available from selected dealers. One North American mail order source is Elderly Instruments, 1100 N. Washington, Box 14210, Lansing, MI 48901.

Stefan Sobell was the early-seventies pioneer of an instrument which resembles an oversized, long-necked mandolin. He called it a cittern (an ancient name for similar medieval and renaissance instruments), and it became a standard of the British/Celtic folk revival. Many leading British Isles musicians, including Andy Irvine, Phil Cunningham, John Renbourn, and Gerald Trimble, play Sobell mandolin-family instruments.

Sobell started making guitars in the early eighties, and now produces about 25 round-hole flattop and archtop models each year. In addition

Martin Simpson with a Stephen Sobell guitar. *Photo courtesy Martin Simpson.*

to the standard models listed below, custom and lefthanded instruments and custom materials and features are also available. Archtop models are made with a brass tailpiece. Built-in Lloyd Baggs pickups and Keir preamps/equalizers are available at additional cost. Standard bindings, position markers, and other fittings are simple and elegant. Prices, which include shipping, insurance, and a hard case, are based on January 1990 exchange rates.

The following features are standard on all 6-string models. Woods are quartersawn. Top is European spruce or western red cedar, with Indian rosewood back and sides. An ebony fingerboard is set in a Brazilian rosewood neck with an adjustable truss rod. Martin-style X-bracing, which may be scalloped if the buyer desires, is standard, along with herringbone purfling.

Model	Size/Shape	Scale	Nut width	Price
Flattop Models 1, 1A	auditorium with wide lower bout; 1A has higher waist (therefore more area to lower bout) than Model 1	25.6	1.73	$1850, $1900
Flattop Models 2, 2A	12-fret jumbo; 2A is 14-fret with higher waist (therefore more area to lower bout) than Model 2	25.6	1.73	$1950, $2000
Flattop Model 3	16-fret guitar with shortened upper bout and 16-inch lower bout	25.6	1.73	$1850
Flattop Model 4 ("Double-decker")	12-fret dreadnought; Nicknamed "Double-decker" because of un-usually deep (5.3-inch) body	25.6	1.73	$2050
6-String Archtop[a]	archtop auditorium with wide lower bout	25.6	1.73	$2000
12-String Archtop[a]	12-string, 12-fret archtop jumbo	25.3	1.85	$2150

[a]Top wood on archtops is offered in European spruce only.

D. W. Stevens

Box 442, Golden, CO 80402

Dennis W. Stevens has made flattop and archtop guitars and mandolins since 1965. He produces eight to 12 guitars annually. Variations, personalized instruments, and custom features (neck width, cosmetic options, etc.) are available in addition to the basic models below. In Stevens's model designations, the initial letter refers to wood and trim specs and the subsequent number to size and shape (the opposite of the more usual Martin-derived designation systems).

Cutaways are offered on many models for an additional $200. Adjustable truss rods are standard. Workmanship and materials are warranteed for the duration of the maker's career.

In addition to the instruments listed below, Stevens offers a U-series priced from $2100–4200, using high-quality woods and offering variable options without requiring a custom order.

Model/ Size	Scale/ Nut width	Top	Back/ Sides	Neck	Fingerboard/ Bridge	Price
M-40 auditorium (with wider lower bout)	25½ 1¹¹⁄₁₆	Sitka spruce	Honduras or African mahogany	Honduras mahogany	ebony	$1075
M-44 dreadnought	25½ 1¹¹⁄₁₆	Sitka spruce	Honduras or African mahogany	Honduras mahogany	ebony	$1075
N-44 dreadnought	25½ 1¹¹⁄₁₆	Sitka spruce	Honduras mahogany	Honduras mahogany	rosewood	$950
J-50 jumbo	25½ 1¹¹⁄₁₆	Sitka spruce	East Indian rosewood or koa	Honduras mahogany laminate	ebony	$1475
J-44 dreadnought	25½ 1¹¹⁄₁₆	Sitka spruce	East Indian rosewood or koa	Honduras mahogany laminate	ebony	$1450
J-40 auditorium (with wider lower bout)	25½ 1¹¹⁄₁₆	Sitka spruce	East Indian rosewood or koa	Honduras mahogany laminate	ebony	$1450
J-30 rounded grand auditorium	24¾ 1¹¹⁄₁₆	Sitka spruce	East Indian rosewood or koa	Honduras mahogany laminate	ebony	$1450
A-40 auditorium (with wider lower bout)	25½ 1¹¹⁄₁₆	Sitka spruce	East Indian rosewood or curly maple	Honduras mahogany with darker center strip	ebony	$1750
A-44 dreadnought	25½ 1¹¹⁄₁₆	Sitka spruce	East Indian rosewood or curly maple	Honduras mahogany with darker center strip	ebony	$1750
A-50 jumbo	25½ 1¹¹⁄₁₆	Sitka spruce	East Indian rosewood or curly maple	Honduras mahogany with darker center strip	ebony	$1775
A-30 rounded grand concert	24¾ 1¹¹⁄₁₆	Sitka spruce	East Indian rosewood or curly maple	Honduras mahogany with darker center strip	ebony	$1750

Timeless Instruments (David Freeman)

Box 51, Tugaske, Saskatchewan S0H 4B0, Canada

Timeless guitars are made by luthier David Freeman, who has been in business making stringed instruments since 1980, and turns out about a dozen guitars a year.

Like most luthiers, Freeman offers several standard models with a variety of options, including 12-string, cutaway, choice of peghead and position marker inlays, built-in electronics, and fretwire width. Scale length on most models is optional from 24½ to 25⅝, and fingerboard width may be varied from the 1¹¹⁄₁₆-inch standard. All instruments have an adjustable truss rod, scalloped X-bracing, and are made of solid quartersawn woods. Woods and features different from those listed are available, and include options of maple, padauk, walnut, and cocobolo. Finished instruments are often available for sale without custom order. Prices are for basic models without custom options.

Model	Size/ Shape	Top	Back/ Sides	Neck	Fingerboard/ Bridge	Price
GM-03	dreadnought	Sitka spruce or western red cedar	East Indian rosewood or mahogany	mahogany or maple	rosewood or ebony	$1395
Monarch	auditorium	Sitka spruce or western red cedar	East Indian rosewood or mahogany	mahogany or maple	rosewood or ebony	$1395
TI-27	concert	Sitka spruce or western red cedar	mahogany (rosewood available)	mahogany	rosewood or ebony	$1295

Intrepid model guitar by Mark Wescott. *Photo by Mario Romo, courtesy Mark Wescott.*

Mark Wescott

301 W. New York Ave., Somers Point, NJ 08244

Originally trained as a cabinetmaker, Mark Wescott began to study guitarmaking in 1980 and has been in business as a guitar maker since 1987. He makes about five acoustic guitars yearly, all influenced by the Kasha soundboard design and Wescott's work with luthier Richard Schneider.

Each instrument is unique and modified to the client's needs. However, the basic design and materials for Wescott's Intrepid model are as follow. Woods are quartersawn and a non-adjustable graphite/carbon fiber reinforcing rod is used. Instruments are warranteed for two years. Price includes hard case.

Model/ Size	Scale/ Nut width	Top	Back/ Sides	Neck	Fingerboard/ Bridge	Ornamentation/ Bracing	Price
Intrepid K-S-X-I[a]	25¾ 1¾	Sitka spruce	Indian rosewood	Honduras mahogany	ebony fingerboard; maple laminate bridge	dyed wood purfling and binding; Kasha-principle bracing with off-center soundhole	$10,000

[a]This has a unique shape roughly between a narrow-waisted dreadnought and an auditorium model.

Glossary of Terms

When a word used in a definition also appears as a glossary item on its own, it is printed in bold type.

Acoustic. Term used to describe nonelectric guitars, or music that is basically nonelectric. An **acoustic-electric, semi-acoustic,** or **electro-acoustic** guitar has built-in electronics intended to make it sound more like a miked acoustic guitar than an electric guitar. See also **Electro-acoustic.**

Acoustic-electric. See **Acoustic.**

Action. Ease of playing as a function of the height of the strings above the fingerboard (see **Setup**). While this may be measured objectively, the player's perception of action is also affected by strings, scale length, and the condition of the frets.

Archtop. A guitar with a wood top arched by carving or pressing, usually thicker than the top of a flattop guitar, and with cello-like f-holes rather than a round soundhole. In f-hole models and some roundholes, the back is usually likewise arched. F-hole guitars are the typical choice of mainstream jazz guitarists. Roundhole archtops, which often had a dark, wooly sound, went out of fashion after Gibson introduced the f-hole model in the twenties. However, lighter-sounding models are now being made by some contemporary luthiers and factories.

Arpeggio. A chord played one note at a time, usually with a rippling sound (Italian for "harp-like," more or less).

Backbow. See **Warp.**

Balance. The relative volume, tonal strength, and sustain of the high and low strings of the guitar. (Beginners often perceive well-balanced guitars as not having a loud enough bass. So do some experienced players.) Also, the distribution of the guitar's weight.

Barrel. See **Peg.**

Bars. Properly speaking, the smaller or secondary struts that make up the top's bracing system, and the braces used on the guitar's back. Most people don't usually make this fine distinction and loosely call them braces anyway, as in "back-braces." See also **Tone bars.**

Bass. The lowest range of notes. Also used to refer to the lowest three strings of the guitar, and short for string bass or bass guitar.

Bass Guitar. (1). Instrument with an oversize acoustic guitar-like body and long 4-string neck, tuned like a bass fiddle. (2). Another name for electric bass. (3). Obsolete name for a 7- to 10-string guitar, where the extra strings are bass strings.

Belly. The area of the top in back of the bridge (toward the endpin), or a bulge in this area caused by string tension on the bridge.

Belly bridge. The standard guitar pin bridge shape, so called because it's basically rectangular with a curved-out portion (belly) along one side.

Bend. To push or pull a string with a finger of the fretting hand along the fingerboard parallel to the frets, in order to alter the pitch for a sliding or bluesy effect.

Binding. Strips of plastic, wood, or nitrocellulose added at the edges of the back and top where they join the sides; sometimes also at the edges of the fingerboard. See also **Marquetry** and **Purfling**.

Blank. A roughly shaped piece of wood, for example for a neck, prior to the final fine shaping and carving and finishing. In fine guitars, the neck blanks are machine-cut but the final shaping is done by hand.

Bookmatched. Term applied to sections of a single piece of wood that has been cut in half down the narrow dimension and then opened out like a book. The resulting symmetrical structure looks good and, more important, minimizes the possibility of cracking. Sides and back of fine guitars are bookmatched. In less expensive laminate guitars, bookmatching the top layer of laminate is cosmetic only, and adds nothing to the instrument's durability.

Bottleneck. See **Slide.**

Bottom block. Another term for **end block.**

Bouts. The upper or lower parts of the guitar's body, separated by the **waist.** (Sometimes affectionately called the bust and hips).

Bow. See **Warp.**

Bracing. The pattern of struts underneath the top of a guitar, which has both acoustical and reinforcing functions. Bracing patterns, explained at greater length in the text, include the **x-bracing** typical of flattop guitars and **fan-bracing** typical of classical guitars.

Brazilian. In casual talk, short for Brazilian rosewood or for a guitar (usually a pre-1969 Martin) with Brazilian rosewood back and sides.

Bridge. The wooden structure, mounted on the soundboard, that holds the strings.

Bridge plate. A flat piece of wood, preferably maple or rosewood, glued for structural support to the underside of the top, beneath the bridge.

Buzz. The sound a string makes when it vibrates against a fret further up the fingerboard than the fret against which it is being depressed. Usually the result of neck **warp** or poorly adjusted action or relief. Often also used loosely for any rattle or foreign sound, for example from a loose brace or tuner.

Carved-top. Another term for **Archtop.**

Center seam. The point at which the two halves of the top or back are joined.

Channel rod. One type of **reinforcing rod,** consisting of a U-shaped or hollow rectangular metal bar. An adjustable truss rod may be run through the inside of the channel rod.

Checking. Small cracks in the finish of the guitar, caused by the different coefficients of expansion of the finish and of the wood itself when the instrument is subjected to sudden or extreme temperature change. (In the wood industry, checking refers to hairline cracks in milled lumber caused by improper kilning.)

Compensated saddle. See **Saddle.**

Cleat. Another term for **stud.**

Clubby. Used to describe the feel of a thick, roundly contoured cut (club-like) guitar neck.

Course. A close-together set of one to three strings that are fretted and plucked as a unit; for example, a pair of strings on a 12-string guitar.

Crazing. The pattern caused by **checking**.

Cross-bracing. A term to avoid, since some people use it to mean **x-bracing** and others to mean **transverse bracing**.

Crown. The top visible portion of the fret. **Crowning** is dressing the tops of the frets with file and emery paper to ensure good tone and smoothness of playing.

Cutaway. Area of the upper bout cut away in a crescent-shaped indentation in order to make the upper frets accessible. A pointy-shaped cutaway is called Florentine; one with a smoothly curved horn is called Venetian.

DI. Pronounced *dee-eye:* see **Direct input.**

Diamond. Another term for **handstop**, because the classic Martin-design hand-stops are carved into a diamond shape. Also sometimes used for **stud** (because most luthiers cut studs in a diamond shape), as well as for the diamond-shaped position markers used on older Martins, and widely imitated by other makers.

Direct input. The technique of running a guitar's pickups directly into the mixing console of a sound system or recording studio, without the intermediary stage of an individual guitar amplifier and speaker. (However, preamps and various equalization and other sound-processing devices are frequently used in the signal path.)

Dobro. Although a trademark for resophonic guitars made by the Original Musical Instrument Company (OMI), "dobro" has become a generic word for any resophonic guitar played Hawaiian style.

Dots. See **Position dots.**

Dreadnought. Name for a large-bodied, narrow-waisted guitar shape developed by Martin in the 1930s, which is now the common shape in the industry.

Dressing. Smoothing and shaping the frets with file or emery paper.

Edge binding. See **Binding.**

Electro-acoustic. This is becoming the standard term to describe a shallow-bodied cutaway guitar with built-in electronics. However, usage is not entirely consistent within the industry. See **Acoustic.**

End block. A block of hardwood placed inside the guitar body at the tail end, to provide a reinforcement for the sides where they join, and to provide an anchor point for the pin that holds the guitar strap.

End joint. An ornamental strip of wood or other binding material joining the two side pieces where they meet over the end block. Not on all guitars; some just have a simple seam.

Endpin. A pin seated in a hole at the lower end of the guitar, for the purpose of attaching a strap.

Equalizer. Short for **parametric equalizer:** an electronic sound-processing device that boosts or suppresses selected frequencies.

F-hole. The soundhole shape of violin-family instruments and most archtop guitars, formed like an old-fashioned script letter f. On some guitars, the holes are shaped with an Art Deco flow to them, more like an elongated teardrop. Also short for a guitar with f-holes. See **Archtop.**

Fan-bracing. A bracing pattern typically found on classical guitars. The pattern of the braces closely resembles the supporting structure of a fan.

Fast neck. A neck with any or all of these qualities: thin contour, low action, or extra-wide frets. More typical of jazz and electric than acoustic guitar necks. "Fast" isn't necessarily better; it's a matter of personal preference.

Figure. The visual design formed by the grain pattern in a piece of wood.

Fingerboard. The strip of wood along the top of the neck in which the frets are seated. Also called the **Fretboard.**

Fingerpicks. Metal or plastic picks that are worn on the thumb and fingers of the picking hand.

Fingerpicking, Finger-style. Any style of playing the guitar in which the strings are plucked by the fingers (either bare or wearing fingerpicks). Sometimes refers more specifically to the spectrum of melodically expressive ragtime-blues through country styles encompassed by, say, Elizabeth Cotton and Chet Atkins.

Flattop guitar. An acoustic guitar with a flat top (and almost always a round or roundish soundhole), as opposed to an archtop guitar.

Floating Pickup. A magnetic pickup mounted on the end of the fingerboard or on the pickguard of an archtop guitar, so it won't interfere with the vibrations of the top.

Folk Guitar. In this book, and often elsewhere, a steel-string flattop guitar. Occasionally elsewhere, especially in materials from the 1960s, the term refers to a wide-necked, small-bodied 12-fret steel-string guitar like the Martin 0-16NY.

Forward bow. See **Warp.**

Friction pegs. Violin-style wooden tuning pegs held in place only by friction. Today used only on flamenco guitars.

14-fret. See **12-fret.**

Fret. T-shaped metal strip with a studded tang seated in the fingerboard, against which the strings are depressed. Most guitars have 20-21 frets, of which 14 are clear of the body. See also **12-fret.**

Fretboard. Another word for fingerboard.

Golpeador. Spanish for tap-plate (literally, "striker").

German silver. (Also called **nickel silver.**) A strong, silvery-looking stainless nickel-steel alloy desirable for frets and other fittings. There is no actual silver content to this alloy.

Graduation. The technique of altering the thickness of a guitar's soundboard in different areas in order to promote a maximum balance of strength and acoustic response.

Handstop. A protruding piece of wood carved into the neck to add extra thickness and reinforcement at its most vulnerable spot, the point where the headstock angles back.

Harmonic. The sound produced by the total length of the vibrating string (the *fundamental*), or any of the sounds of its independently vibrating fractional sections (**overtones**). Also used specifically to refer to the bell-like overtone produced by a plucked string which is touched lightly (not fretted) at one of its exact fractional points; for example, the harmonic produced at the twelfth fret (half the string length).

Harp guitar. A guitar with extra unfretted strings, usually bass strings, attached to an extra neck or neck-like extension of the body.

Hawaiian guitar. See **Spanish guitar.**

Head. Another word for headstock or for tuning machine, as in **tuning head** or **machine head.**

Head Block. A block of hardwood placed inside the guitar body opposite the heel of the neck, to provide a reinforcement for the sides where they join, and to provide a joining point for the neck heel. The neck heel is traditionally mortised into the heel block with a dovetail joint. On cheap guitars and on some good guitars of unusual design, the neck may be otherwise glued or even bolted on.

Head plate. The veneer used to cover the front of the headstock, sometimes (though not necessarily) of the same wood as the sides and back. The head plate is strictly ornamental and may be omitted, or a paint or finish may be used instead (though usually only on cheaper guitars.) This term is rarely used; people usually just speak casually of headstock veneer, etc.

Headstock. The section at the end of the guitar neck that holds the tuning machines.

Heel. The widened-out portion at the base of the neck, where it joins the body. On some instruments the bottom of the heel may be covered with an ornamental piece of wood veneer, ivoroid binding, etc., called the **heel plate.**

Heel block. Another term for **head block.** Sometimes **heel block** is used specifically to refer to a configuration often used in classical guitars, where the block is carved out of the same piece of wood as the neck.

Heel plate. See **Heel.**

Herringbone. A herringbone-pattern purfling strip used on pre-World War II Martin 28-series guitars, and more recently revived by Martin and other makers. Also short for a Martin guitar with such purfling, especially a prewar D-28.

In-line. Parts suppliers' term applied to tuning machines that are mounted three to a **plate.**

Intonation. Ability to play in tune. Bad intonation on a guitar may be caused by improper fret or saddle placement, a warped neck, or worn-out strings.

Jumbo. Name for a common large-bodied, deep-waisted guitar shape.

Kerf. See **Lining.**

Laminate (*noun*). Veneered wood or plywood. Also refers to necks made out of several wood sections glued together. Good multipiece laminate necks are sturdy and, unlike plywood bodies, perfectly respectable. Laminated headstocks are less respectable but quite acceptable.

Lap steel. See **Steel guitar.**

Lining. The strip of wood glued around the edges of the inside of the body of the guitar, to provide support and extra gluing surface where the back and top join the sides. Linings are usually **kerfed,** which means that they have indentations cut into them so they may be easily bent to the shape of the guitar.

Loop bridge. The bridge shape typical of classical guitars, where the string is run through a hole parallel to the fingerboard and then looped around itself to hold it in place.

Luthier. A stringed-instrument maker.

Machine or **Machine head.** The string tuning mechanism, including the knob, gears, and winding post.

Marquetry. Decorative strips of patterned wood inlaid into the guitar's body, usually in rosettes or at joining points such as edge bindings and center seams.

MOP. Abbreviation, especially in dealer's catalogs, for mother-of-pearl.

MOT. Abbreviation, especially in dealer's catalogs, for mother-of-toilet seat.

Mother-of-toilet seat. Fanciful but commonly used term for fake plastic mother-of-pearl, especially the highly iridescent and artificial-looking variety.

Multipiece. Word used of laminated necks. See **Laminate.**

Neck block. Another term for **heel block.**

Neck reinforcement. See **Handstop.**

New York Martin. A Martin guitar made before 1898. In that year, Martin terminated its agreement with the New York-based company that had distributed its guitars since the beginning, and finally changed its guitar imprint from "C.F. Martin & Co., New York" even though the company had been in Nazareth, PA since 1839. The model code suffix "NY" is used by Martin to designate recent models patterned after pre-1898 originals.

Nickel silver. See **German silver.**

Nut. The grooved rectangle of ivory, bone, ceramic, plastic, metal, or hardwood that spaces the strings at the headstock end of the fingerboard, and defines one end of the string **scale.**

Nut extender. A grooved metal collar that sits over the nut, raising the action to a height suitable for slide playing.

Offset saddle. See **Saddle.**

Open tuning. A manner of tuning the guitar strings to the notes of a chord rather than to their usual pattern, which does not constitute a chord. Characteristic of certain blues, Hawaiian, steel, and bottleneck styles, and also used extensively in contemporary British Isles and new-age styles. The term is usually also used loosely to refer to other unusual tunings, even when they don't produce a real chord.

Orchestral guitar. Outmoded term for acoustic archtop guitar, especially loud, heavy models for big-band use.

Overtone. The sound of each vibrating fraction of the string length. (A guitar string vibrates not only along its entire length but along its fractional sections.) These overtones combine with the *fundamental* (the sound of the entire string length vibrating) to give each guitar its unique sound.

Pearl. Among guitarists and luthiers, short for mother-of-pearl.

Pedal steel. See **Steel guitar.**

Peg. The cylinder part of the tuning machine, around which the strings are wound. Also called **barrel, string post, tuning peg, winding post.**

Peghead. Another word for **headstock.**

Pick. Usually short for **flatpick,** though might also refer to a **fingerpick.**

Pickguard. A plate of plastic (rarely hardwood, formerly tortoiseshell) glued to the top near the soundhole to protect it from pick and finger abrasion.

Pickup. An electronic transducer device that converts the sounds of the guitar strings (or, in some cases, the oscillation of their magnetic fields) to electrical signals that are fed into an amplifier.

Pin bridge. The standard bridge style for steel-string guitars. Ball-end strings are run through holes in the bridge into the guitar body. The ball ends are held in place against the bridge plate on the underside of the top, while removeable pins are inserted to hold the strings in position against the bridge plate.

Plate. The strip of metal on which several tuning machines may be mounted (though tuners may also be separate). Also, an obsolete word for **soundboard.**

Plectrum. Flatpick.

Plectrum guitar. Obsolete term for archtop guitar. Also sometimes used to describe an uncommon 4-string guitar design of the twenties era, with neck specs approximating those of a plectrum banjo.

Position dots, Position markers. The dots or inlays located on the fingerboard (usually below frets 5, 7, 9, 12, and perhaps also 3, 15, 17, and 19) to provide visual guidance for the player's fingers.

Prewar. Made prior to World War II. During that war, most manufacturers were involved all or in part in the production of war materials. When they retooled after the war, perhaps with new personnel, quality and/or specifications were usually somewhat different, and often not as good.

Purfling. Ornamental strips of inlay, usually around the edges of the top and/or back where they join the sides, inside of the binding. In casual usage, people may not carefully distinguish the terms **binding, purfling,** and **marquetry.**

Pyramid bridge. A pin bridge design in which the bridge feet are carved ornamentally into pyramid shapes, characteristic of Martin guitars up to the late 1920s.

Quartersawn. Wood sawn so that the edge grain is perpendicular to the cut. The most desirable way of milling wood for guitars.

Reinforcing rod. A steel bar, ebony strip, or similar strengthening device set in a routed-out channel in the neck under the fingerboard to help keep the neck straight under pressure from the strings. Sometimes used synonymously with **tension rod.** A few 19th-century guitars were also made with a completely different form of metal or wood reinforcing rod set banjo-style inside the body, running from the heel block to the end block.

Relief. A small amount of apparent warp deliberately built into the fingerboard to avoid string rattle in certain circumstances, and to make the higher frets more playable. A fingerboard should not be perfectly straight.

Reverse bow or **reverse warp.** Another term for **back-bow.** See **Warp.**

Ribs. A term sometimes used for the sides of the guitar.

Rosette. Ornamental marquetry pattern surrounding the soundhole.

Saddle. The strip of ivory, bone, plastic, or other synthetic material seated in the bridge, across which the string rests. The saddle is usually mounted on an angle ("offset") and/or shaped ("compensated") on an angle so that the lower strings are slightly lengthened to allow for their different coefficient of length-to-mass, in order to help them play in tune.

Scale. Short for *scale length*, the length of the vibrating portion of the string, from nut to saddle. Scale properly refers to the guitar maker's model or template for placing the frets, which is mathematically derived from the length of the vibrating portion of the string. Most guitars are built more or less in conformance with three standards: Martin short scale (24.9 inches, mostly smaller guitars); Martin long scale (today's most common scale length: 25.4 inches), and classical concert scale (26 inches). Also, a musical scale, as in common usage.

Semi-acoustic. See **Acoustic.**

Separation. A quality of an instrument in which the notes played simultaneously in a chord are perceived distinctly and individually, rather than as a homogeneous whole. How much separation you want is a matter of taste.

Set. The precut, roughly shaped sections of wood that will be used for the back and sides of the guitar. In the highest-quality instruments, sets will be quartersawn (to minimize shrinkage and the possibility of cracking) and cut from the same log (to maximize visual and structural uniformity and the symmetry of whatever shrinkage does occur).

Setup. The sum of adjustments that govern the action and playability of the guitar: nut and saddle height, tension-rod adjustment, and choice of string gauge. Other relevant factors, such as neck set, fingerboard planing, and fret dressing, are in the realm of more serious repair work and aren't usually considered part of setup.

Shoulders. The parts of the sides along the top of the upper bout where they abut the neck heel.

Signal path. The path followed by an electrical current carrying sound information; for example, the pathway through the various cables and devices from a guitar pickup through a phase shifter, a digital delay unit, and into an amplifier.

Skewing. Sideways (rather than convex or concave) bowing or distortion of the neck. See **Warp.**

Slide guitar. A style of playing in which the strings are not depressed against the frets, but instead are fretted with a movable, hard object held by the fretting hand. This may be a cut-down glass bottleneck or pill bottle worn on the pinky or third finger, a steel cylinder, a jacknife held between the fingers, a store-bought guitar slide or **steel**, etc.

Soundhole. The hole in the top of an acoustic guitar, which affects tone production of the sound chamber and the elasticity of the top. Usually round (or, at least, roundish) on a flattop guitar. Archtop guitars generally have two f-shaped soundholes like a violin.

Solidbody. An electric guitar with a body constructed of a solid piece of wood, offering no sound-chamber resonance so that its amplified sound is totally produced by its electromagnetic pickups.

Sound chamber. An enclosed or semi-enclosed chamber that amplifies and colors sound vibrations; for example, the body of a guitar.

Spanish guitar. A troublesome, obsolete term that has caused confusion out of all proportion to its innocence. It doesn't necessarily refer to a guitar made in Spain or used to play Spanish music. The term originated in the twenties to distinguish *any* kind of guitar (flattop, archtop, classical, whatever), held in the normal upright playing position, from the **Hawaiian guitar.** A Hawaiian guitar is any kind of guitar as long as it's held flat (face-upwards) across the lap and fretted with a steel bar held against the strings. (Therefore it's possible—and common—for an Hawaiian person to play Hawaiian-style music on a Spanish guitar. However, the nature of the Hawaiian guitar is such that it is unlikely, though theoretically possible, that a Spaniard or anyone else would ever play Spanish-style music on the Hawaiian guitar. The Hawaiian guitar has also been used successfully for playing Indian ragas. Got it? Good.)

Steel. The heavy metal bar or cylinder used to note the strings on a **steel guitar.** Also short for **steel guitar.**

Steel guitar. An electrified instrument consisting essentially of a neck and strings without a body, played horizontally. You note a steel guitar by holding a heavy metal cylinder (the **steel**) against the strings. The **lap steel** is a simple version held on the player's lap. The more complicated **pedal steel** has more strings, the basic pitches of which are altered by pressing different combinations of pedals and levers with feet and knees.

Solid. In the context of this book (and of the guitar industry), "solid" refers to genuine lumber as opposed to veneered laminate or plywood.

Soundboard. The top of the guitar, on which the bridge is mounted.

Spatula. The part of the fingerboard that extends over the body of the guitar (usually beginning at the fourteenth or twelfth fret).

Splint. A shaved sliver of wood glued into a crack to be repaired. Used when the crack is too wide for simple gluing and clamping.

Strap button. A pin attached to the guitar's neck near the heel, or sometimes to the side close to the neck heel, for the purpose of attaching a strap. See also **End pin.**

Struts. Another word for bracing.

Stud. A small rectangular- or diamond-shaped chip of spruce, ideally with bevelled edges, glued in the inside of the guitar body to reinforce a repaired crack.

Sustain. The guitar's ability to keep a string sounding once it's been plucked.

Sympathetic strings. Extra strings that are not plucked or fretted, but that are set in motion by the vibration of the strings that are played. The sitar is a good example of a sympathetic-string instrument.

T-bar. One type of **Reinforcing rod**, consisting of a T-shaped metal bar.

Table. An obsolete word for soundboard, used mainly by classical luthiers.

Tail block. Another term for **end block.**

Tailpiece. A device that holds the ends of the strings on archtop and occasionally older flattop guitars. Conventional on archtops, but usually the sign of a cheaply made flattop (Maccaferri-style guitars being one exception).

Tap-plate. Protective plate of wood, plastic, etc, similar to a pickguard, used on flamenco guitars to protect against percussive effects made by fingernails.

Taro-patch. A variety of ukulele with 4 double-strung courses instead of the ukulele's 4 single string.

Tenor guitar. A small-bodied 4-string guitar tuned like a tenor (4-string) banjo.

Tension rod or Bar. Also commonly called **truss rod.** A steel (sometimes ebony, graphite, etc.) rod inserted under tension in a channel cut the length of the neck in order to inhibit warping of the neck under string pressure. Most manufacturers now use a steel rod in which tension is adjustable to compensate for changes in climate, aging, or string gauge. In this book, as often elsewhere, **tension** or **truss rod** is used loosely of any kind of neck reinforcing rod, including nonadjustable metal or ebony bars.

Terz guitar. (Pronounced "tertz," from German.) A small guitar, fashionable in the 19th century, tuned three tones higher than usual. The smallest-sized antique Martins were terz guitars.

Tiple. A 10-string ukulele strung in four courses. The outer two courses are double-strung in unison. The two courses in the middle are triple-strung, with the center string of each course tuned an octave below the two others.

Tone bars. In a flattop guitar: the ancillary struts under the lower bout of the guitar, other than the two main struts that form the X-brace—though most people usually use the word "bracing" loosely to encompass both the X-braces and the tone bars. In an archtop guitar: the two longitudinal struts that in most such guitars solely comprise the bracing system.

Transducer. The technically correct term for pickup. (A transducer is any device that converts one form of energy to another; in this case, sound into an electrical signal.)

Transverse bracing. An early form of bracing in which a few struts run laterally, or at a very slight angle off the lateral, underneath the belly. Transverse bracing reinforces the top structurally but doesn't help much acoustically.

Treble. The highest range of notes. Also used to refer to the highest three strings of the guitar.

Truss-rod. Another term for **tension rod.**

Tuner or Tuning machine. Another term for **machine head.**

Tuning Peg. See **Peg.** Also sometimes used loosely of the entire **machine head.**

12-fret, 14-fret. These terms refer to the two major neck styles. The number indicates the number of frets clear on the neck before the neck joins the body (ignoring any cutaway)—not the total number of frets on the fingerboard. Classical guitars, a few contemporary steel-string guitars (especially those with wider fingerboards), and early steel-string guitars have twelve frets. Most contemporary steel-string guitars have fourteen frets, to allow greater access to high notes.

Vintage. A term used of high-quality used guitars made far enough in the past to have antique or collector's value (usually pre-World War II for acoustic guitars and pre-Beatles-era for electrics.)

Voicing. The process in which a luthier listens to the sounds of the top and bracing as they are being carved into final shape on a fine handmade guitar. (In music theory and composition, **voicing** refers to the way notes are located within chords.)

Volute. See **Handstop.**

Waist. The narrowest section of the guitar's body, between the upper and lower bouts, where you rest it on your knee.

Warp. Any distortion in the shape of wood, usually in reference to the straightness of the long axis of the neck. Concave distortion is called a **bow** or **forward bow.** Convex distortion is called a **backbow, reverse bow** or **reverse warp,** confusingly, also just **bow** (as opposed to **warp**) by some repairpeople. Sideways distortion or movement is called **skewing.**

Winding. The outer part of a string (usually strings 3 through 6), consisting of a thin metal wire wound around a metal or fiber core.

X-bracing. The bracing system pioneered by C. F. Martin, featuring two main braces crossing in an "x" pattern just below the soundhole. Standard on almost all steel-string guitars.

Zero fret. An extra fret, placed directly in front of the nut, which serves as a de facto nut to determine where the scale begins.

Resources

Further Reading

Cumpiano, William and Jonathan D. Natelson. *Guitarmaking: Tradition and Technology*. (Publisher information not available.) A well-received recent book, which covers both classical and steel-string guitars. However, I haven't yet seen a copy.

Duchossoir, A. R.. *Guitar Identification*. Minneapolis, MN: Hal Leonard, 1983. A short, basic guide to the dating of serial numbers and salient historical characteristics of Fender, Gibson, Gretsch, and Martin acoustic and electric guitars.

George, David. *The Flamenco Guitar*. Madrid, Spain: Society of Spanish Studies, 1969. History, spirit, and sociology of the flamenco guitar as well as flamenco music, flamenco life, and the Gypsy mystique; some details on guitarmaking.

Grunfeld, Frederic V.. *The Art and Times of the Guitar*. New York: MacMillan, 1969. Witty, readable social history primarily of the classical guitar and its music, with some attention to other forms and styles as well.

Kamimoto, Hideo. *Complete Guitar Repair*. New York: Oak Publications, 1978. A readable, reasonable, and comprehensive book. Its price and accessibility make it a likely candidate for your bookshelf. Even though you shouldn't attempt any difficult repairs yourself, and should think twice about making even simple adjustments, a book like this can give you insights into how your instrument works.

Kasha, Michael. *Complete Guitar Acoustics*. Tallahassee, FL: Cove Press, 1973. Currently out of print.

Longworth, Mike. *Martin Guitars: A History*. Minisink Hills, PA: Four Maples Press, 1987. Detailed information on Martin's history, specifications, and production figures from the beginning through the mid-1980s, based on direct access to the company's official records, foremen's logs, etc. Essential information if you're planning to purchase or cultivate an interest in used or antique Martins.

Sandberg, Larry and Dick Weissman. *The Folk Music Sourcebook*, rev. ed. New York: Da Capo Press, 1989. Discography, bibliography, and other information about people, places, retailers, and organizations as well as the music itself. Includes recommendations for instructional materials: books, tapes, videos, records, etc. A good place to get started.

The Guitar. Santoro, Gene (ed.). New York: Quill/Quarto, 1984. Separate sections by various authors on classical, jazz, blues, country, and rock guitarists and styles. Personality-oriented.

Schneider, John. *The Contemporary Guitar.* Berkeley, CA: University of California Press, 1985. In the course of expounding his personal theory of tone production, the author deals with guitar construction, repertoire, and the compositional conventions of the nylon-string and electric guitar in contemporary classical usage. Much information on guitar acoustics in general.

Sloan, Irving. *Steel-String Guitar Construction.* New York: E.P. Dutton, 1975. A useful guide especially for the beginning luthier; includes sources of tools and materials.

Teeter, Don. *The Acoustic Guitar: Adjustment, Care, Maintenance, and Repair.* vols. I and II. Norman: University of Oklahoma Press, 1980. Sensible advice, methods, anecdotes, custom tool diagrams, and controversial, brilliantly idiosyncratic techniques generously shared. Professional-level though interesting to all.

Tyler, James. *The Early Guitar: A History and Handbook.* New York: Oxford University Press, 1980. Scholarly study of the guitar and its musical styles from the 16th through the mid-18th century.

Wheeler, Tom. *American Guitars: An Illustrated History.* New York: Harper & Row, 1982. Covers acoustic, electric, resophonic, f-hole archtop guitars, and more. Good overall view of the subject, organized by company/brand, comprehensively illustrated, with much detail. A good place to start learning more about vintage guitars and industry history.

Young, David Russell. *The Steel String Guitar: Construction and Repair.* Westport, CT: The Bold Strummer, 1987. Methods and techniques of a well-respected Southern California luthier strongly influenced by the traditions of classical guitar making.

Vintage Guitar Blue Book. Portland, OR: Marketwright Publications. Box 40766, Portland, OR 97240. I have not seen this publication. In general I have reservations about blue books (in any field), because they don't take specific or local conditions into account and because any errors or eccentricities on the part of the compilers tend to skew the market. However, they do have their use in providing a starting point, at least.

Magazines

Acoustic Guitar, Box 767, San Anselmo, CA 94960. A magazine that has just gotten under way as this book prepares for press. It promises a broad and interesting range of articles on artists, music, and instruments in all the idioms in which the steel- and nylon-string acoustic guitars are played.

Dirty Linen, Box 66600, Baltimore, MD 21239. A lively publication dealing with traditional music and associated acoustic styles.

Frets. Discontinued in 1989 after a decade of publication. If you can find back issues (some are available from *Guitar Player;* see below), you'll learn a lot from them about contemporary and traditional acoustic music, instruments, and personalities.

Guitar Digest, Box 1252, Athens, OH 45701. Bimonthly with articles, ads, swap offers, etc. Acoustic and electric.

Guitar Player, 20085 Stevens Creek Blvd., Cupertino, CA 95014. Deals mainly with electric and especially rock guitar, but has increased coverage of acoustic guitar since the demise of its sister publication, *Frets*.

National Instrument Exchange, Rt. 9, Box 43, Fayetteville, TN 37334. Instrument sale and swap notices.

Sing Out!, Box 5253, Bethlehem, PA 18015. The voice of the urban folk song community, with its roots in the protest and political song movements of the the fifties and sixties.

Vintage Guitar, Box 7301, Bismarck, ND 58502. Articles, price guides, news of shows, buy and sell ads.

Mail-Order Sources

Most of these businesses will add you to their regular mailing list for a nominal subscription fee, and will send you a sample catalog for the asking. Look in the *Magazine* section and the *Folk Music Sourcebook* listed under *Further Reading* for more names of mail-order sources; this is a basic list to get you started. In addition to book and vintage instrument retailers, I've also included some sources for hard-to-find acoustic music recordings. There's a lot of good stuff available by mail that your record store doesn't have, never had, and never will have.

Alcazar, Box 429, Waterbury, VT 05676. Recordings in many folk and acoustic styles. Large catalog.

Andy's Front Hall, Box 307, Wormer Rd., Voorheesville, NY 12186. Records, books, instruments, etc.

Big Boy Once, Marc Silber and Stefany Reich-Silber, Box 9663, Berkeley, CA 94709. Newsletter with price list of used, vintage, and collectible instruments. Inventory typically includes some obscure and lower-priced instruments, chic junk, and other interesting items off the beaten path, as well as serious goods. For collectors and earnest buyers.

The Bold Strummer, 1 Webb Rd., Westport, CT 06880. A rich source of publications for the classical guitarist, interesting to the steel-string guitarist as well.

Down Home Music Mail Order, 6921 Stockton Ave., El Cerrito, CA 94530. Catalog/newsletter available. Records and books in all areas of traditional and ethnic music, rock, jazz, etc.

1833 Shop, Martin Guitar Company, Nazareth, PA 18064. Good selection of books on instrument lore, as well as accessories and guitar-related gift items, etc.

Elderly Instruments, Box 14210, 1100 N. Washington, Lansing, MI 48901. Separate catalogs available for records, new and used instruments, books and videos, etc. Comprehensive inventory, and a good place to do business.

Gruhn Guitars, Inc., 410 Broadway, Nashville, TN 37203. The major vintage guitar dealer. Newsletter and price list available; send a self-addressed stamped envelope. For collectors and earnest buyers.

Homespun Tapes, Box 694, Woodstock, NY 12498. Instructional tape cassettes and videos for acoustic instruments in many styles of music. Recommended. Specify instrument and style when requesting a catalog.

Lark in the Morning, PO Box 1176, Mendocino, CA 95460. Sells used and new instruments of all types.

Legacy Books, Box 494, Hatboro, PA 19040. Specializes in traditional songbooks, scholarly publications on traditional music and folklore; catalog includes many guitar-related books as well. Serves individuals and institutions.

Roundup Records, Box 154, N. Cambridge, MA 02140. Large, comprehensive catalog of all idioms plus books, videos, etc.

Shanachie Records, 37 E. Clinton St., Newton, NJ 07860. Varied catalog of records, tapes, and videos; strong in Celtic, historical blues, other acoustic guitar, reggae, African, and world-beat music.

Vintage Fret Shop, Box 562, Ashland, NH 03217. Small, friendly quarterly newsletter and price list of used and collectible guitars. For collectors and earnest buyers.

Acoustic Music Shops

The following list includes as many specialty guitar shops, printed music dealers, and other retail resources for acoustic music as I know of. (Remember also to look at the mail order dealer section in this chapter.) Since this list is derived from secondary sources, inclusion does not necessarily constitute a recommendation. There are also undoubtedly many fine shops which have not found their way onto this list, so be sure to consult your local yellow pages and to ask around on the grapevine.

Alaska
Down Home Guitar, 2917 Spenard Rd., Anchorage, AK 99503
Old Time Music Co., Box 4-2294, Elmendorf AFB, AK 99506
M & M Music, Box 32793, Juneau, AK 99803

Alabama
Golden Spring Music, 1306 Greenbrier Rd., Anniston, AL 36201
Guitar Shoppe, 113 Mitcham Ave., Auburn, AL 36830
Fretted Instruments, 2906 Linden Ave., Birmingham, AL 35209
Fret Shop, 502 Pratt Ave. NE, Huntsville, AL 35801
The Guitar Shop, 1108 7th Ave., Tuscaloosa, AL 35401

Arizona
Vallee Guitars, 2630 W. Baseline Rd., Mesa, AZ 85202
The Village Luthier, 1300-B 36th Dr., Phoenix, AZ 85023
Beck Fretted Instruments, 807 S. Ash Ave., Tempe, AZ 85281
Folk Shop, 415 N. 4th Ave., Tucson, AZ 85705

Arkansas
Eureka String Shoppe, 10 Mountain, Eureka Spring, AR 72632
Ronnie's Steel Guitar, 881 Park Ave., Hot Springs, AR 71901
McSpadden Musical Instruments, Box 1230, Highway 9 North, Mountain View, AR 72560

California
Thin Man String Co., 1506 Webster St., Alameda, CA 94501
Lundberg Fretted Instruments, 2126 Dwight Way, Berkeley, CA 94704
Museum Music (Mark Silber), 2923 Adeline St., Berkeley, CA 94703
The Fifth String, 3051 Adeline St., Berkeley, CA 94703
Holcomb's Banjo & Guitar, 548 E. Campbell Ave., Campbell, CA 95008

Blue Ridge Pickin' Parlor, 20246 Saticoy St., Canoga Park, CA 91306

Carmel Music Co., Dolores & 5th, Carmel, CA 93921

Folk Music Center, 220 Yale Ave., Clarement, CA 91711

Hobgoblin Music, 1655 Mission Rd., Colma, CA 94014

The Fret House, 309 N. Citrus, Covina, CA 91723

Blue Ridge Music, 509 First, Encinitas, CA 92024

Fiddles & Camera, Fort Bragg, CA 95437

Foggy Mountain Music, 104 W. Main St., Grass Valley, CA 95945

A. B. Music Studios, 19171 Magnolia St. 10, Huntington Beach, CA 92646

The Guitar Shoppe, 1027 N. Coast Highway, Laguna Beach, CA 92651

McCabe's Guitar Shop, 4209 E. Anaheim, Long Beach, CA 90804

Betnun Music, 403 N. Larchmont, Los Angeles, CA 90004

Westwood Musical Instruments, 2301 Purdue Ave.,
    Los Angeles, CA 90064

Lark in the Morning, PO Box 1176, Mendocino, CA 95460

Shade Tree, 28722 Marguerite Pkwy., Mission Viejo, CA 92692

Bluegrass Music Shoppe, 514 McHenry Blvd., Modesto, CA 95354

South Seas Guitar, 247 Pearl St., Monterey, CA 93940

Acoustic Guitar, 127 Sheridan Rd., Oakland, CA 94618

Psaltery Music, 944 N. Tustin, Orange, CA 92667

Draper's Music Center, 330 California Ave., Palo Alto, CA 94306

Gryphon Stringed Instruments, 211 Lambert, Palo Alto, CA 94306

Norman's Rare Guitars, 6753 Tampa, Reseda, CA 91335

Fifth String, 5522 H St., Sacramento, CA 95819

Tiny Moore Music Center, 1165 48th St., Sacramento, CA 95819

Amazing Grace Music, 111 Redhill Ave., San Anselmo, CA 94960

Blue Guitar Workshop, 1020 Garnet Ave., San Diego, CA 92109

Freedom Guitar, 1053 8th Ave., San Diego, CA 92101

The Fifth String, 5957 Geary Blvd., San Francisco, CA 94121

Premier Music Co., 4102 Vachell Ln., San Luis Obispo, CA 93401

Jensen Music, 2830-F De La Vina, Santa Barbara, CA 93105

Paul Hostetter, Luthiery/restoration, 2550 Smith Grade,
    Santa Cruz, CA 95060

Union Grove Music, 1013 Pacific Ave., Santa Cruz, CA 95060

McCabe's Guitar Shop, 3101 Pico, Santa Monica, CA 90405

Washington St. Music, Box 331, Soquel, CA 95073

Pick 'n' Grin, Box 2186, Truckee, CA 93734

Countrywood Music, 2058 Treat Blvd., Walnut Creek, CA 94598

Colorado

Great Divide Music, 111 S. Monarch, Aspen, CO 81611

Boulder Early Music Shop—Early/historical instruments
    2037 13th St., Suite 16, Boulder, CO 80302

H.B. Woodsongs, 1605 Pearl St., Boulder, CO 80302

The Music Store, 1535 Pearl St., Boulder, CO 80302

Folklore Center, 330 N. Tejon, Colorado Springs, CO 80903

Acoustic Music Revival, 1934 S. Broadway, Denver, CO 80210

John Dillon Sheet Music, 4535 E. Colfax Ave., Denver, CO 80220

Pearl St. Music, 533 E. Ohio Ave., Denver, CO 80209

Back Porch Music, 511 Main St., Grand Junction, CO 81501
Wildwood Music, 136 W. Tomich Ave., Gunnison, CO 81230
Guitar City, 9895 W. Colfax Ave., Lakewood, CO 80215
Rockley Music, 8555 W. Colfax Ave., Lakewood, CO 80215
Virgil Reed Music, 323 Main St., Wray, CO 80758

Connecticut
Melody Music Co., 104 Asylum St., Hartford, CT 06103
Select Guitars, 43 Wall St., Norwalk, CT 06850
Country Folk Music Center, Sharon Mountain, Sharon, CT 06069
Guitar Workshop, 1074 Storrs Rd., Rt. 195, Storrs, CT 06268
The Bold Strummer Ltd., 1 Webb Rd., Westport, CT 06880

District of Columbia
Southworth Guitars, 4816 MacArthur Blvd. NW, Washington, DC 20036
The Guitar Shop, 1216 Connecticut Ave. NW, Washington, DC 20036

Delaware
Mid-Atlantic Music, 2003 Rodman Rd., Wilmington, DE 19805
Vogel Custom Guitars, Birdhaven Rd., Millville, DE 19667

Florida
F-Sharp Music, 10361 W. Sample Rd., Coral Springs, FL 33065
Bluegrass Central, 2088 Central Ave., Fort Myers, FL 33901
Sabine Music, 305 Northwest 13th, Gainesville, FL 32601
The Banjo Shop, 5653 Johnston St., Hollywood, FL 33021
Guitar Czar, 6254 Powers Ave., Jacksonville, FL 32217
Ed's Guitars, 4047 SW 96 Ave., Miami, FL 33165
Fret Factory Discount Music, 133 Mill Spring Pl.,
    Ormond Beach, FL 32074
Old Dixie Pickers, Box 31234, Palm Beach Gardens, FL 33418
Metro Music, 9068 St. Rd. 84, Ridge Plaza, Davie, FL 33224
Blount's Music, 2025 Fernway St., Sebring, FL 33872
Bluegrass Parlor, 4810 E. Busch Blvd., Tampa, FL 33617
Don's Bluegrass Music, 6809 N. Gunlock, Tampa, FL 33614

Georgia
Atlanta Guitar Center, 3130 Make Dr. NE, Atlanta, GA 30305
Jay's Music Center, 927 Broad St., Augusta, GA 30901
Dulcimer Shoppe, The River, Helen, GA 30545

Hawaii
The Music Exchange, 762 Kandelehua, Hilo, HI 96720

Idaho
Third Fret, 116 S. Main, Hailey, ID 83333
Chesbro Music Co., 327 Broadway, Idaho Falls, ID 83402
Guitars' Friend, 309 S. Main St., Moscow, ID 83843
Vintage Guitars, 316 E. 5th Ave., Post Falls, ID 83854

Illinois
Golden Frets, 715 S. Illinois St., Carbondale, IL 62901
Rosewood Guitars, 313 E. Green, Champaign, IL 61820
Andy's Music, 2310 W. Belmont, Chicago, IL 60618

Different Strummer, 909 W. Armitage, Chicago, IL 60614
Hogeye Music, 1920 Central St., Evanston, IL 60201
Jack Moore Guitar, 108 S. Stone, La Grange, IL 60525
Village School of Folk Music, 545 N. Milwaukee Ave.,
    Libertyville, IL 60048
Cisco's Music, 1704 Dunray, Normal, IL 61761
Hank's Country Store, 3025 Kilburn, Rockford, IL 61103
Herb Roth Guitars, 3313 Lee St., Skokie, IL 60076

Indiana
Bluegrass Record Shop, 1250 Highway 31N, Austin, IN 47102
C & K Bluegrass, 447 E. Line, Geneva, IN 46740
About Music, Inc., 911 Broad Ripple Ave., Indianapolis, IN 46220
Mountain Made Music, Box 816, Nashville, IN 47448

Iowa
Ye Olde Guitar Shoppe, 6806 Douglas Ave., Des Moines, IA 50322
Guitar Gallery, 527 S. Gilbert St., Iowa City, IA 52240
Edd's Fretted Instruments, 206 Austin Ave., Maquoketa, IA 52060

Kansas
Acoustic Stringed Instruments, 106 E. Sherman, Hutchinson, KS 67501
Mass Street Music, 1347 Massachusetts St., Lawrence, KS 66044
Richardson Music, 18 E. 9th St., Lawrence, KS 66044
Banjo, Fiddle, Etc., S. George Washington Blvd., Wichita, KS 67218
E. M. Shorts Guitars, 2525 E. Douglas, Wichita, KS 67211

Kentucky
Bluegrass Music Shop & Co., 302 3rd St., Carrollton, KY 41008
Flat Picker's Paradise, 323 E.K. Rd., Greenup, KY 41144
Doo Wop Enterprises, Inc., 1587 Bandstown Rd., Louisville, KY 40205
Pick 'n' Grin, 107 N. 4th, Paducah, KY 42002
Pro Frets Music, 815 N. Wilson, Radcliff, KY 40160
Appalshop, 306 Madison St., Whitesburg, KY 41858

Louisiana
Tim's Guitar Repair, 10808 Greenwell Springs RD 2,
    Baton Rouge, LA 70814
Collingsworth Guitar Service, 413 W. 77th St., Shreveport, LA 71106

Maine
Down Home Music Shop, 43 Main St., Fairfield, ME 04937
Snee Music, 175 Main St., Norway, ME 04268
Buckdancer's Choice, 10 Longfellow Sq., Portland, ME 04101

Maryland
Acoustic Music Resource, 1 Bloomsbury Ave., Baltimore, MD 21228
Appalachian Bluegrass, 643 Frederick Rd., Baltimore, MD 21228
Boe's Strings, 26 S. Market St., Frederick, MD 21701
Veneman Music Co., 1150 Rockville Pike, Rockville, MD 20852
House of Musical Traditions, 7040 Carroll Ave., Takoma Park, MD 20912
Washington Music Center, 11151 Viers Mill Rd., Wheaton, MD 20902

Massachusetts
Acton Music Center, 140 Main, Acton, MA 01720
Fretted Instrument Workshop, 49 S. Pleasant St., Amherst, MA 01810
Wood & String Music Center, 493 Massachusetts Ave.,
      Arlington, MA 02174
E. U. Wurlitzer, Inc., 360 Newbury St., Boston, MA 02115
Jones Vintage & Custom Guitar, 295 Huntington Ave., Suite 304,
      Boston, MA 02115
Briggs & Briggs Sheet Music, 1270 Massachusetts Ave.,
      Cambridge, MA 02138
Music Emporium, 2018 Massachusetts Ave., Cambridge, MA 02140
Sandy's Music, 896A Massachusetts Ave., Cambridge, MA 02139
Strings Attached Music Center, 12 Federal St., The Tannery,
      Newburyport, MA 01950
Fretworks, 74 Lakewood St., Worcester, MA 01603

Michigan
Herb David Guitar Shop, 302 E. Liberty, Ann Arbor, MI 48104
Fiddler's Music Co., 16209 Mack Ave., Detroit, MI 48224
Rainbow Music, 824 Leonard St. NW, Grand Rapids, MI 49504
Elderly Instruments, 1100 N. Washington, Lansing, MI 48901
Gitfiddler Music, 302 E. Main, Northville, MI 48167
Rochester Folk Workshop, 420 East St., Rochester, MI 48063
Pick 'n' Strum, 30081 Greenfield, Southfield, MI 48076
Northern Acoustic Instruments, 1319 Airport Rd. W.,
      Traverse City, MI 49684
Home Grown Music, 117 S. Kalamazoo, White Pigeon, MI 49099

Minnesota
Don's Guitar Repair, 501 Blue Earth St., Mankato, MN 56001
Hoffman Guitars, 2219 Franklin Ave. E., Minneapolis, MN 55404
Schmitt Music Center, 12343 Wayzata Blvd., Minnetonka, MN 55343
Homestead Pickin' Parlor, 6625 Penn Ave. S., Richfield, MN 55423
Cadenza Music Center, 149 N. Snelling, St. Paul, MN 55104

Missouri
Mountain Music Shop, 109 N. Second, Branson, MO 65616
The Blue Guitar, 101 Orr St., Columbia, MO 65201
George's Music, 8101 N. Oak St. Thruway, Kansas City, MO 64118
Luyben Music, 4318 Main, Kansas City, MO 64111
Fazio's Frets & Friends, 1034 Manchester Rd., Manchester, MO 63011
Brentwood Music Co., 2670 S. Glenstone, Springfield, MO 65804
St. Charles Guitar, 1026 1st Capitol Dr., St. Charles, MO 63301

Montana
Bitterroot Folklore Center, 4378 Last Chance Gulch, Helena, MT 59601
Bitterroot Music, 529 S. Higgins St., Missoula, MT 59801

Nebraska
Yanda's Music, 2200 Central Ave., Kearney, NE 66847
Dale London, 2639½ N. 48th St., Lincoln, NE 68504
Browns' Music, 7351 Pacific St., Omaha, NE 68114

Nevada
Bizarre Guitar, 2677 Oddie Blvd., Reno, NV 89512

New Hampshire
Vintage Fret Shop, 20 Riverside, Ashland, NH 03217
Blue Mountain Guitar Center, 2 Colonial Plaza, W. Lebanon, NH 03784

New Jersey
Nolde's Music Box, Hunterdon Shopping Center, Flemington, NJ 08822
Caizzo Music, 181 South St., Freehold, NJ 07728
Guitar Emporium, 104 Brighton Ave., Long Branch, NJ 07740
Guitar Trader, 8 Broad St., Red Bank, NJ 07701
Last Chance Used Guitars, 361 Westfield Ave., Roselle Park, NJ 07208

New Mexico
Pimentel & Sons, 3316 Lafayette NE, Albuquerque, NM 87131
Fiddler's Choice Music, 41 E. Main St., Jaffrey, NM 03452
Candyman, 851 St. Michael, Santa Fe, NM 87501

New York
Lark St. Music, 221 Lark St., Albany, NY 12210
Roxy's Music Store, Genesee County Mall, Batavia, NY 14020
The String Shop, 187 Norwalk Ave., Buffalo, NY 14214
Buck Dancer's Choice, 47 Main, Canton, NY 13617
Fret Shop, 1 Bartlett Ave., Cortland, NY 13045
Banjo Mart, 29 Mechanic, Hoosick Falls, NY 12090
Ithaca Guitar Works, 215 N. Cayuga St., Ithaca, NY 14850
Simpson Guitar Services, Box 4326, Ithaca, NY 14852
Matt Umanov Guitars, 273 Bleecker St., New York, NY 10014
Scognetti Vintage Instruments, 138 Willowpond Way,
    Penfield, NY 14526
Fretted Instruments, 424 Clay Ave., Rochester, NY 14613
Guitar Workshop, 1579 Northern Blvd., Roslyn, NY 11576
Mandolin Brothers, 629 Forest Ave., Staten Island, NY 10310
Tom Hosmer String Instruments, 120 Julian Pl., Syracuse, NY 13210
Andy's Front Hall, Andy Spence, Box 307, Wormer Rd,
    Voorheesville, NY 12186
Folkscraft Instruments, Webcetuck Craft Village, Wingdale, NY 12594

North Carolina
Bluegrass Center, 598 Hendersonville Rd., Asheville, NC 28803
Green River Dulcimers, 31 Carolina Lane, Asheville, NC 28801
Dulcimer Shop, Main St., Blowing Rock, NC 28605
Pickin' Loft, 22½ Park St., Canton, NC 28716
Reliable Music Co., 1001 S. Independence, Charlotte, NC 28202
Harry and Jeanie West, 3815 Tremont Ave., Durham, NC 27705
David Sheppard Instruments, 1820 Spring Garden St.,
    Greensboro, NC 27403
Ray's Music, Norwood St., Lenoir, NC 28645
Hoffman Stringed Instruments, 2660-D Yonkers Rd., Raleigh, NC 27604

North Dakota
Guitarland, 210 E. Main, Bismarck, ND 58501

Ohio
Akron Music Center, 270 S. Main St., Akron, OH 44308
Pavlov Music Center, 632 Wheeling Ave., Cambridge, OH 43725
Famous Old Time Music, 6101 Montgomery Rd., Cincinnati, OH 45213
Goose Acres Folk Music, 2175 Cornell Rd., Cleveland, OH 44106
Bluegrass Musicians' Supply, 1370 S. High St., Columbus, OH 43207
Columbus Folk Music, 4760 N. High St., Columbus, OH 43214
Stanton Sheet Music, 330 S. Fourth St., Columbus, OH 43215
Wildwood Stringed Instruments, 672 N. White Woman St.,
    Coshocton, OH 43812
Drinking Gourd, 4944 Northcutt Pl., Dayton, OH 45415
Blue Grass Corner, 1058 Clark, Holland, OH 43528
Woodsy's Music, 135 S. Water St., Kent, OH 44240
Smart's Music Store, 375 Marion Ave., Mansfield, OH 44490
J.B. Jewitt Co., 11017 Southwind Ct., Strongsville, OH 44136
Durdel's Music, 2628 W. Central, Toledo, OH 43606

Oklahoma
Guitars & Such, 100 S. Mississippi Ave., Ada, OK 74820
Driver Music, 6600 NW 39th Expy., Bethany, OK 73008
Peaches Music, 318 W. Main, Norman, OK 73069
Guitar Center, Box 15444, Tulsa, OK 75115
Medium Rare Guitars, 1305 S. Peoria, Tulsa, OK 74120

Oregon
Cripple Creek Music Co., 40 N. Main, Ashland, OR 97520
Balladeer Music, 296 E. 5th, Eugene, OR 97401
Mountain Music, 111 N. Central Ave., Medford, OR 97501
Artichoke Music, 3522 SE Hawthorne, Portland, OR 97214
Pioneer Music, 505 SW 3rd, Portland, OR 97204

Pennsylvania
Medley Music Corp., 1031–43 Lancaster Ave., Bryn Mawr, PA 19010
The Music Store (Sheet Music), Presser Place, Bryn Mawr, PA 19010
Pickers' Delight Music Store, 412 Chestnut St., Emmaus, PA 19049
MacLaren Music, 1024 Serrill Ave., Fairless Hills, PA 19030
Troubadour Music, Valley Forge Center, King of Prussia, PA 19406
Bucks County Folk Shop, 40 Sand Rd., New Britain, PA 18901
Note-ably Yours, Ed & Judy Ireton, 6865 Scarff Rd.,
    New Carlisle, PA 45344
Barber's Bluegrass & Country Music, RD1, New Freedom, PA 17349
Flop-Eared Muse, 759 S. 4th St., Philadelphia, PA 19147
Vintage Instruments, 1529 Pine St., Philadelphia, PA 19102
Specialty Guitar Shop, 3049 W. Liberty Ave., Pittsburgh, PA 15216

Rhode Island
Silva's Guitar & Banjo, 4 Goulart Ave., Bristol, RI 02809
Vintage Guitars, 2 Ella Terrace, Newport, RI 02840
Providence Guitar, 355 S. Main St., Providence, RI 02903

Music Man, 87 Tillinghast Ave., W. Warwick, RI 02893

South Carolina
Banjo Cason Music Co., 12 Chesterfield Highway, Cheraw, SC 29520
Fifth String Music Studio, 2320 E. North St., Greenville, SC 29607
Low Country Music, 100 N. Highway 52, Moncks Corner, SC 29461
Jerry Tillman Music, 566 Anderson Rd., Rock Hill, SC 29730
Jim Smoak Music, 890 Bacons Bridge Rd., Summerville, SC 29483

Tennessee
Mountain Music Guitar Shop, Rt. 1 Bear Creek Rd, Crossville, TN 38555
Rose Guitar Co., 1080 W. Main, Hendersonville, TN 37075
Blaylock Music Co., 7710 Hixson Pike, Hixson, TN 37343
Pick-N-Grin, 5802 Kingston Pk., Knoxville, TN 37919
Shot Jackson's Guitar Center, 105 Westchester Ct., Madison, TN 37115
Music Town, 4844 Summer Ave., Memphis, TN 38122
McPeak's Unique Instruments, Guill Rd. Rt. 6, Mt. Juliet, TN 37122
Cotton Music Center, 1815 21st Ave. S., Nashville, TN 37212
Gruhn Guitars, 410 Broadway, Nashville, TN 37203
Get-Tar Shop, 718 Parkway, Sevierville, TN 37862

Texas
Guitar Resurrection, 3004 Guadalupe 8, Austin, TX 78705
Guitar Banjo Studio, 4355 Calder, Beaumont, TX 77704
Wood 'n' Strings, 1513 Baker Rd., Burleson, TX 76028
Charley's Guitar Shop, 11389 Harry Hines, Dallas, TX 75229
Frets & Strings, 4451 Lovers Lane, Dallas, TX 75225
Herb Remington's Pedal Steel Guitar Gallery, 2101 Jean,
    Houston, TX 77023
Rockin' Robin, 3619 S. Shepherd, Houston, TX 77098
Old Time String Shop, 216 E. Pillar, Nacogdoches, TX 75961
Guitar Stringer's Music Store, 1406 Shaver, Pasadena, TX 77502

Utah
The Great Salt Lake Guitars, 362 W. Center St., Provo, UT 84601
Acoustic Music, 857 East 400 South, Salt Lake City, UT 84102
Intermountain Guitar & Banjo, 712 East First South,
    Salt Lake City, UT 84117

Vermont
Maple Leaf Music Co., 49 Elliot St., Brattleboro, VT 05301
Calliope Music, Box 300, Underhill, VT 05489

Virginia
Plucked String, Box 11125, Arlington, VA 22210
Picker's Supply, 902 Caroline St., Fredericksburg, VA 22401
Old Time Music Exchange, RD 2, Box 447, Halifax, VA 24558
Mountain Music, RD 1, Box 237, Lyndhurst, VA 22952
Luthier Meadows Musical Instruments, Rt. 1, Box 505-B,
    Natural Bridge Station, VA 24579
Ramblin' Conrad's Guitar, 871 N. Military Highway, Norfolk, VA 23502
Billy Cooper's Steel Guitar Shop, Rt. 2, Box 525, Orange, VA 22960
Don Warner Music, 401 S. Libbie, Richmond, VA 23226

The Fret Mill, 23 E. Salem Ave., Roanoke, VA 24011

Venneman Music, 6319 Amherst NE, Springfield, VA 22150

Washington

Ray's Fiddle Shop, 2131 Lummi Shore Rd., Bellingham, WA 98225

The Folk Store, 5238 University Way NE, Seattle, WA 98105

Lundin's Sound Hole, N. 4326 Maringo Dr., Spokane, WA 99212

Monte Vista Guitar Shop, 8328 S. Tacoma Way, Tacoma, WA 98499

West Virginia

Smakula Fretted Instruments, Box 882, Elkins, WV 26241

A Different Strummer, 150 Pleasant St., Morgantown, WV 26505

Fret 'n' Fiddle, 807 Pennsylvania Ave., St. Albans, WV 25177

Wisconsin

Spruce Tree Music, 851 E. Johnson St., Madison, WI 53703

Freelance Guitars, 181 E. Henry Clay Ave., Milwaukee, WI 53217

Dan's Pick-a-Way, 1011 Milwaukee Ave., South Milwaukee, WI 53176

Wyoming

Snake River Guitar Works, 2300 Teton Village Dr., Jackson, WY 83001

Luthier's Supplies, Woods, and Special Tools

Euphonon Co., Orford, NH 03777

International Luthier's Supply, Box 15444, Tulsa, OK 75115

Luthier's Mercantile, Box 774, Healdsburg, CA 95448

Saga Musical Instruments, Box 2841, 433 Littlefield,
    South San Francisco, CA 94080

Stewart-MacDonald Guitar Shop Supply, Box 900,
    21 N. Shafer St., Athens, OH 45701

Vitali Import Co., 5944 Atlantic Blvd., Maywood, CA 90270

Woodcraft Supply Company (general woodworking tools), Box 4000,
    10 State St., Woburn, MA 01888

Guitar Shows

The big music industry trade shows run by NAMM (National Association of Music Merchants) are open to the trade only. However, regional guitar shows of one to three days' duration, open to the general public, have become a usual feature of the musical landscape. Dallas, Austin, Columbus, Decatur, Kansas City, and Houston are just a few of the cities that have recently hosted such shows; smaller ones sometimes are held in smaller towns. Find out about them by reading the guitar magazines and asking your local dealers.